Palgrave Studies in International Relations Series

General Editors:
Knud Erik Jørgensen, Department of Political Science, University of Aarhus, Denmark

Audie Klotz, Department of Political Science, Maxwell School of Citizenship and Public Affairs
Syracuse University, USA

Palgrave Studies in International Relations, produced in association with the ECPR Standing Group for International Relations, will provide students and scholars with the best theoretically informed scholarship on the global issues of our time. Edited by Knud Erik Jørgensen and Audie Klotz, this new book series will comprise cutting-edge monographs and edited collections which bridge schools of thought and cross the boundaries of conventional fields of study.

Titles include:

Mathias Albert, Lars-Erik Cederman and Alexander Wendt (*editors*)
NEW SYSTEMS THEORIES OF WORLD POLITICS

Barry Buzan and Ana Gonzalez-Pelaez (*editors*)
INTERNATIONAL SOCIETY AND THE MIDDLE EAST
English School Theory at the Regional Level

Oliver Kessler, Rodney Bruce Hall, Cecelia Lynch and Nicholas Onuf (*editors*)
ON RULES, POLITICS AND KNOWLEDGE
Friedrich Kratochwil, International Relations and Domestic Affairs

Cornelia Navari (*editor*)
THEORISING INTERNATIONAL SOCIETY
English School Methods

Dirk Peters
CONSTRAINED BALANCING: THE EU'S SECURITY POLICY

Simon F. Reich
GLOBAL NORMS, AMERICAN SPONSORSHIP AND THE EMERGING PATTERNS OF WORLD POLITICS

Robbie Shilliam
GERMAN THOUGHT AND INTERNATIONAL RELATIONS
The Rise and Fall of a Liberal Project

Rens van Munster
SECURITIZING IMMIGRATION
The Politics of Risk in the EU

Palgrave Studies In International Relations Series
Series Standing Order ISBN 978–0230–20063–0

You can receive future titles in this series as they are published by placing a standing order. Please contact your bookseller or, in case of difficulty, write to us at the address below with your name and address, the title of the series and the ISBN quoted above.

Customer Services Department, Macmillan Distribution Ltd, Houndmills, Basingstoke, Hampshire RG21 6XS, England

---

On Rules, Politics and Knowledge

Friedrich Kratochwil, International Relations and Domestic Affairs

Edited by

Oliver Kessler
Associate Professor for Political Science, Bielefeld University

Rodney Bruce Hall
University Lecturer in International Political Economy, Department of International Development, University of Oxford, UK

Cecelia Lynch
Professor of Political Science and Director of the Center for Global Peace and Conflict Studies, University of California, Irvine, USA

Nicholas Onuf
Professor Emeritus, Department of Politics and International Relations, Florida International University, USA

palgrave
macmillan

First published 2010 by
PALGRAVE MACMILLAN

Palgrave Macmillan in the UK is an imprint of Macmillan Publishers Limited, registered in England, company number 785998, of Houndmills, Basingstoke, Hampshire RG21 6XS.

Palgrave Macmillan in the US is a division of St Martin's Press LLC, 175 Fifth Avenue, New York, NY 10010.

Palgrave Macmillan is the global academic imprint of the above companies and has companies and representatives throughout the world.

Palgrave® and Macmillan® are registered trademarks in the United States, the United Kingdom, Europe and other countries.

ISBN 978–0–230–24604–1 hardback

This book is printed on paper suitable for recycling and made from fully managed and sustained forest sources. Logging, pulping and manufacturing processes are expected to conform to the environmental regulations of the country of origin.

A catalogue record for this book is available from the British Library.

Library of Congress Cataloging-in-Publication Data

On rules, politics, and knowledge: Friedrich Kratochwil, international relations, and domestic affairs/edited by Oliver Kessler ... [et al.].
p. cm. — (Palgrave studies in international relations series)
Includes bibliographical references.
ISBN 978–0–230–24604–1
1. International relations—Philosophy. 2. International law—Philosophy. 3. Kratochwil, Friedrich V. I. Kessler, Oliver, 1973–
JZ1305.O57 2010
327.101—dc22

2010023838

10 9 8 7 6 5 4 3 2 1
19 18 17 16 15 14 13 12 11 10

Printed and bound in Great Britain by
CPI Antony Rowe, Chippenham and Eastbourne

For Fritz

Contents

Foreword

After several years on the faculty at Princeton I remember Fritz Kratochwil most vividly as the first truly intimidating graduate student I had encountered. The phenomenon of intimidation is subtle and elusive. It was particularly so in this instance as Fritz was invariably gracious and receptive to discussion. The intimidation came from his astounding breadth and depth of knowledge, and a super-sophisticated style of articulating his viewpoint as to make it rarely immediately comprehensible, yet always understandable and illuminating if the effort was made. When I finally managed to get beyond these barriers I experienced what is for every dedicated member of the academy a peak experience: The thrill of learning from someone nominally categorized as a student. Adopting a Kratochwilian outlook, the student/teacher language game disguised in our exchange something more fundamental, an existential role reversal. And so I can, with this major qualification, proudly, claim Fritz as my PhD student. It should be obvious that the reality of our pedagogic relationship was far more horizontal, that is, egalitarian, than vertical, that is, hierarchical, and to the extent vertical that it was I who occupied the subordinate status. Perhaps, more remarkably, in my latter 40 or so years of teaching, despite many talented and wonderful PhD students, I never again experienced quite the awe that Fritz's intellectual presence generated. Beyond this, it was not just a personal feeling of intimidation, but one shared with several colleagues, what might be best described as a rare instance of "institutional awe," not a common emotion at a place like Princeton.

And perhaps, as astonishing, Fritz's intellectual identity seemed firmly and fully established from the moment he undertook doctoral studies. Indeed it seemed so deeply inscribed in his intellectual personae that I wondered whether he was not so marked at birth. Even when most of his fellow graduate students were floundering about in search of an identity, Fritz was already a confirmed Humean, as distinct from being a Hobbesian, preoccupied with the actualities of order in world politics that at the time dominated the academic landscape. There was no doubt that Fritz was disenchanted with the several varieties of "realists" vying for adherents. He definitely went his own way, which struck me at the time as very much of his own making, neither realist, nor liberal, nor Marxist, nor utopian.

The Kratochwil methodological turn from my earliest contact with him was to examine how things work in world politics, and to acknowledge with unflinching clarity the complexities of social activity in every domain relevant for his concerns. Given this orientation, it is hardly surprising that Fritz rejected all efforts to organize knowledge about international relations by reference to either "scientific laws," deductively formulated on the basis of the logic of power, or "behavioral laws" statistically compiled by meticulous empirical observation. Immersed in the philosophical traditions of Europe, Fritz was deeply concerned with the philosophical grounding of inquiry, to an extent unusual for students, however talented, having a North American background. More specifically, he was intent on explicating to the extent possible how best to link an appropriate epistemology (what do we know, and how) with an ontology (what, if anything, is real, the nature of truth, reality) in ways that avoid distorting by various forms of reductionism the way things really are. In one respect, the totality of Fritz's entire corpus of scholarly endeavor consists of a series of discernments of the epistemological and ontological implications of an insistence on regarding the perceived substance of specific issues as an array of interpretive challenges.

What seems to most intrigue Kratochwil's incredibly energetic mind are the recurrent puzzles associated with the emergence of ever-evolving forms and shapes of order in a political setting that lacks strong governmental institutions. As has been observed by others, Kratochwil follows in this regard, the path earlier cleared by Hedley Bull and later developed by the English School constituted by his devotees, which seeks to depict the distinctive societal order that underpins international relations in its irreducibly pluralist character. As with Bull, Kratochwil examines the distinctive workings and contributions of law and diplomacy in such settings, taking note of the extent to which the political actors *constitute* the normative order through their *practices*. Both Bull and Kratochwil emphasize the crucial importance of history, giving interpretative specificity to the ways in which behavior is adjusted to the aspirations, perceptions, and shared expectations of those who make the important policy decisions that necessarily give shape to political reality. With such an emphasis there is a turn away from a preoccupation with *enforcement* of norms, and a repudiation of the possibility of finding a "solution" to the issue of effectiveness by an embrace of either a legalistic and formalistic jurisprudence in the manner of Kelsen that is essentially indifferent to the actualities of behavior in world politics or looks to geopolitics to provide the muscle that selectively implements the rules (e.g. as the US tries to do with respect to administering the nuclear nonproliferation regime) without deference to normative protocols and restraints. Bull, in particular, thought that a proper awareness of the societal features associated with an anarchical world order also signaled limits to the role of law, rejecting any effort to hold individually accountable those acting on behalf of sovereign states as was done at the Nuremberg trials after World War II. I am not sure whether Kratochwil would be as critical of such an experiment in the globalizing of legal accountability.

What is important for Kratochwil is the phenomena of world politics as it continuously unfolds, combining pattern based on shared expectations and a variety of assimilated and historically conditioned protocols of right conduct with contingency associated with the changing expectations created by a stream of decisions made within inherently distinctive contexts. He is very clear that there is nothing tangible out there beyond our interpretative discourses to facilitate the reaching of decisions, but only the vectors of expectation and sociability associated with how diplomacy has operated in the past as reconstructed in view of an emergent future. International law, international morality, diplomatic convention are all vast repositories of the interpreter's conscious and unconscious toolkit, which will be manifested via communication and conversation. In this respect there are notable affinities between Kratochwil and Jürgen Habermas as both of these thinkers recognize that we must continuously struggle to find the right approach, but can never enjoy the comfort of having such efforts underwritten with guarantees. In this spirit of postmodern epistemology, Kratochwil reminds us in many ways that grand narratives are not to be trusted or respected anymore than metaphysical pretensions about the nature of truth and reality. We will do better for ourselves and for the world if we abandon such illusionary quests and content ourselves with the more modest dynamics of particularity. In this sense, the old verities as expressed by truths and laws of history were expressions of insecurity and weakness, an unwillingness to live without a God. Kratochwil's worldview is not for children who cannot fall asleep without being told a fairy tale. It is more akin to the kind of absurdity of existence that so entranced such European thinkers as Nietzsche, Sartre, and Camus. We cannot know for sure, but we are condemned to keep trying.

Yet the challenge for Kratochwil is more formidable than becoming emancipated from centuries of illusion. It is also constructivist. Kratochwil also has affinities with John Dewey, and the American pragmatists, as his somewhat prosaic primary concern is to find useful knowledge that is relevant for problem solving. In this sense, although obliquely, there is implicit in Kratochwil's work an ethos of epistemological responsibility.

As far as I know, it is never spelled out, but it demands fidelity to particularity and change, as well as a practical emphasis on how to use our capacity for action and decision to enhance the life experience of all persons on the planet. Perhaps, I am guilty here of superimposing a humanistic protocol on Kratochwil's essentially amoral epistemological journey. But perhaps not. As it seems to me that implicit in the intersubjective sociability from which our constructions of reality derive is embedded ethical/humanistic protocol. When a Hitler, Stalin, or Idi Amin comes along, their widespread repudiation represents a community consensus resting on normative presuppositions about the outer limits of acceptable political behavior, presuppositions given direction by notions of the rule of law, by a certain minimum ethical universalism, and by invoking precedents relating to pariah status. Of course, cynics could point to the verdicts of history being opportunistic in character, with long-term reputations being constructed out of thin air. We tend to overlook the crimes of Winston Churchill against the colonized peoples of Ireland and Africa or of Harry Truman for deciding on the use of the atomic bomb against heavily populated Japanese cities because they led their countries to victory in a war that has been widely interpreted as "just" and "necessary" for the preservation of liberal democracy and humane values. If I understand Kratochwil correctly, his orientation can easily accommodate these apparent departures from legal and ethical assessment by taking note of the interpretative context. But what does he have to say if Germany and Japan had prevailed in World War II? Is there any criterion for judgment that transcends the historical narrative? What about the dispossession of indigenous peoples in the Western Hemisphere and elsewhere as an historical datum? These questions linger even for the most devoted admirer of Fritz's numerous accomplishments as heuristic interrogator.

What makes this volume in celebration of Kratochwil's achievement so special is the high degree to which their content is impossible to imagine without its engagement with the substance of his work. This is unlike most collections of this sort that exhibit a vague kind of appreciation of the individual being honored, but then the various chapters themselves are on disparate topics reflecting the distinctive concerns and outlook of each author, and without any significant connection to the honoree. Also, there is not much spillover of interest from one chapter to the next. In contrast, here as one reads through the text there exists both an organic and inspiration linkage to one or more of Fritz's preoccupations, as well as an implicit conversation among the chapter authors who in a variety of interactive ways address items on a shared epistemological agenda. It is a great tribute to Fritz's impact that he has not only inspired such a disparate group of theoretically inclined scholars but that his approach commends itself to very diverse applications and explorations. Fritz is never an easy read, and those who stay the course have generally found it valuable enough so that there own work bears the impact of the experience.

In the end I think the Kratochwil legacy, preliminarily foreshadowed by this volume, will be most associated with a normative turn toward constructivism in IR theorizing and with a late modern formulation of vintage American pragmatism. This strikes me as a happy marriage (or is it merely a civil union?) suitable for our historical situation. We are no longer tied to the persistence of the Westphalian template of sovereign states, which as Kratochwil explains, was never as clear and essentialist as such a shorthand suggested, nor should we waste our time and energy playing probabilistic word games based on measurement and observation that generate little useful knowledge about how to meet the formidable challenges of the twenty-first century lifeworld. What is more, this kind of normative constructivism encourages an illuminating reincorporation of the study of international law and of compliance with behavioral and diplomatic norms into the wider field of international relations.

Consistent with his epistemological integrity, Fritz neither offers us hope nor condemns us to despair, but seems to counsel struggle for as much clarity and understanding as can be obtained through the sharpening of our interpretative skills. We can never expect to get unconditional guidance as to optimal problem solving but must always remain ready to adapt and innovate in recognition of changes in context, and in this foundational sense must learn to live with radical uncertainty as a pervasive feature of the human condition. What may be most impressive about this Kratochwil legacy is its uncompromising honesty about the limits of our knowledge together with an unwavering seriousness about the quest for usable knowledge. And so at the end of the day, this quest is a refinement of the Enlightment ethos rather than a reaffirmation of Kierkegaard's insistence that "fear and trembling" is the last best hope of humanity.

Richard Falk

Acknowledgments

The editors organized a day-long symposium celebrating Fritz Kratochwil's life and work ("Fritzfest" to one and all) at Columbia University, in New York City, on February 14, 2009. We thank Robert Jervis for enabling Fritz's friends to meet with him on this joyous occasion. We asked participants to present short papers, written for the purpose and circulated in advance; we thank everyone who was able to join us for their presentations and ensuing discussion. We also thank Ingrid Gerstmann, of Columbia's Saltzman Institute of War and Peace Studies, for her help in making the day a complete success. Dan Deudney made useful suggestions in planning Fritzfest.

From the beginning the editors envisioned a book based on the Fritzfest papers. We are grateful to Stefano Guzzini for advice on the editorial process and Hannes Peltonen for editorial assistance. As one of the editors of the series in which this book appears, Audie Klotz expressed an early interest in the project and gave close attention to its execution. We thank Alexandra Webster, Liz Blackmore and Manavalan BhuvanaRaj at Palgrave Macmillan for their patience. We very much appreciate the cooperation of contributors in revising their chapters and readying them for publication. At Fritzfest, Chris Brown took the picture of Fritz which appears as the frontispiece, and Devora Yanow suggested a better title for the book than the editors then had in mind—better because it reaches beyond the field of International Relations, as does Fritz's work

Oliver Kessler, Rodney Bruce Hall, Cecelia Lynch
and Nicholas Onuf

List of Contributors

Mathias Albert is Professor of Political Science, Bielefeld University. His latest publications include *The European Union and Border Conflicts: The Power of Integration and Association* (ed. with Thomas Diez and Stephan Stetter, 2008), *Transnational Political Spaces* (ed. with Gesa Bluhm et al.), and *New Systems Theories of World Politics* (ed. with Lars-Erik Cederman and Alexander Wendt).

Chris Brown is Professor of International Relations, London School of Economics. He is the author of *Sovereignty, Rights and Justice: International Political Theory Today* (2002), *Practical Judgement in International Political Theory* (2010) and *Understanding International Relations* (4th edn, with Kirsten Ainley, 2010) and co-editor (with Terry Nardin and N. J. Rengger) of *International Relations in Political Thought: Texts From the Ancient Greeks to the First World War* (2002).

Mlada Bukovansky is Associate Professor of Government, Smith College. She is the author of *Legitimacy and Power Politics: The American and French Revolutions in International Political Culture* (2002). Her next book is titled *Vices and Virtues in Global Governance.*

James W. Davis is Professor for Political Science and Director of the Institute for Political Science, University of St. Gallen. He is the author of *Threats and Promises: The Pursuit of International Influence* (2000) and *Terms of Inquiry: On the Theory and Practice of Political Science* (2005).

Richard Falk is Albert G. Milbank Professor of International Law and Practice, *Emeritus*, Princeton University, and Visiting Professor, Global and International Studies Program, University of California, Santa Barbara. Among his many books are *The Declining World Order: America's Imperial Geopolitics* (2004), *The Costs of War: International Law, the UN, and World Order after Iraq* (2007) and *Achieving Human Rights* (2008).

Jörg Friedrichs is University Lecturer in Politics at the Department of International Development, Queen Elizabeth House, University of Oxford. He is the author of *European Approaches to International Relations Theory: A House with Many Mansions* (2004), *Fighting Terrorism and Drugs: Europe and International Police Cooperation* (2008), and, with Friedrich

Kratochwil, 'On Acting and Knowing: How Pragmatism Can Advance International Relations Research and Methodology', *International Organization* (2009).

Stefano Guzzini is Professor of Government, Uppsala University, and Senior Researcher, Danish Institute for International Studies. He is the editor of *Constructivism in International Relations: Wendt and his Critics* (with Anna Leander, 2006) and *Geopolitics Redux? 1989 and the Revival of Geopolitical Thought in Europe* (forthcoming), as well as the author of *Realism in International Relations and International Political Economy: The Continuing Story of a Death Foretold* (1998) and *Power Analysis and International Relations* (forthcoming).

Rodney Bruce Hall is University Lecturer in International Political Economy and a Fellow of St. Cross College, University of Oxford. His books include *National Collective Identity: Social Constructs and International Systems* (1999) and *Central Banking as Global Governance: Constructing Financial Credibility* (2008).

Oliver Kessler is Associate Professor for Political Science at Bielefeld University. He is the author of *Die Internationale Politische Ökonomie des Risikos: Am Beispiel der Asienkrise* (2008) and many journal articles. He is currently working on a book titled *Uncertainty, Politics, Risk.*

Rey Koslowski is Associate Professor of Political Science, Public Policy and Informatics, University at Albany (State University of New York). He is the author of *Migrants and Citizens: Demographic Change and the European State System* (2000), the editor of *International Migration and the Globalization of Domestic Politics* (2005) and the director of the 'Global Mobility Regimes' research project.

Yosef Lapid is Professor and Head, Department of Government, New Mexico State University. He has edited *The Return of Culture and Identity in IR Theory* (with Friedrich Kratochwil, 1996) and *Identities, Orders, Border: Rethinking IR Theory* (with Mathias Albert and David Jacobson, 2001).

Deborah Welch Larson is Professor of Political Science, University of California, Los Angeles. Author of *Origins of Containment: A Psychological Explanation* (1985) and *Anatomy of Mistrust: US-Soviet Relations During the Cold War* (1997), she is currently doing research on the use of intuition and analysis in American foreign policy decisions and on Russian and Chinese identities and their search for status.

Richard Ned Lebow is James O. Freedman Presidential Professor of Government, Dartmouth College, and Centennial Professor, London School of Economics. His recent books include *The Tragic Vision of Politics: Ethics, Interests and Orders* (2003), *A Cultural Theory of International Relations* (2008) and *Forbidden Fruit: Counterfactuals and International Relations* (2010).

Michael Loriaux is Professor of Political Science, Northwestern University. His latest book is *European Union and the Deconstruction of the Rhineland Frontier* (2008) and his current book project is titled *European Union and the Phenomenon of Power*.

Cecelia Lynch is Professor of Political Science and Director of the Center for Global Peace and Conflict Studies at the University of California, Irvine. Her books include *Beyond Appeasement: Interpreting Interwar Peace Movements in World Politics* (1999) and *Strategies for Research in Constructivist International Relations* (with Audie Klotz, 2007).

Nicholas Onuf is Professor *Emeritus* of Politics and International Relations, Florida International University. His most recent books are *Nations, Markets, and War: Modern History and the American Civil War* (with Peter Onuf, 2006) and *International Legal Theory: Essays and Engagements, 1966–2006* (2008).

Nicholas Rengger is Professor of Political Theory and International Relations, University of St. Andrews, and editor of the *Review of International Studies* (2006–10). He is the author of *International Relations, Political Theory and the Problem of Order: Beyond International Relations Theory?* (2000) and *Dealing in Darkness? Political Theory, International Relations and the Pursuit of the Idea* (forthcoming). He is currently preparing study of the Anti-Pelagian imagination in Political Theory and International Relations.

Jens Steffek is Professor of Transnational Governance, Technische Universität Darmstadt. He is the author of *Embedded Liberalism and Its Critics* (2006). He has edited *Civil Society Participation in European and Global Governance* (2008) with Claudia Kissling and Patrizia Nanz and *Legitimacy in an Age of Global Politics* (2007) with Achim Hurrelmann and Steffen Schneider.

Antje Wiener is Professor of Politics & Global Governance, University of Hamburg, and a founding editor of the journal *Global Constitutionalism* (to be published by Cambridge University Press). Her most recent publications include *The Invisible Constitution of Politics: Contested Norms and International Encounters* (2008), *European Integration Theory* (edited with Thomas Diez, 2nd edn, 2009), and *Contested Norms in International Relations*, special issue, *Journal of International Law and International Relations* (edited with Uwe Puetter, 2009).

Introduction

Oliver Kessler, Rodney Bruce Hall, Cecelia Lynch and Nicholas Onuf

As scholar and teacher, Friedrich Kratochwil has had an enormous impact on the field of International Relations (IR), first, with his celebrated book, *Rules, Norms, and Decisions: On the Conditions of Practical and Legal Reasoning in International Relations and Domestic Affairs* (1989a; see the complete list of Kratochwil's published work for references); second, with a steady stream of incisive essays on important topics; and third, through colleagues, teachers and students who have been awed by his learning and critical powers, and inspired by his focus, discipline and integrity. Over the course of Kratochwil's academic career in the US (1975–95) and Europe (1995 to the present), changes in international relations have troubled many scholars in the field. As the field itself has globalized, young scholars everywhere have engaged in what will certainly come to be seen as a grand project to open the field to diverse perspectives and give it better moorings. In this grand project, they have turned to Kratochwil, perhaps more than to anyone else, for guidance and inspiration.

Origins of this book

As Richard Falk notes in the Foreword, Kratochwil is himself skeptical of grand projects and easy generalizations. Indeed, he has made a career of documenting complexity and ambiguity, while making unexpected connections and following suggestive lines of inquiry. This book reflects such a disposition. Following on a symposium, held at Columbia University in February 2009, to honor Fritz (as he is known to all) and his work, this book extols his contributions by showing their impact on contributors, all of them established scholars in their own right. Most contributors expressly acknowledge their debts to Kratochwil. All of them reveal their debts in the questions they ask, the arguments they pursue, and the conceptual difficulties they identify.

The title, *On Rules, Politics, and Knowledge: Friedrich Kratochwil, International Relations, and Domestic Affairs*, plays on Kratochwil's 1989 work (which he dedicated to his friends) and points to this book's relevance for political scientists and other theoretically inclined students of social relations. It also points to the three large questions that he has posed for himself and the rest of us over the course of his career:

(1) How do rules and norms work, how is their "force" related to the reasons we offer for our conduct, what results from rules in force?
(2) How do speech, practice and practical reason make social reality so pervasively political?
(3) How can anyone know anything certain about the world?

How Kratochwil's intellectual path intersects with chapter topics

Before we describe the book's organization and preview its chapters, we tie our organizing questions into a discussion of Kratochwil's intellectual development, the genealogy of the field of International Relations (IR), and the Euro-American political context. Kratochwil's sense of complexity and indeterminacy in social life, his subtle inquiries into the way rules work, his emphasis on argument and interpretation, his skepticism about grandiose claims of any kind undoubtedly have multiple sources. He was born in 1944 in Lundenburg (Břeclav), a small city in what is today the Czech Republic, into a world of dislocation and privation. He often projects a world weariness typically associated with Central European intellectuals, but as so many of us know, it is one that is always mediated by an ironic, altogether infectious sense of humor and belied by his capacity for warm and enduring friendship.

When Kratochwil was a child, Plato kept him company while tuberculosis kept him indoors. He earned an *Abitur* in 1963 from the Maxmiliansgymnasium in Munich, where he mastered Greek and Latin, and then studied Classics, Philosophy and Political Science at Ludwig-Maxmilians-Universität in Munich. His knowledge of and fascination with the ancients has continued throughout his career, inspiring parts of his 1989 book as well as several contributions to this volume, notably that of Michael Loriaux.

When he was ready to begin a thesis under Eric Voegelin's supervision, Voegelin ordered him to subject a single passage from a secondary classical text to exhaustive examination. Instead Kratochwil took his leave. It is inconceivable, as Richard Falk points out, that Kratochwil could ever have been anyone's disciple; he apparently played the role of "gate-breaker" instead of a "gate-keeper" (as Mathias Albert and Yosef Lapid call it in Chapter 17) from early on. Voegelin's unceasing, notoriously idiosyncratic preoccupation with order and transcendence in Western political thought was at odds with Kratochwil's already-developing sense of complexity and contingency in social relations.

In 1967 Kratochwil enrolled as Fulbright Fellow and doctoral student in Georgetown University's Department of Government. One of the editors of this book (N. O.) was teaching international law and organization at Georgetown when Kratochwil arrived, the two sharing interests in the theoretical intersection of international politics, law and organization, not to mention, as political scientists, a keen sense of disciplinary irrelevance. With political realism's rise in the preceding two decades, departments of political science had systematically eliminated international law and organization courses from their curricula. While Kratochwil and Onuf each pursued paths connecting international relations, social theory, and international law, they have always articulated differing conceptions of rules and practice, a difference that is not often understood and that Onuf touches on in his contribution to this volume.

After two years, Kratochwil left Georgetown for Princeton University. There he pursued doctoral studies with Richard Falk. As a political activist in fraught times and a principal in the World Order Models Project, Falk was then a theoretically inclined international legal scholar with strong normative commitments. Kratochwil would later say (1978: 2) that his own work was "normatively informed" without being "reformist" in the way Falk's work was then (and continues to be). Yet Falk's influence on Kratochwil is obvious in those early years, not least in their shared focus on the problem of order—international order, legal order, world order. The contemporary contours of this problem Chris Brown and Antje Wiener address in their contributions to this volume.

For Kratochwil, the problem of order called for "rigorous international relations analysis" (1978: 2) to avoid falling in the binary of apology or utopia, as most international lawyers do (Koskenniemi 1989). At Princeton, Kratochwil studied international relations with Robert Gilpin (then revitalizing realism), Leon Gordenker (well known for his work on the United Nations), Jeffrey Hart, Ronald Rogowski and Oran Young (all of them adept with formal theory, including game theory, bargaining theory and public goods theory). Reading deeply in sociology (in particular, the work of G. H. Mead, Erving Goffman, Herbert Blumer and Peter Berger and Thomas Luckmann), he concluded that an appropriately rigorous analysis should show how symbolic interaction is related to strategic interaction, exemplified in Thomas Schelling's immensely influential analysis of mixed games of conflict and cooperation. Were this not challenging enough, showing how interaction of any sort relates to the problem of order would seem to provide an even greater challenge in the form of the level of analysis problem (Singer 1961). As Kratochwil pointed out (1978: 15–17, 1981a: 15–19), Hobbes offered an attractive solution to the problem of order—a solution grounding liberal thought and embraced by political realists—by supposing that rational agents decide among themselves to exchange their freedom for collective security. Nevertheless what the Hobbesian solution to the problem of order cannot account for is the effect of ongoing interactions of self-interested agents on the production and distribution of order in any such system of relations.

Kratochwil has always acknowledged the relevance of agency and intentionality in human affairs and, with reservations (e.g. 1982), granted that agents are rational and self-interested in their conduct. He has always had an interest in systems and their properties (1972a, 1986b, Kessler and Kratochwil 2010). He understood that the level of analysis problem in IR mapped onto the agent-structure problem long before the latter became fashionable in social theory and catalyzed the constructivist moment in IR. He recognized that the rational choice perspective could get us to interaction but not all the way "up" to the system, and that the system perspective could help us find patterned limits on interaction but could not get us all the way "down" to agents' choices. That is why open-minded rational choice scholars have found his work to be so fruitful (see Deborah Larson's contribution to this volume), and why other contributors (Stefano Guzzini, Nicholas Rengger) note that rational actor perspectives ground an important component of his point of departure in understanding agency.

Hobbes alone, however, could not resolve the problems of either order or agency. Early on, Kratochwil found in Hume what he needed to develop a perspective on international order (1978: Chapter 1) and power politics (1981a). The Humean perspective shows how rational agents can and frequently do interact in such a way as to settle on conventions, or mutually acceptable outcomes, that "structure expectations" about future outcomes as interaction continues (1981a: 16, drawing from Hume's *Treatise on Human Nature*, III, II, ii). Consequently, the Humean perspective, which "is concerned with the importance of perception and the embodiment of experience in rules," "provides valuable insights, since its problem-set concerning the conditions of order results in a wider research program" than "Hobbes's analysis of order" does (1981a: 19).

Rules in this perspective are not just objects with fixed causal properties. As Hume taught, "constant conjunctions" do not permit definite conclusions about causal relations. Least of all can we establish cause when these objects, as prescriptive statements, tell agents what they *should* do. Much of Kratochwil's early work is dedicated to clarifying "the 'grammar' of rules" (1978: title, Chapter 3—quite possibly the first time any scholar in IR turned to Wittgenstein's late work for guidance), as well as their exercise in speech acts (see Rodney Bruce Hall's development of Kratochwil's treatment of promises and trust in this volume). To this end, he addressed a question long vexing international lawyers—"Is international law 'proper law?'" (1983: title)—and sought to explicate "the force of prescriptions" (1984b, title) in terms that political scientists could appreciate. Whatever the audience, he insisted that rules can never be dissociated from their use: choosing to follow rules (or not) changes them in content and force, and the agents making these choices are themselves changed; the world changes. Many of his students, including Cecelia Lynch and Mlada Bukovansky, employed this essential insight in their own work, although in this volume they also push Kratochwil, in different ways, to be more open to ethical intentionality, motivation and contingency on the part of agents.

As must any perspective oriented to interaction, the Humean perspective starts and ends with process. Agency and order are passing points of reference calling for attention on normative grounds. Other processes figure in this equation. Agents invoke, and respond to, "rule-like" phenomena, such as doctrines, historical analogies, metaphors (here preceding Lakoff and Johnson 1980, which made talk of metaphors fashionable in IR) and myths (1978: 4). All such phenomena suggest a return to Aristotle's concern with practical reason and rhetoric (1978: 64–6). In these early years, Kratochwil had already begun to enrich the Humean perspective—itself a model of simplicity and explanatory economy—with the alterations and extensions that make his later work at once so compelling and so demanding.

Kratochwil moved to Columbia University in New York in 1981, an appointment that provided him with stimulating colleagues, such as Robert Jervis, Deborah Larson, John Ruggie and Jack Snyder, as well as doctoral students, including one of the editors of this book (C. L.). The 1980s had seen the first signs of a postmodern movement in international law (Critical Legal Studies) and in IR, where Richard Ashley was its most visible proponent. Kratochwil had already pointed out (1984a) that Ashley's epistemological position mirrored weaknesses in the standard positivist epistemology he attacked with such polemical vigor. Nevertheless Kratochwil and Ruggie (1986a) sensitized a large number of scholars to "the need for an epistemology that does justice to the *practical* aspects of human interaction," just as Ashley insisted (Kratochwil 1984a: 306, emphasis in original). Their much discussed essay, "International Organization: A State of the Art or an Art of the State" (1986a), pointed up the difference between positivist and interpretive epistemologies while explicating the many deficiencies in the study of international regimes. Thanks to Kratochwil and Ruggie more than anyone else, terms such as *intersubjectivity, interpretation* and *meaning* entered the vocabulary of many liberal internationalists, preparing them for constructivism as an alternative to both positivist and postmodern weaknesses.

Kratochwil left Columbia for the University of Pennsylvania's political science department in 1988. Among his colleagues in the department were Daniel Deudney and John Ikenberry, among his doctoral students one of the editors of this book (R. B. H.). Soon after Kratochwil arrived in Philadelphia, *Rules, Norms, and Decisions* appeared. Unsurprisingly, Kratochwil drew extensively on earlier work (1989a: x). Humean conventionalism remains as a scaffolding (Chapter 4), now complemented by a substantial, highly original discussion of legal reasoning—"the path of legal arguments" (Chapter 8, title)—in order to clarify the relevance of rhetoric and practical reason to social life. Additional discussion reached from Pufendorf's conception of natural law to Myres McDougal's configurative jurisprudence in order to establish "a much closer conception between reason and choice than the original Humean perspective implied" (1989a: 131). While Kratochwil used Habermas to good effect in *Rules, Norms, and Decisions*, subsequent work in the German Idealist tradition of IR seems to have forgotten Kratochwil's grounding of communication in intersubjective rules that govern persuasion and argumentation, as Jens Steffek points out in his contribution to this volume. Such a grounding cannot guarantee that norms will diffuse through social interaction.

By now fully recognized for his scholarly accomplishments, Kratochwil emerged as a leading voice for the constructivist movement in IR just as the Cold War ended and the problem of "understanding change in international politics" (1994a: title) prompted many scholars—especially those just entering the field—to favor constructivism over realism (see Rey Koslowski's contribution to this volume for an inquiry into whether recent and impending technological change will have an even greater impact on world politics). In 1995 Kratochwil returned to Munich as professor in the Lehrstuhl für International Politik der Ludwig-Maxmilians-Universität. There he taught courses in IR theory, epistemological problems and international governance to advanced students, one of whom (O. K.) is an editor of this volume.

Kratochwil's move coincided with a dramatic expansion of IR outside of the US. In Europe and the rest of the world, scholars have increasingly come to view IR as a discipline drawing on social theory and a variety of postpositivist philosophical resources. Meanwhile IR remained a field of positivist political science for a majority of scholars in the US. Many political scientists credit rational choice theory with a scope and explanatory power that suffices for the study of international relations. Their dogmatic self-assurance offends many Europeans, including Kratochwil (2001b: 13: "when you are equipped with a hammer, the whole world looks like a nail"), and inspires charges of Foucauldian disciplining and Gramscian hegemony (see also Richard Ned Lebow's contribution to this volume). Perhaps Kratochwil's departure from American shores marked not just the growing distance across the Atlantic Ocean but also the possibility that few scholars can stand on both continents and be heard above the fray. By advocating "constructivism as an approach to *interdisciplinary* study" (2001b, title, emphasis added), Kratochwil has signaled his skepticism about disciplinary claims, whether on behalf of political science or IR, *and* his faith in "a research program . . . which outflanks the Humean fork rather than denying its existence" (2001b: 34). Constructivism is not just an enriched version of the Humean perspective. Philosophically speaking, it is, or should be, a post-Humean perspective, but not necessarily an anti-Humean one. Moreover, as James Davis points out in his contribution to this volume, interdisciplinary interpretive strategies for investigating norms can still move from case-specific to general claims, providing a type of "explanatory power" concerning how rules and norms can be appraised across a range of circumstances.

From 2000 to 2005 Kratochwil edited the *European Journal of International Relations* at a time when that journal soared in prestige by showcasing theoretical diversity and innovation. In 2003 he assumed the Chair in International Politics at the European University Institute, where he continues to influence numerous students and colleagues. He also continues to write about epistemological issues (2007a, 2007b, 2007f). "Without a clearer understanding of why and how we can circumvent fruitless meta-theoretical traps when going about our research, the old spectres are likely to haunt us sooner or later" (2007a: 2). In this work, Kant's first *Critique* affords him a "foil" and pragmatism offers "a good bet" in avoiding traps.

Kratochwil's growing enthusiasm for pragmatism—a philosophical stance that arose in the US as a response to the rigid certainties of Continental philosophy and remains an antidote to the aridity of Anglo-American analytical philosophy—suggests that he has found a way to outflank Hume and his fork while maintaining a good measure of Humean skepticism. "A pragmatic approach reminds us that 'truth' and meaning are . . . not problems of simple reference but problems of relation with other concepts in a semantic field and of linking the problem under investigation to actions and practices which are the stuff of 'politics'" (2008d: 25; see also Jörg Friedrichs' discussion of "substance" in this volume). In short, pragmatism presumes that all reason is practical reason and implies that subjectivity is always social. For any scholar whose concern is international relations, understood as an especially complex, porous and consequential set of social practices, a pragmatic approach is sufficiently open and flexible to get on with the task at hand.

Organizing this book

Chapter topics (*topoi*, a favorite term of Kratochwil's and a key to his Aristotelian predilections) generally blend more than one of the three central questions animating his work, just as Kratochwil himself has consistently refused to draw boundaries around any of them. Indeed, quite a number of chapters show that, for Kratochwil at least, treating speech, practice and practical reason (question 2) and the quest for certain knowledge (question 3) as distinct themes misses the point: given his carefully worked out position on what "knowing" is all about, these questions are inseparable. Also inseparable are questions of "theory" from those of "practice"—or, more aptly, "politics." All of the chapters draw attention to the importance that Kratochwil attaches to politics. Politics in its many, often ambiguous manifestations constitutes not the just the overarching theme in Kratochwil's life work, but the very reason—the sustaining rationale—for his tireless labors. In Kratochwil's case, politics is most directly manifested when people come together to deal with the problem of order and change in their affairs.

The book's organization reflects the substantive concerns we, in the process of editing, increasingly realized are complementary parts of Kratochwil's work as a whole. We identify these concerns in the three parts of the book as speech, reason, and knowledge; rules, norms, and ethics; and persuasion, order, and change. Additionally, we suggest that each of these concerns has fostered a characteristic response from contributors. Those whose primary concern is *speech, reason,* and *knowledge* tend to be thinking along lines closely related to Kratochwil's way of thinking. Contributors whose primary concern is the way Kratochwil writes about *rules, norms,* and *ethics* identify their disagreements with him on various points. Finally those for whom *persuasion, order,* and *change* are primary concerns build on Kratochwil's work but also bring other influences to bear on those concerns. We believe this three-part scheme gives readers an overview of Kratochwil's enduring concerns, clarifies contributors' reasons for taking up these concerns up in their chapters and will persuade at least some readers that these concerns effectively constitute an agenda for contemporary scholarship in IR and cognate fields of study.

Part I suggests that Kratochwil's concern with speech, reason and knowledge informs what has now become a collective undertaking. All seven chapters affirm, as Kratochwil has expressly, Aristotle's dictum that speaking (and understanding what people mean by what they say) makes us social beings unlike any other living beings. Without language we would have habits but not norms, futures but no sense of the future, interaction but not practice, cognition but not reason, passion but not compassion. To think the way Kratochwil does is to acknowledge that understanding is an exceedingly complex activity of the mind—of individual minds. Yet what we (think we) understand also constitutes an enormously complex social whole, which we rather loosely call knowledge. Over the years, Kratochwil has increasingly devoted himself to the problem of understanding these complexities and found himself engaged in debates no less fierce for their philosophical sophistication. On the evidence of these several chapters, Kratochwil settled on the guiding premises for his work on speech, reason and knowledge early in his career, thereby anticipating and even precipitating later debates.

Chapter 1, Stefano Guzzini's chapter, more than any other in the book, reviews the way Kratochwil has dealt with all three themes and shows how they are inextricably linked in his work. What links them is Kratochwil's conviction that politics broadly conceived suffuses not just social relations of every sort but any effort to understand the human condition. In short, political practice and practical reasoning are inseparable. Guzzini illustrates this central concern of Kratochwil's with close readings of Kratochwil's early work on post-World War II politics and his recent work on what science can, and cannot, tell us. The early work on politics acknowledges both the impediments to common action and the possibilities inherent in ongoing conversation (themes also explored by Jens Steffek, Antje Wiener and Chris Brown in their chapters). Kratochwil's work on science is critical of the foundationalist assumptions most scientists never trouble to examine and is most clearly revealed in their views on causality. For Kratochwil, the conundrum of causality is not just a recurring theme but a point of access to the epistemic, and latently political, priorities of knowledge-seeking communities. Guzzini concludes that Kratochwil's lifelong preoccupation with the political—and his hostility to "political engineering"—stems from a sense of responsibility and reveals a humanist ethical sensibility.

In Chapter 2, James Davis demonstrates how Kratochwil's concern for the particular can help lead us to general knowledge that nomothetic reasoning, whether inductive or deductive, can never provide. In this he follows Hume and Popper: a finite number of observations does not warrant general knowledge claims with any certainty. Davis argues that, from Kratochwil's perspective, we must "move away from a single logic of inference toward a diversity of explanatory logics" that also capture the generative (or constitutive) capacity of norms, institutions and contingent social and historical context. The ordering functions of norms, their counterfactual validity and generative or constitutive capacities necessarily defeat attempts to construct or "test" general propositions through the kind of procedures, so prevalent in quantitative, statistical work in IR and political science, that Lakatos would have called "naive falsification." While the conventional wisdom "equates scientific knowledge with nomothetic knowledge," general knowledge would be better built upon the application of interpretive methods, such as discourse analysis, that are proper to the study of unobservable mental states. As the social universe is an intersubjective realm, actors give "reasons" for compliance or noncompliance with social norms, and Kratochwil has resoundingly demonstrated why reasons are not causes. Collective beliefs and motives must be studied to provide a coherent account of such reasoning, and "reconstructive and interpretive methods" are wanted for this purpose. Davis concludes by suggesting that scholars using these methods are yet to develop adequate "communal standards" for the evaluation of their accounts.

Deborah Welch Larson, in Chapter 3, draws upon Kratochwil's game theoretic development of the social concepts of "trust," "obligation" and particularly "reciprocity," as well as his critiques of the limitations of game theoretic investigation, to advance her own work on the effects of the notion of reciprocity between states in the context of diplomacy.

She draws crucially on the constructivist emphasis on the importance of the social meanings of social concepts, such as reciprocity, that mediate interaction and exchange. She thereby illustrates that the meaning of reciprocity depends on disparate cultural norms and perceptions in the absence of a common "standard of value" in exchange, such as money provides in economic exchange. Varying notions of reciprocity among states have different implications for the notion of equity in exchange. The relative status relationship of the donor and recipient of an exchange is also crucial. Guided by varying cultural norms, the status relation of the parties helps each party to determine "what counts as reciprocation." The familiar constructivist linguistic formula (*x* counts as *y* in context *C*) clearly indicates that the "constitutive rules" of reciprocation in a given exchange are thereby constructed. Larson explores the prescriptive and normative force of norms of reciprocity on those who have internalized them and the relationship between trust and reciprocity. To do so, she draws on the resources of social psychology and illustrates her conclusions with brief vignettes of diplomatic exchange during the Cold War.

Chapter 4 finds Rodney Bruce Hall developing the utility of Kratochwil's work on language and the social institution of "promising" for international political economy, and in particular for the analysis of money and the social relations of credit and debt. Hall's chapter is largely focused, however, on the normative effect of the illocutionary force of speech acts, thus extending Kratochwil's work on speech act theory. Promises are social institutions constituted by performative speech acts, and they are rule-governed activities performed through speech, with important perlocutionary effects on the recipients of the promise. Not the least of these is the social "obligation" to give credence to the promiser, even if she or he doubts the sincerity of the promise. The illocutionary force of the promise similarly imposes an obligation on the promiser to discharge the obligations she or he incurs in promising to redeem the claim of social and moral agency she or he has made in the utterance. Hall emphasizes the importance of social context in a discussion of social valid "reasons" one might give in abrogating a promise. Following Kratochwil, he argues that it is the social salience of performative speech that lends prescriptive force to norms, and the counterfactual validity of the latter leads us into adjudicative procedures for addressing the question of valid reasons for abrogating a promise. Trust and reputation emerge as social institutions addressing the Hobbesian problem of order. Hall concludes by showing how money depends on the social institution of promising.

Chapter 5, by Jörg Friedrichs, returns our attention to the question of knowledge and the process of reasoning through which we might fruitfully seek it. In elaborating on Kratochwil's frequent calls for a return to substantive analysis of politics, Friedrichs provides an excellent case that IR has been largely devoid of substance from its inception. Friedrichs argues that, as a consequence, the analysis of substantive political questions in IR has been supplanted by three "diversionary moves": scholarship is theoretically and methodologically driven; problems of interest to like-minded communities of scholars are devoid of social relevance; the investigation of social life as a realm of intersubjective meaning is sacrificed on the altar of "scientific objectivity." Friedrichs claims that the political realm is the realm of "obligatory voluntarism" and it is the duty of political scientists to vouchsafe the centrality of this realm in their study. Otherwise they are subject to colonization by other disciplines, such as economics, with other substantive concerns at their centers. Whether we accept "obligatory voluntarism" as the common ground for political inquiry, it is difficult to quarrel with some of Friedrichs' conclusions, namely, that IR has been impoverished by a lack of substance, its substantive delimitation remains "completely up for grabs," and it has suffered all three diversionary moves. In short, "the problem is structural."

In Chapter 6, Oliver Kessler examines the "practice turn" in IR theory. Even though Kratochwil is himself a principal in the practice turn, Kessler draws on Kratochwil's writings on the utility of practical reason as a "healthy corrective" to deficiencies, and even banalities and redundancies, dominating recent discussion of the turn. Kessler criticizes the turn's advocates for a binary conception of knowledge ("knowing that versus knowing how") and their willingness to dispense with intersubjectivity in the analysis of social life. He argues that the question of the relationship between language and the physical world is thereby dismissed, as is the important matter of our knowledge of our "non-knowledge." The latter's existence is beyond doubt, for we actually have coherent histories of its evolution and transformation. Kratochwil's notion of practice, he argues, avoids these deficiencies by providing "an account of how language and reality relate to each other." The centrality of intersubjectivity in social life is thereby not lost in Kratochwil's analytics of practical reason. Nor is the focus on the constitutive rules of social life that are generated in language. Communication is a prerequisite for human sociality, let alone politics.

The last chapter in Part I, by Richard Ned Lebow, picks up the on the claim that science produces certain knowledge. He illustrates the problem with this claim by recapitulating Kratochwil's ironic tale of Galileo's bad experience with good science (Kratochwil 2007e: 29–31). With Kratochwil, Lebow argues that today as much as in Galileo's day the rules governing science—rules telling a community of practitioners what commitments and presumptions constitute "good practice" for their community—are constantly evolving with developments in practice. Good science depends on debate and dissent. Yet political science as "science" has developed a ruled set of practices foreclosing debate and prescribing methods in ignorance (or defiance) of their demonstrable inadequacies. These tendencies are especially evident in the US, as Lebow makes evident from his own experience. The tyranny of "science" also fosters a climate of disregard for an ethics of responsibility, as manifest in the polemical uses of bad science.

Part II, "Arguing with Kratochwil: Rules, Norms and Ethics," features five contributions that raise questions about the way Kratochwil handles normative phenomena. These chapters raise questions about important thematic threads in his body of work without suggesting any danger of the whole cloth unravelling. On the contrary, these chapters suggest that, by inspiring argument, Kratochwil's life work has become a collective enterprise. These issues, regarding practice and especially ethics, take up issues that Kratochwil himself has not chosen to work through in any detail. Yet they all reflect a scholarly ethos or sensibility that Kratochwil has done so much to create, thus building on his pioneering inquiries and enlarging the collective enterprise in which he has figured so prominently.

If contributors to Part II raise questions about topics that have drawn Kratochwil's attention, then it should be said straightaway that his decision in *Rules, Norms, and Decisions* to consider *rules* and *norms* separately and Nicholas Onuf's decision in *World of Our Making* (1989) to call all normative phenomena *rules* do not set the terms of argument—any argument—whether between Kratochwil and Onuf, or Kratochwil and any other scholar contributing to this volume. It should also be said that Kratochwil's decision to highlight normativity by using the term *norm* did far more to shape constructivism and reconfigure IR than any other conceptual *démarche*. By accommodating the sociological distinction between informal norms and formal rules, Kratochwil's choice licensed scholars in the field to explore empirically a large segment of world affairs simply ignored by liberal institutionalists in law and IR. None of this is to say that Kratochwil has answered all possible questions about normative phenomena in practice—or, more specifically, in relation to agents, power, compliance and legitimacy. When such questions are raised, scholars have vast resources from many fields to draw on, often leading to subtle discussions of other major contributors to social, political and ethical thought.

Onuf's contribution to the book (Chapter 8) leads off Part II. He begins his discussion of rules in relation to practice by making clear how his scholarly practices differ from Kratochwil's. While Kratochwil resists efforts to fix meanings and form models, Onuf teases two models of practice out of a literature that goes back to Aristotle. One emphasizes informal rules, or norms, and tacit knowledge (as does Kratochwil; also see Kessler's contribution to this volume), and the other emphasizes powers, or human faculties, turned into skills and put to use. Onuf then asks, as a philosophical problem, whether the "shared ideational stuff" of the first model can have the causal properties the second model stipulates; he dispatches the problem by insisting that we have to conceive of practice as a process rather than a condition. For Kratochwil, there is no problem; to his way of thinking, process always trumps content. Onuf suggests instead that his conception of practice as a process points to agency and choice as conditions, captured in models, decisively affecting this process.

Michael Loriaux's contribution (Chapter 9) distinguishes between "behavioral" and "historicist" contructivism and identifies Kratochwil as an antifoundationalist historicist who refuses to treat norms, or indeed the power behind norms, the way behavioralists do—as "things." Yet this same stance leaves the concept of power "largely untouched." Loriaux suggests that the best way to conceptualize power is not as a "transhistorical essence" but as having an essence nevertheless, which a phenomenological reading of Thucydides' *History* would locate by coming at the concept from a variety of directions and angles. Throughout this process, the reader suspends judgment, abjures definitions and defers any conclusion. On Loriaux's subtle reading of Thucydides, power is seen as movement, captured by verbs and only those nouns that have aesthetic implications. While it is by no means clear that Kratochwil would ever think of power, as a "choreographic performance" or an "artful indulgence," it is clear that he has no great affinity for extended textual readings or indeed the pursuit of essences, however conducted.

In Chapter 10, Cecelia Lynch also directs our attention to the way Kratochwil conceptualizes norms, but she is primarily concerned with the moral sensibility that actors bring to their situations and how this affects the particularly *constitutive* nature of norms and power, including the way Loriaux conceptualizes it. While Kratochwil would never deny that agents have goals and that they make and use norms to achieve these goals, he has been reluctant to use the language of intentionality very much at all in his work. As a result, he has had little to say about the limits and possibilities of agency except insofar as these conditions are expressed in immediately relevant norms or in philosophical constructs. In other words, Kratochwil has tended to overlook the moral and ideological backdrop affecting agents and their choices, except perhaps (as in his recent work) when he makes a point of identifying agents, such as lawyers, by their professional vocations. Lynch sets about to remedy this omission by tracing the moral sensibilities and ideological proclivities of nonstate actors with humanitarian concerns. That she does so for nineteenth and early twentieth century activists and then again for today's "NGO world" tells us a great deal about shifting moral and ideological concerns that most discussions of norms simply overlook. Yet she also makes it clear that the relation between moral action and more immediate normative phenomena—what we have come to call global governance—brings IR theory back into play. In this case, Foucault's work on governmentality provides a useful corrective—although not all the answers—to the liberal assumptions informing the global governance perspective.

In Chapter 11, Mlada Bukovansky addresses yet another feature of normative phenomena to which Kratochwil has drawn attention. Norms call for conduct that complies with their requirements. Agents do not always comply and, as Kratochwil has emphasized, noncompliance is not always self-serving. While he asks what reasons agents offer for their conduct, Bukovansky asks what standards observers use to judge noncompliance. She offers three possibilities—legalistic, cosmopolitan and identity standards—which she finds deficient because scholars invoking them, including Kratochwil, think they have evaded the problem of moral incommensurability by ignoring purpose in practice. Bukovansky uses Alasdair MacIntyre's virtue ethics to assess the moral incoherence of modern liberalism, and thus of legalistic, cosmopolitan and identity standards, and to articulate a "practical teleological standard" as an alternative. To ground her position in practical politics, she uses Indian noncompliance with nuclear nonproliferation regime as a running illustration of her argument.

Nicholas Rengger brings us back in Chapter 12 to Kratochwil's groundbreaking work on the distinctive properties of normative phenomena. On Rengger's account, *Rules, Norms, and Decisions* develops three claims: people make choices, they use norms when making choices and their choices depend not just on what norms say but on reasoning and interpretation. These claims situate Kratochwil in a philosophical setting framed by Anglophone analytic philosophy and radically reframed by Ludwig Wittgenstein. The latter dispelled the claim that "all forms of meaningful human action are rule-governed"—a claim that Kratochwil might well say Rengger is just a little cavalier in assigning to him so starkly. For Rengger, Michael Oakeshott (whose distinction between practical and purposive association Bukovansky discusses in her chapter) provides an antidote by claiming that people actively pursue moral ideals as well as follow immediately available moral rules. Rengger then turns to legal rules, which raise additional issues about rule following. What makes such rules legitimate? If their legitimacy depends of the authority of those who issue them, then the kind of moral considerations that Kratochwil underplays call for attention.

The chapters making up Part III, "Building on Kratochwil: Persuasion, Order, Change," take up Kratochwil's political concerns in ways that enrich and extend what he has had to say, but they also require us to situate Kratochwil in contexts where his distinctive voice blends in with many others, including those of the chapters' authors. In *Rules, Norms, and Decisions*, Kratochwil offered a landmark discussion of persuasive speech—speech that uses not just content but its own properties to change people's minds. He did so as postmodern humanists rediscovered rhetoric, Michel Foucault drew attention to discourse and Jürgen Habermas worked out the relation between speech and contestation; anyone following up on Kratochwil's arguments about argument will also take other sources of inspiration into account. From the beginning, Kratochwil has been deeply concerned with the properties of order in a world of states. In this respect he joins many other scholars who bring many converging perspectives to bear on the problem of order and, especially after 1989, the dynamics of unforeseen change. Discussions of order and change, such as we find in this part of the book, will also blend many voices that resonate with Kratochwil's.

In Chapter 13, Jens Steffek takes a critical look—one that is informed by Kratochwil's perspective on knowledge claims—at the work of empirically oriented constructivists, mostly German, who draw on Habermas to distinguish between communicative and strategic action, and therefore between rational and norm-guided choice. According to Steffek, these mainstream constructivists, as he calls them, argue that identifiable norms can induce actors to choose courses of action with demonstrable causal effects. He then dismantles three "idealizations" that these constructivists have adapted from Habermas: first, actors can switch between communicative and strategic interaction at will; second, persuasion causes norms to spread among actors engaged in communication;

third, when actors agree on their choices, it is because their normatively conditioned motives also coincide. Steffek concludes that turning to Habermas for an idealized conception of how norms work may broaden rational choice theory, but it unduly narrows our view of what goes on in the world. Celebrating the reciprocal relation of norms and persuasion may lead us to ignore the actual content of norms, the persuasive advantages of superior resources and strong convictions, or the strategic element in normativized social interaction. The point is not to forget Habermas but to start with Kratochwil in any discussion of norms.

Antje Weiner is also interested in how norms work. In Chapter 14, she starts not with the norms as such but the social group that makes and uses them. The more diverse the group, the less likely it is that norms will be implemented without conflict or the need for time-consuming Habemasian deliberation. In today's world, the increasing volume of international encounters—occasions in which individuals in different governments are obliged to deal with each other—increases the diversity of backgrounds and thus the likelihood of conflict over the application and interpretation of international legal norms. For an empirical assessment, Wiener disaggregates norms into three types (fundamental norms, organizing principles and standardized procedures) and the "normative baggage" we all carry around with us into three evaluative components (we use formal validity, social environment and individual cultural associations for reference points). The formulation of fundamental norms and agreement on formal validity point to a global constitutional framework, but this development does not lessen the need for social recognition and the relevance of individual experience in reducing normative conflict. Contrary to liberal expectations, recent studies show that social environment and individual cultural associations resist change even with repeated encounters; when transnational arenas do form around specialized norm clusters, they resist widening. Diversity is here to stay, and so is normative conflict as a constitutive feature of international order. Wiener sees this as all the more reason to pursue a research program that asks Kratochwil's question: How do norms work?

Chris Brown puts international order front and center in Chapter 15, just as Kratochwil did in his earliest work (1978). And just as Kratochwil emphasized the political conditions that shaped institutional arrangements in the post-World War II international order, so does Brown in sketching the emerging international order of the twenty-first century. Brown assumes that US military primacy will go unchallenged, but that the rising political importance of China, India and even Brazil, and the continuing importance of Russia, Japan and Western Europe will reconstitute some semblance of the balance of power. He then asks what effect this development will have on the normative foundations of the emerging international order. After showing that realists would call this question a nonquestion, he turns to liberal pluralists who believe that newcomers are socialized to support the new order's normative foundations for practical reasons. Like Wiener, Brown is dubious about socialization. Sovereignty and nationhood constitute a powerful normative complex which, with stress and turmoil in the world economy, foster the kind of relations in the new order that realists see as dominating the old order.

Chapters 14 and 15 pick up on Kratochwil's enduring concern for the normative foundations of international order and raise serious questions about degree and direction of change in such an order. In Chapter 16, Rey Koslowski reminds readers that, as he and Kratochwil argued (1994a), the end of the Cold War was a fundamental change in the old order, thanks to the way superpower practices changed the old order's basic rules. Since many observers ask how fundamental this change may have been, Koslowski broadens the question to include not just the September 11 attacks and the so-called war on terror but more generally the "revolution in military affairs," the information revolution and economic globalization. His constructivist review of technology emphasizes the interplay of perceived political imperatives, practical knowledge and sheer contingency, and points to the inevitability of unanticipated consequences, some of which have revolutionary implications. To reinforce the point that "the social construction of technology" is unpredictably dynamic and potentially transformative, Koslowski discusses nanotechnology ("the study, design, creation, synthesis, manipulation and application of functional materials, devices and systems through control of matter at the scale of one billionth of a meter") and more especially the design of self-replicating nano-devices. Such a development could open the door to "knowledge-enabled mass destruction" in the not-so-distant future—a transformative event that science fiction aficionados might anticipate but no one would wish on the world.

Chapter 17 ends the book by drawing together many of the concerns identified in earlier chapters with Kratochwil and his work. In this chapter, Mathias Albert and Yosef Lapid point out that Kratochwil has had an overriding concern—they all call it a "sustained fascination"—with the "inter" in International Relations. This concern reflects Kratochwil's conviction that a better understanding of the "inter" means a richer understanding of the political in any ongoing boundary-crossing set of practices. Much of Kratochwil's work is devoted to historicizing the "inter" as an ever-shifting set of political practices. Yet Albert and Lapid also emphasize Kratochwil's interest in space as well as time, and in particular in the "space" simultaneously setting territorially defined units apart and holding them together. As they say, politics is always particular and contingency always at work. It follows that, for Kratochwil, to ask whether the world is fundamentally changing is a nonsensical question. Change is all there is. That change comes at various speeds and happens in complex semantic fields means that scholars can never keep up with the elusive "inter," the quest for precise definitions is futile, disciplines are subject to constant renovation, and "cracks in the foundations" demand the kind of attention that Kratochwil has always granted them.

The book's three parts cover a great deal of ground, yet the chapters keep coming back to the same constellation of concerns that have animated Kratochwil's work over four decades. Taken together, the contributions have much to say about the ways in which knowledge, normative phenomena and politics are linked to each other and expressed in practice. They also show that, for their authors as much as for Kratochwil, there is nothing neat, deeply ordered or easily explained about a world that we, as social beings, have made for ourselves. Our politics, the ways we see and talk about the world—all our practices—consist of innumerable, intricately related elements that are themselves substantially indeterminate.

We think we know quite a bit about the world, but we cannot agree on what we know or even on what counts as knowledge. We respond to uncertainty with unearned conviction. We argue, endlessly and, one might even say, compulsively. Whatever we say is subject to multiple interpretations. We pick and choose among possible interpretations of what others say to suit ourselves. We give reasons for what we do; we tell others what we think they should do; we formulate guidelines that others often follow for their own reasons; we force people to do our bidding. The cluttered contingency of such a world masquerades as order, nourishes liberal hopes for improvement and induces positivist fantasies of control. There can be no greater tribute to Kratochwil than a book that reflects his skeptical sense of the world we have wrought, for better or for worse.

Part I

Thinking with Kratochwil: Speech, Reason and Knowledge

1

De gustibus (valoribus) est *disputandum*: Friedrich Kratochwil *contra* Realpolitik without Politics, Theory without Reflexivity, Science without Judgment

Stefano Guzzini

> Actors reproduce and change by their practice the normative structures by which they are able to act, share meanings, communicate intentions, criticize claims, and justify choices. Thus, one of the most importance sources of change . . . is the *practice of the actors* themselves.
>
> Friedrich Kratochwil (1989a: 61)

Intrigued by politics and its nature, and the demanding challenges of post-1945 international politics, Friedrich Kratochwil turned early to philosophy. Yet his engagement with philosophy ended in disappointment because of philosophy's tendency to look for an Archimedian neutral point, a quest ultimately vain and logically self-contradictory to him. Turning eagerly to Political Science, he was quickly disheartened by its denial of the normative nature of things political and the similarly vain quest for some scientific, objective point from which to inform what cannot be but a reduction of politics to political engineering. For him, what is missing from both is an understanding of actually existing human practices. These practices are the cornerstone for his understanding of world politics, International Relations (IR) theory and the social sciences.

Hence, this chapter claims that, for all Kratochwil's prose, often abstract and theoretical, the practice of politics in its widest sense is at the core of his scholarly work. It is not because of his view of science, his meta-theory, so to speak, that he developed a certain vision of IR theory and political practice. If anything, it is the other way round—not top-down, but bottom-up. Because of his interest in and understanding of political practice, and the need to achieve coherence of thought between political, theoretical and scholarly action, Kratochwil takes his understanding of practice to develop his positions in IR theory and the philosophy of the social sciences.

As such, Kratochwil stands out as one of the very few thinkers in IR whose work tries to understand the implications of thinking and making assumptions about ontology, social theory and science in tandem. And by making the analysis of human (or social) practices the pivotal point for understanding politics, theory and science, his work testifies to the need to relate these levels to one another in order to achieve a more coherent and richer understanding of "politics." This chapter deals with the relationship between the nature of political practices, their theorization and the philosophy of science in Kratochwil's work, in that logic and order.

International politics: Symbolic communication and the problem of order

What is politics? Very early Kratochwil was disenchanted with the way leading political theorists understand and conceptualize politics. He quickly moved beyond the futile attempt to define what politics really "is," since almost anything can, dependent on the situation, be considered "political." Hence, the conceptual analysis has to start the other way round and approach "the political" from the way it is expressed in practice.[1] Having thus ruled out the typical positivist conceptual analysis,[2] Kratochwil's quest can draw little succor from prevailing political theories, which reduce politics to some version of utilitarianism or an authoritative allocation of (scarce) values. Whereas the first tradition errs by reducing politics to maximizing behavior, the second suffers from the assumption of a scarcity of values which is not necessarily appropriate. Moreover, the "authoritative allocation of values," already an ideal type for political systems in their domestic environment, ends up excluding the international altogether from the understanding of politics.

Instead, Kratochwil has taken the international realm as his frame of reference, in which the "political" is most visible. For the study of politics is, as he will later write, an "attempt at illuminating the problem of order" (Kratochwil 2000b: 53). And the specifically political emerges when action takes place in a situation in which no reference to a *common* value system can be established.[3] This is reminiscent of

Max Weber's eternal clash of Gods (Weber 1988: 605). Let me use it to introduce the fundamental role of practice in Kratochwil's thought.

Weber and Kratochwil share a sense for, and fear of, the totality of conflicts since the turn of the twentieth century. But Kratochwil is not essentializing "value systems." In fact, for him, or so I would argue, it is as thinkable that no common reference system evolves between actors, despite allegedly common values,[4] as it is that apparently diverse actors can find a common language. Indeed, this is the guiding idea for his analysis of the Cold War. Moreover, he avoids essentializing the role of value systems because, according to his understanding of politics, they are not to be defined in theory but by the way they work themselves out in human practices. However abstract the level of his analyses, it is the way practices unfold to which his analyses almost inevitably return. Hence, to approach the abstractly put question of politics (how to deal with collective choice with no common value system), an abstract answer would not do—be it the liberal philosopher's quest for some general neutral position from which agreement would rationally follow,[5] or the alleged need of some Schmittian decisionism to impose a solution, a position to which Weber was tempted at times.[6] For Kratochwil, both ways eschew the "political," either by reducing it to an eschatology of reason or to the determinacy of a reified enmity.

Instead, Kratochwil has no closed and fixed history in mind; all is played out in practice. For him, social practices are fundamentally characterized by the human capacity of creating symbols:

> Symbols create meaning by structuring our universe, building up images far removed from the immediacy of sense perceptions. Because symbolic structures cannot be unequivocally tested against reality—reality itself being a creation of the symbolizing activity that endows perceptions with certain meanings—deception but also persuasion are possible.[7]

Hence, exactly because of this creativity and open development of symbolic systems, the encounter of different value systems neither guarantees nor excludes the possibility of a mediation between them. Even if such systems might seem logically unbridgeable, political practice can create bridges. The "world political process is an ongoing 'conversation,'"[8] and diplomacy is about establishing and using a common language (Kratochwil 1971: 122), or, perhaps more precisely, commonly accepted translations.

Kratochwil developed this role of practices in his understanding of the world politics of the time, that is, against the background of the Cold War and its diplomacy. Here, he used Kissinger's study of international order and gave it an intersubjective—symbolic and linguistic—twist. Kissinger (1957: 1–3) had argued that a stable order required shared rules of the game ("legitimacy" is Kissinger's term), as well as an equilibrium, "both moral and physical" (Kissinger 1957: 12). These two aspects can be teased out to mean far more than the usual textbook realism which is often applied to Kissinger. First, shared rules of the game imply that interstate relations are analogous to social relations. There is a kind of international society, not only when these rules of the game are tacitly shared but also when they are debated. From this it follows, secondly, that most of realist politics, such as the balance of power, appear not (just) as a cause of order, but as its effect, deriving from "a framework of shared conventions with normative status,"[9] thus becoming an institution of the society of states.[10] In their symbolic interaction, practitioners generate conventions and symbols, which, if successfully shared, stabilize meanings and hence enable decisions. Before diplomats can count, they must first agree on what counts. International politics has a social ontology.

Secondly, Kissinger's peculiar definition of equilibrium adds a historical and cultural dimension to this order. He repeatedly castigates a mechanical understanding of equilibrium, that is, one which is purely based on force and not a "reconciliation of historical aspirations" (Kissinger 1957: 147), as noted by Kratochwil (1978: 201). In a passage mined by more than one constructivist, Kissinger (1957: 146) wrote that

> an exact balance is . . . chimerical, above all, because while powers may appear to outsiders as factors in a security arrangement, they appear domestically as expressions of historical existence. No power will submit to a settlement, however well-balanced and however "secure", which seems totally to deny its vision of itself.

While Kissinger did not pursue this matter of identity ("vision of itself"), in Kratochwil's hands it adds a further layer to the social ontology of international order. Such identities reveal themselves and evolve through historical analogies and collective memory,[11] through "myths" and "metaphors," which actors mobilize when trying to make sense of a situation. Together with legal rules (later: norms) and actual doctrines, these are part of the "rule-like inference-guidance devices" which form the background knowledge of international order.[12] Diplomacy is called upon in this ongoing conversation of international politics to find shared translations, eventually establishing a common system of references while accommodating diverse historical identities. It is helped by the fact that political practice comes with an added, and crucial, time factor through which principled disagreements *can* be bridged in the course of iterated "conversations." And it is to this political practice to which Kratochwil returns when showing how shared background knowledge developed through the Cold War between the two superpowers.

Kratochwil's early insistence on the role of practice and on the evolution of common references during the Cold War prepared him well for coming to terms with the end of the Cold War. Not that he would have "predicted" it.[13] However, by having focused on the origins of norms and their possible changes in the practices of actors, and expecting such a change only when a more shared reference system had come into place, he saw that 1989 could not just stand for some shift in the balance of power or sanction-induced change of the Soviet incentive structure. Just as with the change that took place after the Cuban Missile Crisis,

> a redefinition of the game on the basis of mutual role-taking was sought. . . . Putting oneself into the shoes of the other leads to sharing of aspirations, fears, and weaknesses that not only reassures the opponent but makes a rediscovery of a common sociality possible.[14]

Contrary to disenchanted lawyers like Morgenthau,[15] Kratochwil was not impressed by the allegedly ultimate role of sanctions—and the analogy with criminal law—for the understanding of how law (and rules) impinges on actions (Kratochwil 1978: 46; see also Kratochwil 1998a: 200–1). A purely capability-based understanding of how the Cold War came to an end therefore appears profoundly misleading (Kratochwil and Koslowski 1994a). Indeed, although such capability-based analysis ostensibly alludes to the realist tradition, Kratochwil's earlier work on containment had shown him that the more diplomatic wing of realism, as represented by George F. Kennan, offered a far better starting point for understanding actual politics (Kratochwil 1993a).

Kratochwil's earlier studies also provide an important basis for understanding the problem of how the international order would play out after 1989. There is the basic problem that the diversity of historical aspirations and understandings held by the multiple actors who take part in ordering the world inhibit the development of a common language. But that diversity itself is not static. While there is no guarantee that common translations will be found (and even disagreements can be on common terms), solutions are not foregone *by definition* because of alleged civilizational or other differences. Only political practice will tell. Diplomats are surely well advised not to rule out the possibility of unbridgeable value systems or lifeworlds, not least to refrain from conceiving or imposing one's own system as the universal one, thus preventing the curse of self-righteousness and hubris. But diplomats are equally well advised to assume they have common background knowledge (which can anyway not be ruled out), since such an assumption feeds into the ongoing conversation which can recursively produce it as a social fact. Human practices are shot through with institutional facts; they are performative.

Theory: Interpretative practice and reflexivity

This central role of human practices has clear implications for the kind of social theory that is possible and the role of the theorist in it. Social theory cannot predominantly be of the positivist kind in which efficient causality applies. Theorizing must start from the social ontology of human practices, which feature the role of language and interpretation, background knowledge and symbolic communication, open systems of meaning and an open history—one that is nonteleological and noncyclical. Theory must be reflexive. Let me take up here the issue of causality in relation to systemic and historical openness.

Kratochwil repeatedly condemns any attempt to turn ideational phenomena (such as ideas, norms, values and regimes) into antecedents which "cause" behavior. This misconstrues the intersubjective nature of these phenomena and wrongly fits them into an objectivist explanation where they are assumed to exist independently of an actor's interpretations: a classical mismatch between ontology and epistemology.[16] Such efforts also misunderstand the nature of the antecedent in the explanation of human behavior, which is the actor's motives, not an external cause. And so the motive, that is, the antecedent, is not independent of its effect. In fact, "the causal arrows run from our (or the agent's) understanding to the world and not from 'the world' to our understanding or theory" (Kratochwil 2006b: 14). Hence social causality, even when it is an insufficient but nonredundant part of an unnecessary but sufficient condition, is profoundly different from natural (efficient) causality.[17]

But the problems of causality in the social world go even further. Social reality is influenced by human understanding. Institutional facts, such as conventions, are actually dependent on it. Hence, a crucial part of any social theory must be the understanding of the *recursiveness* between understanding and reality, whether for the macro level of institutional facts or for the actor's identity, which is profoundly shaped by what others make of it.[18] This focus on the evolution of background knowledge (and culture) and identity formation is necessary for all social theory, IR theory included (Kratochwil and Lapid 1996a). Moreover the content and coherence of background knowledge has to be "discovered and understood, not assumed and inflicted" (Hopf, Kratochwil and Lebow 2001: 12887). Nor can recursiveness be understood in terms of causes; rather, it is about co-constitutive relations. Here, the "why" question, already redefined above in terms of meaningful action, is replaced by the "how," "how possible" and even "what" questions.

This understanding of social reality affects science at yet another level. There is no reason to see the social field of scientific observers as being qualitatively different from the social fields of other social groups. Rather than conceiving of scientific observation as taking place at a meta-level or Archimedian point from which to look down on the social world, science is just another social field which (horizontally) interacts with the social reality it interprets. As a result, truly constructivist theorizing must include this *reflexivity*—the relationship between observation, social reality and actors' understandings—in the effort.

When applied to the study of politics, Kratochwil's solution is to invoke practical reasoning (and the logic of practices) as the common element in all social spheres in which the political can be analyzed. Not just language in general but also law is to be understood in pragmatic, not semantic terms, just as with politics and science. Hence, Kratochwil's practice of thinking through assumptions about ontology, social theory, science and politics in tandem is not a question of choice but an implication of and resource for his way of thinking.

This has a series of corollaries. One is that all these social practices are open. Whereas semantic, deductive or teleological logic asks for closure already at the level of our theories, a pragmatic approach sees closure occurring only in the actual application (Kratochwil 2005a: 117), or, put differently, in practical, not pure reason. Reason is what reason(ing) does. For this very openness, the attempt to reach universal theories of action may be appealing but is eventually futile, if not counterproductive: it is the "*fata morgana* of a transhistorically valid theory" (Kratochwil 1998a: 195, n. 9). Instead, Kratochwil reserves a special place for conceptual history as a way of revealing the collective memory of international politics and its evolution: "precisely because social reality is not simply 'out there' but is made by the actors, the concepts we use are part of a vocabulary that is deeply imbricated with our political projects" (Kratochwil 2006b: 11). Last but not least, reflexivity also has implications for the theorist because it cuts short the debate about whether or not the language of science should be closer to the language of practice from which it has become increasingly divorced, or vice versa. Scientists, just like political practitioners, need to be multilingual and translate between languages. Only this provides the necessary hermeneutic bridge, allowing understanding for the scientist and reflective distance for the politician.

Science and judgment

The fundamental role of language and human practices define Kratochwil's approach to science in what is a nonfoundationalist or conventionalist position, one which has been regularly challenged for its alleged relativism. For Kratochwil, antifoundationalism is the idea that our knowledge claims cannot be ultimately justified by reason itself, or by recourse to method, ontology, or even the world (Kratochwil 2007e: 28). This does not mean that reality does not exist. It means only that the fact of its existence has few implications for our understanding of what it is.

The reason for this stance lies with the idea that language is not representational but constitutive: our knowledge of the world is not a passive registration, impossible outside of language; it is an active conceptualization. And this, in turn, makes our observations theory- and concept-dependent: all scientific laws contain theoretical terms (Kratochwil 1984a: 314). Consequently when we conduct research by asking the social world a question, the answer cannot be provided independently of the system of meaning (language in a wider sense) in which we have asked the question. There is no direct access to the world. Therefore truth cannot be a property of the world, and we cannot test the validity of our claims against reality. "Things or entities cannot be true, only assertion about them can!" (Kratochwil 2007e: 45). This involves doing away with a classical correspondence theory of truth, not to mention the infamous but fashionable instrumentalism attributed to Friedman (1953), which claims that the plausibility of theoretical assumptions does not matter as long as the explanations have an empirical fit. Instead, we can only "test" against other theories, which we can use to uncover blind spots, or provide a different perspective (Kratochwil 2008b: 82).

At the same time, it is not the case that "anything goes."[19] Scientists have to be analyzed as a group of practitioners. We need "an epistemology that does justice to the *practical* aspects of human interaction" (Kratochwil 1984a: 310, his emphasis). Science is a practice and, as such, organized according to its own conventions—conventions that indicate which kinds of theories might be more appropriate in particular contexts. Kratochwil uses the analogy of a game of scrabble to show the path dependence and yet open evolution of this practice (Kratochwil 2007e: 49–50). For here the progress in our understanding is not so much as an accumulation of more and more facts but a newly acquired capacity to "formulate new questions that *could not even be asked previously*" (Kratochwil 2007a: 12, his emphasis).

Therefore, Kratochwil's use of Kuhn relates not so much to the possible incommensurability of paradigms but to the behavior of its practitioners and hence to the context-dependent criteria for the appropriate judgment of validity (Kratochwil 1984a: 314). Indeed, like Kuhn himself (1970a: 180), Kratochwil does not see incommensurability as an insurmountable barrier to debate or proofs, since, as scientific practice shows, translation between paradigms or theories is possible (Kratochwil 2007e: 52, n. 12). But then, he needs to qualify what exactly goes on in such deliberations, and how best to think of the discourse of scientific proofs. And here, Kratochwil uses the Kantian metaphor of a court in which the rules for appropriate proofs provide the basis for judgment. A court's judgments establish what is right, not true. Just as legal practice shows, such judgments can be determinate, but they need not be unique, in that cases can be judged differently (although not arbitrarily so) (Kratochwil 2007a: 12).

And so Kratochwil proposes a (Pascalian) bet. Just as with political practice, where actual interactions show a propensity to uncover and establish common background knowledge which informs individual acts, scientific practice can achieve something similar. In other words, it would be premature and imprudent to give in to "Cartesian anxiety" (Bernstein 1983), which is, in any event, a positivist blackmail: something is either true according to positivist standards or it must be denying the existence of any truth whatsoever. Rather, scientists do make scientific judgments to the best of their knowledge by applying the appropriate rules, and indeed should be doing so. Whether or not this brings us closer to "truth" in any positivist sense is perhaps less important than its capacity to achieve increasingly more appropriate judgments for understanding and dealing with the world.

Hence, science is what scientists do. But this opens a possible breach. If science is convention all the way down, then in principle anything still goes, even if in practice scholarly communities have come to agree on conventions which rule this out. Inversely, why does scientific practice come up with conventions which impose limiting conditions on scientific debate and empower reasoned argument? Is there not a reality constraint, which, however indirectly, is responsible for the development of such conventions?

Scientific realists have asked these questions, among them Colin Wight most forcefully in a debate with Kratochwil. But, as I see it, the difference between these two positions is actually not that great. First, both Kratochwil and Wight agree that there is an indirect contact with reality, both social and material, which influences the scientific process. Neither of them sees the material as ultimately foundational for social explanations. Nor can Wight say precisely how much the material matters, if at all, and in what way (Wight 2007b: 302). This means that one needs to have a better sense of how this "indirect contact" is to be understood.

My guess is that Luhmann's solution could be agreeable to both sides: scientific systems build up expectations which the environment answers (Luhmann 1990). This means that the questions scientists ask, as much as the decoding of the response, are driven by the system or scientific discourse—and not by the environment. Yet the environment does influence the system's reproduction by answering to the expectations built up by the system. In that regard, constructivists can rightly claim that science is theory-dependent observation and interpretation, truth not being a property of reality. Yet the existing feedback from reality would be validating Wight's critical realism. This view also implies that the important word for Kratochwil in the phrase, "theories are not tested against reality, but against other theories" is not "reality," the ontological vacuity feared by Wight, but "tested." And here their epistemologies meet: there *is* contact with the world, but that contact is insufficient to provide a final "test," as Wight also confirms, since every test is an interpretation in the light of competing interpretations.

Second, social facts have often a material substratum. Again, this is something on which both Kratochwil and Wight seem to agree, although perhaps they weigh the consequences differently. For Kratochwil, since this "rump materialism" is most of the time of little interest to the social scientist, it can be dispensed with (Kratochwil 2007b: 74). Wight might leave a greater role to a (usually biological) rump materialism.[20] Indeed, the role of the material may need to be established case by case, suggesting that its actual significance is an open question. Here again, I think both would agree.

Third, Wight charges that a constructivist epistemology, in which the rules of the scientific community ultimately define the truth value of an explanation, will lead to relativism. In the face of several such scientific communities, and with no cross-community meta-language or criteria (and no ultimate reality check), either the more powerful community prevails, or we are left without possible judgment, hence relativism (Wight 2007a: 49). But this is hardly self-evident. Oddly enough, it is not entirely clear whether Wight's own solution is any different from Kratochwil's. Since the world is not the ultimate arbiter for either, and since both agree on the interpretivist turn, Wight's endorsement of Habermas' recent statement on the matter (Habermas 2004) could well be acceptable to both. Since we have all experienced the resistance of the world to some of our *actions* which were based on our interpretations of it, there is a "pragmatic presupposition" of a language-independent world out there, although its meaning is not presumed to be language-independent. Hence, for Wight (2007a: 47), "although the linguistically constituted intersubjective world has an epistemic priority, the language-independent reality that resists our activity has ontological priority." Yet we still do not know what that resistance exactly entails. Reality cannot speak for itself; there is contact with reality but no correspondence to truth. So the solution of a "pragmatic presupposition" of an ontology seems not too far from the Pascalian bet we started with, all the more since Kratochwil sees a social ontology working in all practices, scientific ones included. Indeed, he openly endorses Habermas's pragmatic argument.

Conclusion: A humanist ethics

In our meta-theoretical discussions, critical realists tend to reprimand constructivists for putting the epistemological cart before the ontological horse (Patomäki and Wight 2000). It is, so the story goes, this obsession with our understanding of knowledge which leaves constructivists agnostic about the world out there, and this agnosticism cannot be sustained because ontological assumptions inevitably slip in. Kratochwil may then not be a constructivist, since this is surely the opposite of his approach. His very starting point is a social ontology. And it is because of this social ontology that he argues for a certain understanding of international politics, IR theory and the philosophy of science which is usually dubbed "constructivist."

Kratochwil's social ontology is based on human practice. His analyses almost inevitably return to the way practices unfold, at whatever level. Human practices are fundamentally characterized by the human capacity to create symbols (Kratochwil 1978: 20) and to engage in meaningful communication. Moreover, "man is not determined by nature but transcends nature by transforming it" (Kratochwil 1981b: 120). It is an ontology borne out in diplomatic *and* scientific practice.

But underlying this view is an ethical commitment which Kratochwil has not really thematized. Kratochwil often refers to Popper—not only to tease those who quote him without having really read him. But besides some meta-theoretical sympathies with the late Popper, Kratochwil shares Popper's commitment to the idea of debate and communication, of critique and openness. A liberal antitotalitarian ideal meets a post-structural sensitivity in a suspicion against all meta-narratives or grand historical designs. His plea that we look at practices is also a plea that we keep them open, lest an all-encompassing ideology, grand theory or grand method takes over. Kratochwil is a theoretical scholar who spends his time opposing the grand-theoretical scheme as much for its general impossibility (Behnke 2001) as for its normative undesirability. He resists both the teleological visions which quickly box new data into preexisting schemes, whether functionalist, evolutionist or other, and the rationalist simplifications which reduce human practices to causal action. Both are but reductionisms that fail to further the understanding of actors' understandings or their background knowledge, thereby killing any curiosity in the specifically human—and in the human other.

It is the defense of this ultimate curiosity about the diversity of the human, of the human encounter in practice, which seems to drive Kratochwil's project. Here, *de gustibus* est *disputandum*, not necessarily to agree, but at least in the understanding that the terms of disagreement can be found. And this asks for a classical mind, able to translate, to be multilingual, in time and culture. It is a hermeneutic worldview for both scientific observation and diplomatic practice. It is a defense of politics against the social engineer (although in ways different from classical realists) and the technocratic, anti-humanist vision of the world, as well as the misconception of responsibility such a vision fosters.

For it is nonsense to assert a priori that disputes between value systems are meaningless. For the translating and hermeneutic actor they are not only possible; they are necessary for the practical establishment of a common horizon.

> What is needed is a different approach that investigates more closely the process by which people can adjust their differences without resorting immediately to violence. I maintain that the theory of communicative action is helpful in this respect. Within a normatively secured framework of communication, actors can air grievances and debate value choices, even if such debates are no longer limited to instrumental questions alone.
>
> (Kratochwil 1989a: 16)

But, of course, this process provides no guarantee. And still, Kratochwil places his bet on it. In call for personal responsibility, there is some resemblance to Camus' understanding of the absurd. For Camus (1942), the absurd does not lie in the fact that life is ultimately meaningless. Instead, it stems from the ongoing attempt to uphold simultaneously the human aspirations for harmony and meaning, and the understanding that it will never be achieved. Camus asks of himself not to betray this tension of the absurd, not to start repudiating any side of it. It would be cowardly and wrongheaded to deny humanity its aspirations for harmony, as cynics do, or believe in the possible realization of harmony through transcendence by Reason or God or any other leap of faith. Neither reductionism is admissible if we take our humanity and our historical responsibility seriously. Just like Sisyphus, we roll that stone up the hill, knowing it will never stay on top, but roll down again. But we do this of our own will, almost as the last credible sign of human dignity. Pretending to be a happy Sisyphus despite the absurd, trying again and again, may be the best bet we have—and, for Kratochwil, making good on this bet is the scholar's vocation (Kratochwil 1995c).

Notes

For comments, I wish to thank the participants at the *Fritzfest*, February 14, 2009, at Columbia University, as well as Andreas Behnke, Felix Berenskötter, Barry Buzan, Piki Ish-Shalom and Colin Wight. My gratitude goes to Fritz.

1. For these ideas, see Kratochwil (1971: 114). More generally, for a discussion of the pragmatic, and not semantic, understanding of language and concepts, see Kratochwil (1989a: 28ff.).
2. For an example of such an analysis, see Oppenheim (1981).
3. Kratochwil (1971: 121), taking this approach from Bertrand de Jouvenel.
4. The point was explicitly made by Raymond Aron (1962: 111).
5. It is in this sense that Kratochwil invites philosophers to "forget Kant." See Kratochwil (1998b).
6. See the discussion in Walker (1988–9).

7. Kratochwil (1978: 20). Note that it is the social and interpretivist ontology which drives a certain understanding of science here, not the opposite. For more on this, see below.
8. Kratochwil (1978: 39). See also the stress on communication (p. 22).
9. Kratochwil (1983b: 347). See in particular Claude (1962, 1989) for the classical treatment of the paradox that realists need a balance of power to establish an order, which, in turn, is necessary for the balance of power to function.
10. The classic account of the institutions of international society in the English School is Bull (1977). Bull (1980) also notes the similarities in his book review of Frederick [*sic*!] Kratochwil (1978).
11. For "the link between historical reconstruction and identity," see Kratochwil (1978: 61).
12. This is the basic theme of Kratochwil (1978), quoting p. 4.
13. See Kratochwil (1989b) for his discussion of how to understand Gorbachev's initiatives, which was surely not written with the expectation that things would change so quickly.
14. Kratochwil (1989a: 50). For the role of "alter-casting" in Wendt's account of change, see Wendt (1999: 329).
15. Morgenthau (1933, 1935). The same critique could apply to Luhmann (1975), whom Kratochwil often refers to.
16. For the locus classicus of this argument, see Kratochwil and Ruggie (1986a).
17. Kratochwil (1984a: 316–17). See also Kratochwil (2008b: 94–7). This, however, does allow for the treatment of reasons as causes in the manner of many scientific realists. For a treatment in many ways congenial to Kratochwil, but by a critical realist, see Patomäki (1996).
18. Kratochwil's standard references here are to speech act theory. For the interaction effect on the personal (identity) level, see Hacking (1999).
19. One should perhaps add that these words, taken from Feyerabend, are frequently used out of context. Feyerabend was rather more a disciple of Popper than sometimes acknowledged. Concerned with the way methodological strictures could preempt the critical and open spirit necessary for scientific debate, Feyerabend preferred to allow some "going."
20. Wight also mentions Marxist materialist concerns that would be excluded by fiat by Kratochwil, or so he claims. But these are social, not natural, facts, and hence their being considered "material" by Marxists should not exclude them from Kratochwil's scheme.

2

From Logic to Logics: The Relationship of Particular Cases to General Patterns in Social Life

James W. Davis

> *Um zu begreifen, dass der Himmel überall blau ist, braucht man nicht um die Welt zu reisen.*[1]
>
> Johan Wolfgang von Goethe

> *Seltsamer Zufall, dass alle die Menschen, deren Schädel man geöffnet hat, ein Gehirn hatten.*[2]
>
> Ludwig Wittgenstein

With roots in a widespread revulsion to the catastrophe of the First World War, the contemporary discipline of international relations (IR) from the very beginning sought to uncover general relationships, or indeed causal laws, governing political relations that transcend the borders of territorially defined states. Ideally, such causal regularities would display a high degree of contextual independence. *Ceteris paribus* they would exhibit transhistoric validity and as such would appear unlikely ever to be transcended. Knowledge of the set of valid general laws, it was hoped, would help political actors at least to avoid the worst mistakes of the past (Morgenthau 1966a).

The intellectual history of the discipline is in large part the story of debates among its practitioners over precisely how to reach the common objective—the discovery of *general* knowledge. For early giants of the field such as Hans Morgenthau, the answer lay in part in intuiting constant features of human nature through an examination of recurrent historical patterns. But the persuasiveness of arguments that appealed to imputed and unobservable constants of human nature was short-lived. On the one hand, the range of outcomes of interest to scholars of international relations seems too broad to be attributable to a constant of human nature. Variations in outcomes suggest variations in causes, or variables that indeed *vary*. At least for an explanation of the diversity in the proximate features of international life, constants would seem to drop out. Or to put it another way, if conflict and war are to be ascribed to an innate *animus dominandi*, how do we account for periods of cooperation or indeed peace? On the other hand, proponents of the "scientific approach" to the study of social phenomena rejected outright explanations that relied on intuiting the putative effects of unobservable and immeasurable antecedents such as human nature or individual motives (Kaplan 1966: 1–20).

Having prevailed in the ensuing debate with adherents to the "traditional approach," the proponents of social science were, however, themselves uncertain with respect to the best route to the attainment of general knowledge. Skeptical of the ultimate status of unobservables, behaviorists focused their efforts on discovering relationships between precisely measurable variables in an effort to explain observable behavior. The most productive scholars in this genre produced large empirical data sets and through the application of newly developed tools borrowed from statistics, hoped to derive the sorts of general laws to which the scientific approach was committed (Singer 1969: 62–86). But the essentially inductivist foundations of the behavioral approach produced heated debates within the scientific school and led to rather odd alignments among scholars who shared little more than their methodological commitments.[3] By the 1970s the behavioral revolution had largely given way to deductive approaches to explanation and theory development. Although much more willing to appeal to unobservable entities for the explanation of political outcomes, deductively oriented scholars continued the behaviorists' emphasis on the importance of precision and measurement in an effort to establish general, cause and effect, relations.

Today it is widely accepted that precision is an essential feature of progress in IR, and the utility of concepts is routinely argued to be a function of their specification in terms of precisely measurable empirical referents without which valid inferences are thought to be impossible (King et al. 1994: 26–7; Bueno de Mesquita 1985: 133; Snyder 1984/5: 89–108). As a result of such thinking, however, contemporary IR would appear to be mired in a dilemma. For if the goal of science is to generate general laws and explanations, then we will necessarily be required to sacrifice a great deal of precision, for generalizability implies a high level of analytic abstraction (Sartori 1970: 1033–52). If, however, science is about precision, then the prospects for achieving general explanations would appear to be rather limited.

The dilemma, however, is more apparent than real. It is the result of an overly rigid and fundamentally flawed commitment to the possibility of precision in the social sciences as well as blindness to variety in the types of explanations to which one can legitimately affix the label "general." Elsewhere I have elaborated grounds for skepticism regarding the possibility of achieving high degrees of definitional and operational precision in the study of social phenomena (Davis 2005). My objective here is to demonstrate how a concern for the *particular* can lead to *general* knowledge. The argument I will develop owes its inspiration to the work of Friedrich Kratochwil and takes as its point of departure the notion that purposeful social action occurs against a backdrop of institutions and must be understood in terms of intersubjectively valid rules, norms, and principles (Kratochwil 1989a). It is not an outright rejection of the insights provided by an application of the strictures of deductive logic to social science theorizing. Indeed, these have contributed to our understanding of international relations and helped clear the field of a number of incoherent arguments.

Yet the use of deductive logic in pursuit of explanations for social phenomena is not without limitations. For whereas the application of deductive procedures within an axiomatic system of reason can often tell us what must be the case, and (for the development of theory more importantly) what *cannot* be the case, it does not provide sufficient insight into what *could* be the case, because the scope of deductive analysis is defined and limited by initial assumptions. If, however, the rules, norms, and principles that govern international life are generative, then we need to develop methods and procedures appropriate to the task of explaining the emergence of innovative and novel behaviors.

Indeed, in its rather single-minded search for causal laws, mainstream political science would appear to have forgotten the essence of politics. For whether we define politics as "the authoritative distribution of values," "who gets what when and how," or "distinguishing friend from enemy," the *decision* is central (Lasswell 1936; Easton 1953; Schmitt, 1963). Decisions, of course, imply choice and therefore deliberation. But as Aristotle reminded us, no one deliberates about things that are invariable or which he regards to be impossible (Aristotle 1908, book six). If this is the case, then it would seem prudent that we direct our collective efforts not only toward explaining the recurrent or the invariable but also to accounting for the novel. As political scientists, we should uncover not only the causes of what has been but also the antecedents of what might be. To do so, however, requires us to move away from a single logic of inference toward a diversity of explanatory logics.

Nomothetics

Modern science begins from the basic metaphysical assumption that there is order to the universe. Although it may appear to us as varied, irregular, or indeed chaotic, the universe is believed to be governed by a set of (probably simple and) general relationships or laws. Indeed, Newtonian mechanics managed to show that all variety of motions is consistent with a small set of general physical laws. Similarly, thermodynamics comprises a set of general laws explaining the large variety of ways physical bodies behave when heated. Thus a simple and generally accepted definition for science is the search for general laws governing the universe.[4] And from the seventeenth century to the present, scientific practice has pursued two paths in search for general laws: inductive empiricism and deductive logic.

The inductivist argument maintains that observation alone provides a secure basis on which to build an edifice of truth. The discovery of law-like regularities is thus a matter of generalizing from individual observations to universal propositions. For the inductivist, it is legitimate to generalize from a finite set of singular observation statements provided that the number of observations is large, the observations have been conducted under a variety of conditions, and no accepted observation statement contradicts the universal proposition. Briefly stated, if a large sample of cases of some phenomenon *x* has been observed under a wide variety of conditions, and if, in all cases and without exception, phenomenon *x* possesses the property *y*, then *all x* possess the property *y* (Chalmers 1976: 1–21).

The weaknesses of the inductivist position, already pointed out by Hume, are well known and require little elaboration (Hume 2000). The basic point is this: On the basis of a finite number of observation statements, one can never conclude that a relationship is universally valid. If the set of all possible observation statements is infinite both in time and space, then even a "large" number of observation statements is by comparison quite insignificant. One simply cannot infer a general law on the basis of a finite set of observations. Moreover, the fallback position of contemporary adherents to multivariate regression analysis—that one can replace universal generalizations with probabilistic statements—is subject to the same criticism Hume directed at induction in general. On the basis of a finite number of successes in the application of probabilistic statements there is no logically compelling reason to believe that all applications of the principle of probability will lead to conclusions that are probabilistically valid. Yet, despite its limitations and some 30 years after Professor Young argued induction to be "one of the most wasteful, debilitating, as well as pervasive diseases of contemporary political science," many empirically oriented colleagues continue to collect "raw data" in a rather blind search for those general laws, toward which, it is said, all of science should aim (Young 1969: 490).

Whereas the inductivist begins from singular observation statements and attempts to infer universal statements or empirical laws from them, deductivists propose the theoretical assertion as the proper point of departure in the search for general knowledge. The inductivist confronts the problem that a conclusion derived from even a very large number of observations can be refuted by a single accepted observation statement. The logical asymmetry between the verifiability and falsifiability of universal statements was recognized by Popper and led him to propose falsifiability as the defining characteristic of scientific propositions.

Observations, he argued, may give rise to theories about the world, but no manner of inductive inference can produce from these the sorts of general propositions we seek. Marrying the criterion of falsifiability to deductive logic, however, Popper proposed a different route. By means of logic, general statements can be deduced from propositions and then subjected to tests through which they might be shown to be false: "the method of falsification presupposes no inductive inference, but only the tautological transformations of deductive logic whose validity is not in dispute" (Popper 1968: 42).

From this perspective, general statements, and the theoretical systems from which they are deduced, cannot be proven true, but they can be falsified. Tests of theories lead to singular observation statements, or strictly existential statements, of the "there is" sort. Thus a strictly existential statement, if accepted, can falsify a universal statement. The statement "I see a black swan" would serve to falsify the universal statement "all swans are white."

By contrast, strictly existential statements—for example, "There is life beyond earth!"—cannot be falsified. We cannot search the entire universe to establish that life does not exist. Owing to the limits of observation in an endless universe, we cannot establish the veracity of universal statements nor can we falsify existential statements, or as Popper put it: "Whenever it is found that something exists here or there, a strictly existential statement may thereby be verified, or a universal one falsified" (Popper 1968: 70). Because they cannot be falsified, Popper regarded strictly existential statements to be nonempirical or metaphysical. Hence Popper's approach to deductive theorizing is not aimed at the formulation of "if . . . then" propositions but rather statements that take the form of prohibitions or prescriptions:

> They do not assert that something exists or is the case; they deny it. They insist on the non-existence of certain things or states of affairs, proscribing or prohibiting, as it were, these things or states of affairs: they rule them out. And it is precisely because they do this, that they are *falsifiable*. If we accept as true one singular statement which, as it were, infringes the prohibition by asserting the existence of a thing (or the occurrence of an event) ruled out by the law, then the law is refuted.
>
> (Popper 1968: 69)

From this perspective, science progresses as much if not more from the clearing away of statements demonstrated to be false as from the collection of statements verified by means of observation.[5]

Science has thus provided two answers to the question of how to relate the particular to the general in pursuit of nomothetic explanations. For adherents of inductivist procedures, the individual observation or "case" is of quite limited value in this regard; a mere "data point" in a universe of cases that should be randomly sampled and compared in an effort to control and estimate the effects of individual variables (King et al. 1994: 66–74, 208–28). General knowledge requires the observation of variables, or constellations thereof, across a large number of cases and contexts. For deductivists, general statements are derived from initial assumptions by means of logic. Correctly applied, logic leads to general statements that are *true by definition* (or tautological as Popper argued), their truth being a property of the axiomatic system or theory within which they are embedded. Here too, particular historical cases or individual observations play but a limited role in the search for general laws. They are useful only insofar as they can demonstrate that logically necessary relationships are empirically invalid.[6]

If general statements are narrowly defined as law like, or if the only explanations to which we can legitimately affix the term "scientific" are nomothetical, then the utility of the particular in pursuit thereof is indeed rather limited. Moreover, a narrow understanding of what constitutes a general statement and a corresponding singular focus on nomothetical explanations would be warranted if the universe we are trying to explain is characterized by causal homogeneity, which is to say that any given cause will produce, *ceteris paribus*, the same effects across a population. But if the latter condition does not obtain, then our understanding of general statements and the possibilities for explaining the universe in terms of general laws will have to be reconsidered.

The generative potential of social institutions

In a number of path-breaking contributions, Kratochwil has demonstrated the limits of both inductivist and deductivist approaches to explaining social phenomena. Beginning from the proposition that humans act in social contexts, the focus of his scholarship has been on the defining or constitutive features thereof. Defined by the seemingly permanent condition of structural anarchy, IR would not appear to be the most promising terrain for a research program devoted to uncovering the underlying features of sociality. Clearly inspired by the work of Hedley Bull and other "English School" theorists, however, Kratochwil turns this apparent weakness into a strength (Bull 1977). Precisely because of anarchy, IR presents us with a "least likely" case for a truly social explanation of human behavior. By demonstrating the effects of rules and norms in IR, Kratochwil not only has persuaded skeptics in the field, he has established himself as a major figure in contemporary social thought.

For Kratochwil, social behavior takes place against a backdrop of institutions, defined in terms of rules and norms. From this perspective, to 'explain' a specific behavior is to demonstrate how it is intelligible in terms of institutional logics. If social interactions appear ordered, then some part of the explanation for this will require an appeal to norms and the three distinct "ordering" functions they fulfill: (1) the prohibition of certain methods of individual goal seeking; (2) the regulation of individual or joint enjoyment of scarce goods; and (3) the facilitation of argument or a discourse on grievances (Kratochwil 1989: 70).

That an incorporation of norms into explanations of international outcomes is incompatible with a conception of science defined in terms of the search for universal laws has been pointed out time and again; the implications for deductivist approaches to theory building meanwhile are well known. Norms frustrate efforts to test general propositions deduced from theories because they can enjoy counterfactual validity. Evidence of noncompliance in any particular case is insufficient to falsify claims to general validity (Kratochwil 1989a: 96–102; Kratochwil and Ruggie 1986a: 753–65; Davis 2005: 143–5).

Less widely appreciated is the fact that because norms are generative, they render efforts to test for their effects by means of statistics invalid.

For although norm-based explanations assert the general validity of norms across a class of situations, the borders of the class are not given naturally, nor are they discernable by means of deduction.

By way of example, it is unlikely that the signatories of the Washington Treaty meant to imply that an attack by a nonstate terrorist organization on US territory could justify the invasion of a South Asian state under the terms of Article 5. The experience of the past years suggests, however, that the universe of cases to which NATO's norm of collective defense might apply is simply unknowable *a priori*. Rather, as they are applied by processes of analogical reasoning and according to judgments of similarity in novel fashions, often to novel situations, norms *create* facts and cases (Kratochwil 1989a: 223–36; Davis 2005: 136–53). Hence, the first issue at stake is not the probability that a norm will be observed by actors in a given population of cases but rather the question of to which population a given "case" belongs. Because the applicability and meaning of general rules and norms often is not straightforward, they must be established through deliberative processes. The result is an open or expanding class of cases or events within which individual instances cannot be assumed to be interchangeable or homogenous units. When, however, the members of a set are not "substitutable instances of the same thing," efforts to establish causal effects through statistical procedures produce results of dubious validity (Ragin 2000: 52).

Recognizing the difficulties associated with establishing the effects of social institutions by means of either deductive or inductive procedures, Kratochwil has often asserted a preference for context-specific over general knowledge; for an understanding of the particular case rather than the statistical mode: "If I want to know why someone drowns, it does not help me much if I know that the average depth of the water was two inches!"[7] Although sympathetic to the basic point, I nonetheless suspect that such statements reinforce the conventional wisdom that equates scientific with nomothetical knowledge, and ultimately undermines the larger project of expanding our understanding of what constitutes a valid scientific—and indeed general—explanation (Kratochwil 2008b: 80–98).

Moving from particular to general

Even critics of efforts to generate nomothetic knowledge of social outcomes tend to juxtapose general explanations and particular knowledge, thus reinforcing the notion that particular knowledge is of little use in generating general explanations. For example, in the late-nineteenth and early-twentieth centuries, the neo-Kantians of the so called Baden School, with Wilhelm Windelband at the fore, argued knowledge could be *either* general and nomothetic *or* specific and historical. The social and historical sciences, he argued, should direct their efforts toward understanding the particular way in which concrete individuals ascribe values to events and institutions under unique and never-to-be repeated constellations of historical circumstances. In pursuit of "idiographic" knowledge, the cultural and historical sciences thus seek to understand these particular and concrete "historical individuals" (Windelband 1894). But how do individuals affix values to events and institutions and are the processes and outcomes necessarily historically unique?

Without access to mental states and processes and realizing that observable behavior can be the product of a variety of antecedent factors, the proper focus of such investigation is discourse, namely the reasons that are given and accepted by social actors as a sufficient justification for compliance or noncompliance (Kratochwil 1989a: 97). The giving of reasons involves discursively linking some particular features of the case at hand with a general rule, and thus constitutes a mode of reasoning *from the particular to the general*. And although we cannot predict the path an argument will take, and even if ultimate judgments regarding the meaning of a rule or norm in a particular context are in this sense "path dependent," it does not follow that the process and result of arguing is arbitrary (Kratochwil 1989a: 236–47). Hence, analyzing and evaluating the path and outcome of arguments over the applicability of norms in a particular historical case can lead to general knowledge, albeit of a different sort than is the focus of adherents to statistical or deductive reasoning.

It bears emphasizing, that explanations of this sort are directed at uncovering the collective—that is intersubjective—meanings attached by actors in specific historical circumstances, which is accomplished by means of reconstructive and interpretive methods. These, in turn, focus more on the constitutive than causal features of the case under examination. Again, the basic argument is relatively well known. Yet skeptics and even some adherents to reconstructive methods are not free from some rather common misconceptions and thus overlook or discount their inherent potential for generating general knowledge.[8]

One widespread misconception is that the validity of an explanation based on the reconstruction of arguments somehow must distinguish "sincere" from "manipulative" arguments, which is to say one must somehow evaluate the "true" motives of those engaged in the discourse.[9] But the quality of an argument by no means is linked necessarily to the motives that gave rise to it (although Lynch's chapter argues that the ethics of an argument are linked to intentionality). Distinguishing among pretexts, *mere* rhetoric or propaganda, though perhaps useful for some purposes (see the chapter by Bukovansky), is not central to an appraisal of whether and how a rule or norm is to be judged applicable to specific circumstances. A simple and fictional, although thereby no less real, example should suffice as evidence in favor of the general claim.

Consider the case of the racist judge who sentences a black man convicted of rape to execution. The arguments of the prosecution rely to a large extent on circumstantial evidence, such that the judge is certain a request for appeal will be reviewed by a higher court. When issuing the death sentence, the racist judge will go to great lengths to argue in terms generally accepted as justifying execution.[10] The persuasiveness of the legal opinion is thus independent of any racist motive. Moreover, the opinion may persuade even if the appellate judge is an opponent of the death penalty.[11]

The example serves to demonstrate that the force of normative arguments and their effects on behavior are *general* in that they cannot be reduced or decomposed to the beliefs or motives of individual actors. Indeed, an argument may be collectively persuasive even if it does not reflect the individual preferences of any of the participants to it!

A second misconception of the explanations derived by means of historical reconstruction is that they somehow of necessity are bounded temporally. In some cases this may be correct, but properly understood, a reconstruction not only returns us to the past in order to provide a description of the overall context of an historical event from the perspective of the actors involved. Rather, it also allows the analyst to experience, or "re-experience," events from a novel perspective. Re-experience has the effect of moving historically bounded arguments forward in order to follow their development and uncover their inherent social or institutional logic. Extending arguments across time and space, such interpretive methods can lead to a fuller understanding of an argument's effects than was enjoyed by the historical actors themselves. As Wilhelm Dilthey once argued, social analysis thus resembles an engagement with the arts: "A lyrical poem makes possible, through the sequence of its verses, the re-experience of a nexus of lived experience—not the real one that stimulated the poet, but the one that, on its basis, the poet places in the mouth of an ideal person" (Dilthey 2002: 235). In his magisterial review of classical realism, Richard Ned Lebow recently reached a similar conclusion. Knowledge of the human condition and the ends of human activity, he argues, is approached by integrating the understandings we derive from theory, experience and the arts. Some of this knowledge is reflective, and some takes the form of understandings that go beyond words. Knowledge of both kinds can feed back into our theoretical inquiries and help create a positive, reinforcing cycle of discovery.

(Lebow 2003: 360–1)

Moving forward

The argument I am developing has now progressed in three broad steps. I began with the assertion that the field of political science confronts an artificial dilemma. Although the twin goals of precise and general explanation would appear to run in different directions, the problem may dissolve if we abandon a narrow understanding of what constitutes a general explanation. In a second step I argued that neither inductive nor deductive procedures are adequate to the task of generating general explanations of norm-guided behavior because of the generative potential of social institutions. Thus, in a third step, I asserted the value of analyzing the discursive practices whereby social institutions derive meaning and guide behavior in specific historical contexts. Reconstructing the path of arguments in specific cases, this form of analysis nonetheless leads to a form of *general* explanation because the meanings uncovered are held collectively and are extendable (if also subject to new interpretations) in time and space by virtue of the same process of argumentation. The effects of such arguments flow from their *logical coherence* and cannot be inferred by means of inductive or deductive logic.

A common critique of such interpretive approaches is the lack of standards according to which one might distinguish good from bad analyses. Though vigorously disputed (Lynch 2005; Yanow and Schwartz-Shea 2006; Klotz and Lynch 2007), this criticism is not without merit and points to a rather embarrassing irony. For how can one argue that processes of argument and persuasion are central to explaining much of social life without providing some criteria according to which one might recognize the better argument?

Although recent years have seen an explosion of publications that place argumentative processes in the center of their analyses (Crawford 2002; Deitelhoff 2006; Payne 2001; Schimmelfennig 2003), and important voices assert the "importance of argumentation, deliberation and persuasion" in the field (Hurrell 2002; Checkel 2002), the study of international relations suffers from a lack of a well-developed methodology of discourse analysis (Milliken 1999). To some extent this reflects a failure to theorize and develop key concepts. Most striking in this regard is the lack of a core definition or exemplar of the term "argument" in the German "debate" on "argumentative rationality," now in its 15th year. As a result, "we theorize about the possibility of arguments changing the deep structure of international relations, but have not theorized the structure and content of the arguments to begin with" (Heppt 2007; see also Crawford 2002). Given such deficiencies, humility would appear more appropriate than zealous proselytizing.[12]

Although I believe the field would be well served if proponents of reconstructivist and interpretivist analysis would devote some modicum of attention to articulating some communal standards according to which one could evaluate the product of their scholarship, I am not suggesting we thereby discipline the discipline. For any such rules and standards will themselves be open to collective reinterpretation in accordance with the community's procedural notions of rule following. They will not "determine" our practice, but will "constrain and enable us in our activities" and most important of all, "allow us to go on" (Kratochwil 2007a: 13).

Notes

1. One need not travel the entire world to comprehend that the sky is blue everywhere (my translation).
2. Strange coincidence, that everyone whose skull was opened had a brain (my translation).
3. See Levy (1969), Young (1969), and Waltz (1979).
4. The implications of quantum physics for this generally accepted view of science have yet to be fully appreciated. See Bohr (1984: 156–62), DeWitt (1970: 30–5), and Stapp (1972).
5. For a critical evaluation of the prospects for conclusive falsifications, see Davis (2005: 107–31).
6. For Lakatos, a theory's ability to anticipate "new facts" is an important evaluative criterion. Hence, confirmatory observations can play an important role in establishing the veracity of general propositions. But although such "discoveries" may be psychologically significant, from a logical positivist standpoint, whether a fact that fits a theory was previously known or observed is beside the point. For the argument, see Lakatos (1970: 118).
7. Personal communication.
8. Apparently accepting the proposition that knowledge is either general and nomothetic or particular and idiographic, King et al. (1994: 34–41) have characterized analyses devoted toward reconstructing the constitutive features of human behavior as the search for particular historical knowledge through the summary of historical detail and as such not a valid approach to explanation.

9. My own thinking on this issue has evolved. See, for example, Cortell and Davis (2000: 71–2).
10. On the importance of depersonalized arguments see Kratochwil (1989a: 142).
11. I thank Alexander Heppt for the example and our discussions of its implications.
12. Thomas Risse (2000) has assumed the role of missionary, championing the German debate in a leading US journal.

3
Game Theory and Reciprocity: Toward a Social Perspective

Deborah Welch Larson

Reciprocity is fundamental to political life. Reciprocity makes possible enduring social and political relationships by giving the parties an incentive to continue the interaction. People are unlikely to continue making political deals or exchanges of favors unless they perceive that they are receiving a fair return. This raises the question of how the parties know that other has reciprocated. In political transactions, there is no common standard of value fulfilling the function of money.

In this chapter I shall argue that reciprocity and related social norms serve as an alternative to the market in determining whether an exchange is fair. In the international system where there is no superior authority to allocate values according to some criteria of justice, states have accepted mutual give and take as an alternative rough form of justice for many types of interactions.

International Relations (IR) theorists (Axelrod 1984; Keohane 1984, 1986; Oye 1985; Snidal 1985; Kydd 2005) have also noted the importance of reciprocity in fostering and institutionalizing cooperation among states. The theoretical literature in political science is strongly influenced by game theory and microeconomic models (see also Jervis 1978; Stein 1983). But game theory could be usefully supplemented with the much richer research tradition on reciprocity conducted by social exchange theorists, biologists, and social psychologists.

Friedrich Kratochwil (1989a) used simple game models to develop complex concepts such as trust, obligation, and reciprocity (for other treatments of Kratochwil's use of game theory, see the contributions by Rengger and Davis in this volume). At the same time, however, he emphasized that these concepts cannot be divorced from their political, social, and psychological contexts. The meaning of an action depends on understanding the framework of conventions and rules established in society. Norms are "guidance devices which are designed to simplify choices and impart 'rationality' to situations by delineating the factors that a decision-maker has to take into account" (Kratochwil, 1989a: 10).

I will discuss some limitations of using game theory to analyze international reciprocity, limitations which were identified by Kratochwil even as he used simple models to illustrate the idea. First, the preferences of players are shaped by the social context of interaction and the parties' perceptions. Accordingly, the objective game matrix as viewed by a hypothetical observer may differ considerably from that viewed by the players. Foreign policymakers, like everyone else, evaluate alternative outcomes using a complex calculus, including social norms and their relationship with other states. The meaning of reciprocity varies, depending on cultural norms and the perceptions of the parties. Second, as a theory of choice, game theory ignores *process* variables, such as a player's attempt to understand the reasons for the other's defection or cooperation. In the real world, choices are influenced by policymakers' efforts to explain and interpret the actions of other states, and the prior history of the interaction on which those explanations are based.

Limitations of game theory

IR theorists view the Prisoner's Dilemma game as paradigmatic for explaining the difficulties that states have in reciprocating cooperation in such issues as arms races, tariff wars, the Cold War (Jervis 1978). In the well-known PD game, both sides would receive substantial benefits from mutual cooperation, but there is a temptation to exploit the other player and receive even higher payoffs. Therefore, both players defect, with the result that they are worse off than they would have been had they collaborated. In a PD game, a cooperative move is risky, and will not be made unless a player expects that the other will reciprocate. Game theoretic models (Taylor 1976: Chapter 5; Shubik 1970; Axelrod 1984) suggest that contingent cooperation, that is, tit for tat, is a rational strategy when a PD game is indefinitely iterated.

In the real world, however, people may not behave "rationally" because their values differ from those depicted in the game. Recognizing the discrepancy between the meaning of the matrix as understood and processed by the player and the objective distribution of payoffs, social psychologists formulate hypotheses about the intervening cognitive and affective variables that cause reality to diverge from theory. Kelley and Thibaut (1978) distinguish between the *given* and the *effective* or subjective utility matrix, which may be influenced by perceptions, social norms, motives attributed to the other player, or communication.

The gap between payoffs and people's actual behavior is caused by a variety of factors. For one thing, because of role, personal sentiment, or mutual interdependence, a person's evaluation of the outcomes may be affected by the payoffs of the other player. The extent to which players take the other's payoffs into consideration varies by individual and situation. It matters who people play against. Some research shows that people do not optimize because they are often motivated to obtain higher *relative* gains than the other player (Chadwick-Jones 1976: 8, 76–7; McClintock and McNeel 1966a, 1966b; Wyer 1969). This has important implications for international politics because, according to offensive realists, much international competition is for relative gains.

The problem of measurement

Keohane (1986) defines reciprocity as "exchanges of roughly equivalent values in which the actions of each party are contingent on the prior actions of the others in such a way that good is returned for good, and bad for bad." Even the minimal standard of "rough" equivalence implies that the goods and services exchanged are somehow comparable. But it is impossible to measure social exchanges without a common standard of value such as money. Aristotle (1953: 184–5) went so far as to argue that there could be no reciprocity without a measure of value like money by which to make the products exchanged commensurable. Keohane (1986: 7) acknowledges that "in international relations as in personal social relations precise measurement is often impossible." But the problem is more fundamental. In all social and political exchanges, there is no commonly accepted standard of value fulfilling the function of money in economic transactions (Baldwin 1971: 594–6). As Blau (1964a: 95) points out, "it is not just the social scientists who cannot exactly measure how much approval a given helpful action is worth; the actors themselves cannot precisely specify the worth of approval or of help in the absence of a money price."

When there is no common standard of value, what is equivalent depends on the *perceptions* of the parties to the exchange (Gouldner 1960: 172). But the parties may differ on the value of what has been transferred. As Aristotle (1953: 283) observed: "the recipients assert that what they received cost their benefactors little and could have been had from other sources—thus trying to minimize their indebtedness; the donors on the contrary insist that their services were the greatest that lay in their power, and could not have been had from elsewhere, and were rendered in the face of danger or some such emergency."

Similarly, two states may have differing conceptions of what reciprocity implies. The US and the Soviets disagreed in the early 1970s over the meaning of "political equality," recognized by Nixon and Brezhnev in the 1972 Basic Principles Agreement (George 1983: 115–16). To the Soviets, "political equality" meant that the US was prepared to treat them as a diplomatic equal; Nixon and Kissinger were prepared to give only lip service to Soviet equality, particularly in the Middle East (Jervis 2010: 39–40).

That disagreements may arise over what is reciprocal does not mean "anything goes." A reciprocal exchange is a transaction that the parties regard as "fair" (Blau 1964a: 155–6). When there is no counterpart to money as a common standard of value, judgments of fairness are mediated by social norms, such as equity and social responsibility.

Common norms of justice function as media of exchange, analogous to money in economic transactions (Blau 1964a: 255, 268–9; Blau 1964b: 197; Heath 1976: 116–17; Baldwin 1978: 1240). In interactive relationships, several competing norms of justice may guide behavior, and social psychologists argue that the situation largely determines which is most appropriate or functional. In general, what is considered to be reciprocal by the parties to the exchange depends on the status and relationship of the donor and recipient.

A great power may provide benefits which other states cannot repay to obligate them to reciprocate by complying with the superior state's wishes. An important purpose of US foreign and military assistance programs is to create an obligation on the part of the recipient countries to maintain pro-US policies (Baldwin, 1985: 326). On the individual level, a person may accumulate a credit of unrepaid favors so that subordinates will have to defer to his wishes in order to reestablish reciprocity in the exchange (Blau 1964a: 26, 28–9, 336). In the movie *Godfather*, the Mafia don played by Marlon Brando is introduced by showing him granting the requests of community residents—presumably in return for future compliance. President Lyndon Johnson did not *want* the "books" of favors senators owed him to be balanced, because he would lack political capital for influencing their votes. Thus, in real life, cooperative reciprocal exchanges may be more or less asymmetric, yet still conform to intuitive notions of reciprocity. Reciprocity is a continuum, not a dichotomous variable (Gouldner 1960: 164). Game matrices do not allow one to specify varying degrees of reciprocity; either a player makes the C choice or he does not. Because norms help to determine what counts as reciprocation, explanations can be used to offer praise or assess blame (Kratochwil 1989a: 100).

Norms and obligations

In game theoretic models, players learn to cooperate when they realize that they will gain more in the long run from mutual cooperation than from defection. Having a reputation for being a cooperator can be useful in getting mutual cooperation established, since one party has to take the initiative and risk being suckered. Kratochwil (1989a: 108–9) adduces several examples to show that rational considerations such as reputation and the "shadow of the future" cannot explain why people follow rules. It is necessary to consider emotions and norms, as Durkheim recommended.

In a seminal theoretical statement, sociologist Alvin Gouldner (1960) defines the norm of reciprocity as the belief that (1) people should help those who have helped them, and (2) people should not injure those who have helped them. Gouldner hypothesized that a norm of reciprocity is a cultural universal, and subsequent experimental psychological and anthropological research has provided evidence that children and people from a variety of cultures act consistently with the norm (Mauss 1954; Staub and Sherk 1970; Gergen et al. 1975; Walster et al. 1978).

This raises the question of how norms work, how they exert their "force," one of Kratochwil's (1984b) central preoccupations. Once a norm has been internalized, people feel guilty or suffer shame when they violate it. The norm of reciprocity obligates one to repay favors to avoid internal sanctions. Greenberg (1980) hypothesized that "indebtedness" is an aversive state with motivational properties similar to cognitive dissonance. In support, a number of studies (Berkowitz 1968; Berkowitz and Friedman 1967; Morris and Rosen 1973; Greenberg and Shapiro, 1971; Gergen et al., 1975) have shown that people are reluctant to accept favors or help when they know that they cannot reciprocate.

Because there often is a strong obligation to reciprocate favors, a political actor may take advantage of the norm to induce another person to comply with his/her will. In international negotiations, a diplomat may give up exaggerated, fake demands to pressure the opponent into making a substantive concession (Ikle and Leites 1962).

Trust and reciprocity

Hobbes argues that it is inadvisable for a person to observe a covenant of restraint with another individual in a state of nature without a sovereign because performance must be sequential:

> For he that perform first, has no assurance that the other will performe [*sic*] after; because the bonds of words are too weak to bridle men's ambition, avarice, anger and other Passions, without the fear of some coercive Power . . . but in a civill [*sic*] estate, where there is a power set up to constrain those that would otherwise violate their faith that fear is no more reasonable; and for that cause, he which by the Covenant is to performe first, is *obliged* to do so.
>
> (Hobbes 1968: 196, quoted in Kratochwil 1989a: 103)

Kratochwil (1989a: 113–14) points out that the passage does not, as usually assumed, suggest that reciprocal exchange requires a sovereign able to coerce compliance. Because continual enforcement would be impossible, reciprocity must be based on trust—trust in a system of expectations (see also Hall's treatment of money in this volume). In this context, trust does not mean confidence placed in a person whom we have reason to believe is credible or well intentioned; that form of trust is personalistic. The type of trust that is relevant to international relations or other complex social systems is not personal, moralistic trust (Lieberman 1964), but a more generalized trust in the system (Luhmann 1979). The trust that US leaders place in Britain does not vary with the identity of the prime minister. Since we cannot know our banker, meat packer, or milk producer personally, we have to trust in the impersonal workings of the economic system to ensure that the currency handed over by a teller is not counterfeit, the meat uncontaminated, and the milk unspoiled.

Sequential exchange not only requires but also builds trust. Swinth (1967) found that it was easier to build trust in a Prisoner's Dilemma Game when players had an opportunity to demonstrate their good faith in a preliminary trial of sequential moves, by taking the risk of cooperating first and having their cooperation reciprocated by the other player. To build trust, the person beginning the process must expose himself to the risk of personal loss. When a cooperative move is potentially costly, the other person is more likely to perceive it as sincere and worthy of reciprocation (Brickman et al. 1979; Pruitt 1981; Komorita 1973). Thus people usually develop an exchange relationship gradually, by granting small favors (Blau 1964a: 94, 98). As they become more committed to the relationship and develop greater mutual trust, the scope of the obligations each is willing to assume widens.

In international relations, one can find examples of reciprocal interactions in which the obligation created by a state's concession or favor is nonspecific even between adversaries. Tacit bargaining is a good example of sequential, implicit exchange (Schelling 1960: 72–3). In his June 1963 American University Speech, President Kennedy announced that the US was unilaterally suspending all nuclear tests in the atmosphere and would maintain the moratorium until another country resumed testing first. Soviet Premier Khrushchev reciprocated by making a speech announcing that the Soviet Union was suspending production of strategic bombers. In the United Nations, the Soviets withdrew their objections to sending observers to Yemen. The US reciprocated by agreeing to admit the Hungarian delegation to the United Nations. As Etzioni (1967: 369) points out,

> [w]hile these matters are not readily measurable, it seems that the Russian reciprocations were "proportional" to the American ones. Khrushchev's speech might have been somewhat less elegant than Kennedy's, but it would be difficult to defend the proposition that announcing a halt to the production of bombers is lower in value than the declaration of cessation of tests, both basically psychological gestures. Spies were exchanged for spies; the test treaty and the space ban involved substantively identical, strategically similar, commitments. In short, neither side seemed to have made a disproportionate gain.

Motives and reciprocity

Game theory also does not consider the role of perceptions of the other person's motives in influencing a player's decision whether to cooperate or defect. As Schelling (1968) points out, game theory's concern with "choice and consequences" excludes motives from the strategy of decision, on the assumption that the other player's motivation is revealed in the structure of payoffs. This omission is significant because in the social world the other person's perceived motives and intentions are extremely important in determining one's response.

Whether, and how much a gift will be reciprocated is determined by three factors, originally hypothesized by Gouldner (1960) and substantiated by later experimental research. The first condition is the costliness of the concession (Kratochwil 1989a: 58). People give more in return if the gift was a greater percentage of the donor's resources (Tesser et al. 1968; Gergen et al. 1975). Pruitt (1968) found that subjects gave more in return when the other person had granted them 20 percent of $1, than 20 percent of $4 even though they had received *four times* as much money in the latter case. Similarly, costly concessions are more likely to be reciprocated.

A second important variable is whether the benefactors' motives as perceived by the recipient are benevolent. If the donor is believed to have ulterior designs, then the receiver does not feel obliged to return the favor (Nemeth 1970; Schopler and Thompson 1968). Perceptions need not mirror reality to influence behavior. An "inherent bad faith" image of someone denies the possibility that the individual's behavior could have anything but Machiavellian motives. Tit for tat assumes that "niceness" will be correctly perceived and cooperates on the first move. But if the other side has an inherent "bad faith" image of the tit for tat initiator, then a single cooperative act will be ignored, reinterpreted to conform to preexisting beliefs, or discounted as a trick to lull the target into lowering his guard (Larson 1997: 22; Jervis 1976: 77–8, 117–202, 288–315). This assimilation of cooperative moves to preexisting beliefs and images contributed to prolonging Cold War tensions between the US and the Soviet Union, particularly when John Foster Dulles was secretary of state.

In his influential study of Secretary John Foster Dulles' belief system, for example, Ole R. Holsti (1967) showed that Dulles attributed conciliatory Soviet gestures to economic weakness and the bankruptcy of their foreign policy as a way to preserve his image of the Soviet Union as an implacable enemy, hostile, immoral, and calculating. There was virtually nothing the Soviets could do to change Dulles' mind about the dangers of negotiating with communists.

After Stalin's death in March 1953, the Soviet leadership made numerous unilateral overtures to the West: for example, they apologized to the British for shooting down a plane and proposed three-power air safety talks, agreed to the exchange of sick and wounded prisoners from the Korean War, and finally accepted Dag Hammarskjold's nomination as secretary general of the United Nations. Contrary to the norm of reciprocity, these concessions made Dulles *less* willing to seek a rapprochement with Stalin's successors. At a 31 March National Security Council meeting, Dulles explained that "the current peace offensive is designed by the Soviets to relieve the ever-increasing pressure upon their regime." "Accordingly," he said, "we must not relax this pressure until the Soviets give promise of ending the struggle" (US Department of State 1952–4: 268). On 10 July 1953, Dulles told the cabinet that "the big thing is to exploit Soviet weakness." "This is the time to CROWD the enemy and maybe FINISH him once and for all" (Hughes diary).

While Dulles is the paradigmatic case of the "bad faith" image, the Reagan administration was very slow to reciprocate the unilateral concessions made by Soviet leader Mikhail Gorbachev from 1985–6, even though the Soviet leader's policy is used as a model of a "costly signaling" strategy (Kydd 2000, 2005). Gorbachev launched a 17-month unilateral moratorium on nuclear testing, offered to cut strategic weapons by 50 percent, and proposed "new thinking" in international relations that emphasized cooperation and interdependence. The Reagan administration responded by abrogating the informal SALT II limits and by sending two naval reconnaissance ships within six miles of the Black Sea, at a time when Gorbachev was staying in the area at his dacha (Larson 1997: 209–12). One problem is that actions in international relations are not clearly labeled as "cooperation" or "defect." The same action may be interpreted differently, depending on perception of the underlying motives and intentions.

If one side has a "bad faith" image of the other, then securing the cooperation of the other state in relaxing tensions may require a dramatic, unilateral concession, involving some costs or risks, to shake rigid beliefs and undermine mistrust (Pruitt 1981; Komorita 1973; Swinth 1967). For example, when Gorbachev allowed Eastern Europe to go free and the Berlin Wall to fall, the Bush administration, which had regarded the Soviet leader with some skepticism as a "drugstore cowboy," changed its mind about his sincerity (Larson 1997: 224, 227, 229).

Third, the gift must have been given out of the donor's free will. People do not feel compelled to reciprocate favors unless they were given intentionally, and not simply as a routine behavior (Kratochwil, 1989a: 58). Similarly, states do not feel obligated to reciprocate actions that they believe the other state would have taken anyway, as a matter of course. Thus, in 1955 and 1956, when the Soviets cut their conventional troop strength by over 1,000,000, the US did not feel obligated to respond. US officials felt that the Soviets were reducing their forces for economic reasons, to devote more manpower to agriculture. Since the Soviets would have made the troop reductions in any event, the US did not perceive them as an index of Soviet good faith or of peaceful intentions (Larson, 1997: 68–9).

It follows that the extent to which a concession or benefit will be reciprocated depends on how the target explains and interprets the initiator's behavior. Psychological research suggests that the strategy of tit for tat (Axelrod 1984) will not be successful in eliciting cooperation in the real world unless the recipient perceives the donor's concession as voluntary and motivated by benevolent intentions. These conditions need to be incorporated into a theory of reciprocity and contingent generalizations formulated.

In sum, game theorists are not concerned with *how* or *why* the players reached their decision to cooperate or defect. Game theory focuses on the *outcomes* of strategy choices. In studying international relations, we should determine how statesmen come to value outcomes in particular situations. We should also examine how policymakers explain and interpret concessions, if the theory is to be useful in explaining cooperation in real-world mixed motive conflicts.

Conclusions

If a valid theory of reciprocity is to be developed for the domain of world politics, some effort should be made to depict the process by which policymakers infer others' motives and how this affects their preferences. The process of attribution is likely influenced by the cultural context, by the expectations for behavior that are part of the fabric of society. As Anatol Rapoport (1970: 41) points out, "the chief value of game-theoretic analysis is that it points to questions beyond its scope."

Analyzing the determinants of reciprocity would permit dialogue and cross-fertilization with scholars in the fields of sociology, anthropology, and social psychology. This would follow the example of Kratochwil, whose work is rich in its references to law, philosophy, sociology, and psychology, as in his path-breaking work on the nature of international law and the evolution of norms (Kratochwil 1978, 1984b, 1987b, 1989a, 1994b, 2000a). Reciprocity is found in international political economic exchanges as well as in security issues, and the concept provides a means of bridging the gap between findings and hypotheses in these subdisciplines of international politics. Finally, reciprocity provides a means of grasping the interweaving of cooperation and competition found in international politics.

4

'Trust me, I promise!': Kratochwil's Contributions toward the Explanation of the Structure of Normative Social Relations

Rodney Bruce Hall

My contribution to this celebration of the career and scholarship of Friedrich Kratochwil will demonstrate how Kratochwil's analytic development of the social institutions of "promises" and "trust" are particularly helpful in explaining the social relations of credit and debt, so central to emerging critical topics in International Political Economy—which subdiscipline he has never subjected to sustained attention, but might have done, and with great success.

The immense transdisciplinary value of Kratochwil's work on the normative bases of social life is rooted in the focus in so much of his scholarship on fundamental, explicitly social relations. Even a casual perusal of Kratochwil's scholarship reveals an intensive investigation into the basic conceptual attributes of social actors that give rise to social relations that find application across a broad array of behaviors of the myriad social actors that we encounter in the study of social relations. Among Kratochwil's fundamental contributions to our understanding of the social bases of international relations are intensive and fruitful investigations into such topics as "the notion of interests" (Kratochwil 1982), "the notion of right" (1989a), "the force of prescriptions" (1984b), "the question of law" (1989a), "the discourse on grievances" (1989a), and "the problem of knowledge" (1994d).

I argue in this chapter that another underrecognized fundamental contribution of Fritz Kratochwil's scholarship to our understanding of the centrality of the structure of normativity in international relations, and across the social sciences, are his investigations of the social structure of duties and obligations arising from social institutions and conventions. The questions of "promises," of their obligatory nature, and of "trust" among subjects, are not least among the human social institutions that feature prominently in Kratochwil's scholarship but which are called out less prominently in his titular summaries of his own work, and by others.

Kratochwil's work is paradigmatic to social analysis, particularly because he labors so effectively to develop our fundamental understanding of the nature of social institutions, their relationship to social practice, and the foundational relationships between these social institutions. I have found his work on the relationships between the social institutions of promises, trust, and reputation to be particularly useful in this context. It has been invaluable in the conceptual development of my own work on the consequences of the social character of money and the social construction of monetary institutions (Hall 2008).

In Kratochwil's work, it is often the illocutionary force of an utterance (a speech act) that is found to generate a social institution. His specification of the generation of these institutions, often via the performative effects of speech, is essential to their proper analysis in social interaction, and for explaining both the causal and constitutive social effects of these social institutions. He illustrates effectively why it is in vain to attempt to draw, as does rationalist causal analysis, upon Popper's (1959) fact/value distinction, in analysis of the effects of norms on social interaction. This distinction proves particularly inapplicable to analysis of, as an example to be developed in this chapter, the problem of social obligation and it's attendant social effects.

Kratochwil demonstrates why the problem cannot be analyzed effectively within a rationalist framework. In promising, for example, articulating the utterance "I promise" we have "neither a statement about facts nor about values" (Kratochwil 1989a: 8). Intentionality of the promiser is not relevant to the act, nor does the manner in which the speaker reasons regarding the effect of the promise on the hearer, nor the values s/he holds or imparts in generating the promise relevant to the ensuing obligation. As Kratochwil argues,

> to construe this sentence about the speaker's state of mind is missing the point, since insincere promises are "obligatory", we cannot reduce the deontic component of a statement to an indication of the psychological state of the speaker. It is here that speech act theory provides us with more appropriate tools. It distinguishes between the *locutionary* dimension of the utterance (saying something), the *illocutionary* force of the utterance, (doing something in saying something as such as, for example, making an assertion, promise etc.), and the *perlocutionary* effects of a statement (i.e., the impact it has on hearers). (1989a: 8, his emphasis)

Importantly, Kratochwil points out that promises are social institutions constituted by performative speech acts. Unlike rationalist accounts of institutions, promises are not obligatory in terms of individual utility calculations of the material consequences of failing to keep one's promise, in part because "promises and precepts (assertions of truth) have important other-regarding dimensions . . . [that] transcend the boundaries of simple prudential choices" (1989a: 130). Neither are promises obligatory for fear of sanctions from an enforcing institution (1989a: 144). Nor are promises obligatory due to the expectations of the party who has received the promises. Both threats and promises are rule-governed activities performed through speech. Both have perlocutionary effects, but the perlocutionary effect of threats is crucial to their social effectiveness. As Kratochwil suggests,

> a threat is obviously in vain . . . if the addressee is not moved by it. However, promises are not simply invalid if the promissee does not give too much credence to a promise. . . . [I]t is exactly the 'uptake' of the obligation, i.e., *illo*cutionary force rather than the *per*locutionary effect, which is crucial in this respect. . . . [W]e cannot simply belittle the illocutionary effect. Doing so would mean that we do not take the person seriously, that we deny him/her the status of a moral agent by discounting his/her utterances, or that we may imply that he/she is like a child or an imbecile who does not know what he/she is doing.
> (1989: 147, footnote deleted, his emphasis)

The institution of promising as social and moral agency

Why should we keep our promises? Kratochwil draws upon Durkhiem, Hume, and also Searle in synthesizing an analytical reply that develops the social practice of promising as a social institution. From Durkheim he draws the distinction between "moral authority" and the "material authority of physical supremacy" (Durkheim 1982) noting that "moral facts expressed in rules of conduct are valid not because of threatened deprivations but because of their duty-imposing character which are in turn the precondition for the legitimacy of physical sanctions" (Kratochwil 1984b: 700). The duty-imposing character of promises results from the performance of the promise as a speech act, not from the expectation of the hearer that the promise will be kept. Kratochwil draws upon Hume's assertions that in promising "the hearer's expectation . . . must be based on the belief that, *ceteris paribus,* the act will be performed even if the hearer does change his mind (i.e. his inclinations, etc.).

It is because this expectation is so strong, that people rightly come to rely on promises in a way they don't on statements of intent" (Hume 2000, quoted in Kratochwil 1989a: 147).

However, it is not simply the expectation of the hearer that establishes the obligatory nature of promises. It is the illocutionary force of the self-representation of the speaker, as we have noted previously, that renders the promise impossible to dismiss, thus establishes both the obligation of the speaker to make good the promise, and the normative obligation on the part of the hearer to at least feign expectation that the promise will be redeemed. Kratochwil quotes Warnock (1971) to good effect in this context, that in promising "I give my word, so that what is at stake . . . is not so much the truth and reliability of what I said, as the truth and reliability of me" (Kratochwil, 1989a: 148). This is why individuals (and collective social actors) have the capacity to generate social agency in generating social institutions, in this case through performative speech acts. As Kratochwil elaborates:

> It is our notion that there is a "self" that remains the same despite a variety of changes in desires, moods, intentions and circumstances, that is at stake as much as the possible harm we do to others by misleading them or inducing them to rely on us. To that extent promising is constitutive of "agency" and our ability to bind or commit ourselves by an act of will.
>
> (1989a: 148)

Thus Durkheim's distinction between "moral facts" as a special category of social facts with "duty-imposing" characteristics becomes essential in explicating the deontologies arising from certain speech acts. Kratochwil argues that "precisely because the uptake of an obligation is so fundamental to our basic moral conceptions, promising is most probably paradigmatic for a wide variety of rule-based actions, including the institution of asserting something (telling the truth)" (1989a: 149). It is the presumed intentions of the hearer who is to be presumed to rely on the offered promise, not the intentions of the promiser, that establish the obligation to perform the subject of promise. Or as Kratochwil argues, "even in the case of promising and contracting, which require consideration of the intentions of the parties, intentions defined as validating conditions of the performance are not the same as mental states accompanying the performance" (Kratochwil 1984b: 706).

In other words, it is due to the performative nature of promising (and contracting) as a speech act, on the part of the speaker, that private reservations amid the speech act do not invalidate the obligation that has been acquired in the performance of speaking. The speaker has claimed social agency in constituting a social institution of a promise. S/he has asserted, "I am a moral agent, and you may rely upon me to perform what I have promised." If s/he entertained private reservations regarding her/his intention or ability to perform the promise when speaking, the obligation remains, because the hearer is entitled (even obligated) to give credence to the assertion. Asserting is another social institution constituted by performative speech, for example, "I assert this. It is the truth!" By implication, in failing to fulfil the promise, the promiser surrenders both the social and the moral agency asserted in generating the promise. Thus while no material sanction may result from abrogation of the promise—of interest only because this is the only consideration that a rationalist analyst might examine, leading her/him to posit a "puzzle" of why we keep our promises when rational-instrumental, material sanctions for failure to do so may be absent—the social sanctions that the promiser calls down upon her/himself in abrogating a promise may be quite severe. The "deadbeat" promiser has effectively admitted that "I am not, after all, a moral agent. The social institutions that I generate to establish my moral and social agency are as void as Hobbes' covenants without the sword."

One may be excused from delivering on one's promises only if exceptional circumstances arise that would tend to mitigate the illocutionary force of the institution of promising. Importantly, the nature of these exceptional circumstances, that might obviate the illocutionary force of the promise, are not a result of rational deliberation or calculation of utility but are a structural feature of the normative order. Kratochwil argues:

> Actors . . . have to resort to norms when they want to air their grievances and establish the various obligations that result from general prescriptions and the utilization of certain speech acts. Thus when Bill promises Jane to look after her terrier . . . in her absence, he has an obligation. It can be overridden only by exceptional circumstances . . . which [make] Bill leaving town necessary. His claim that he has changed his mind simply will not do.
>
> (1989a: 9)

So in this example, Bill must evidently resort to the agreement inherent in the structure of normative expectations that it is not reasonable for Jane to hold him to his promise to look after her terrier if he learns subsequent to instituting the promise he also must be out of town on a matter of more importance than Jane's inconvenience and expense in consequently lodging her terrier with a kennel. The structure of the normative social order rescues Bill's reputation (more anon) as a moral agent who may be relied upon to make good his promises *unless exceptional circumstances render it infeasible to do so.* Of course the norms to which Bill has resorted to extricate himself are implicit and subject to variable interpretation. Thus resort to norms to obviate promises can still be destructive of specific social relationships, even while the tacit nature of these particular norms are unlikely to be destructive of Bill's wider reputation. Kratochwil (1989a: 27ff) parleys this example into a broader, quite illuminating discussion of the consequences of the distinctions between conventional and intentional promising in international relations, which space limitations unfortunately constrain me to pass by here.

The institution of promising as performative speech act

Promising is a social institution, the force of whose prescription is generated by the illocutionary force of a speech act. The importance of the fact that promises are obligatory in the absence of intervening circumstances, normally accepted as both intervening and exceptional in the normative structure of the social order, is that it is a rule-governed activity. And it is governed by quite simple practice-type rules. This follows from the nature of its social institution, which is constituted by speech. Kratochwil observes that the "institution of promising is relatively simple in its rule structure; it seems one only has to use the words 'I promise' in order to make clear that one is performing the act of promising. More elaborate rules are required to make a contract" (1989a: 91). Moreover, drawing on Pufendorf (2005), Kratochwil notes that in addition to requiring more elaborate rules to contract, importantly, "promises can be unilateral, while contracts involve *mutual* promises" (1989a: 152, his emphasis).

Kratochwil describes the characteristics of practice-type rules in a fashion that gives us a strong clue of their role in regulating social institutions and their relationship to the social capacities inherent in those institutions, as developed in the institutional philosophy of John Searle. Kratochwil notes that practice-type rules

> usually concern performances, and thus specify the condition under which a given action—often characterised by such terms as "hereby",

> "therefore", etc.—shall be held valid. They try to limit the circumstances which might serve for defeating reasons for the validity of such an act.
>
> (1989a: 91)

Searle similarly characterizes all human institutions in accordance with the linguistic device by which their social salience is invoked. Searle argues:

> Human institutions are above all enabling, because they create power . . . a special kind of power . . . marked by such terms as rights, duties, obligations, authorizations, permissions, empowerments, requirements and certifications. I call all of these deontic powers.
>
> (2005: 10)

Deontic powers, deriving from the collective assignment of status functions, "thereby" (if I may) constitute social structures of power relations by generating institutional facts that function as structures that generate "desire-independent" reasons for action (Searle 2005: 11). As Kratochwil argues, "what acquires here the status of an 'objective' fact is not the thing described but rather the intersubjective validity of a characterization upon which reasonable persons can agree" (Kratochwil 1989a: 229). Both Kratochwil and Searle describe the social salience by which the institutions that concern them are invoked with the linguistic formulae by which the deontic powers employed by the actor or institution (these can be coterminous) are invoked. These formulae designate speech acts, and designate that the speech in question is intended to be performative. And it is their social salience that lends prescriptive force to norms (1984b: 691).

Returning to our discussion of the reason the expectations alone cannot be the source of the obligatory nature of promises, Kratochwil reasons that it "is precisely this puzzle that speech act theory appeared to solve. It was the utilization of the institution [of promising] that created the obligation." Thus "expectations cannot be the sole reason (or even perhaps the main reason) for the obligation incurred" (Kratochwil 1989a: 147).

To summarize, the promiser has invoked the illocutionary force of a social institution through the utterance of a speech act. The promiser has represented her/himself as a moral agent. The promiser's discrepant intentions or private reservations in performing the speech act have no bearing on the obligation incurred in invoking it. The promiser has to resort to norms extant in the social order to be released from the obligation to perform the promise. The social institution of promising is governed by practice-type rules. Consequently "it is through analysing the reasons specific to a given rule or norm type that the intersubjective validity of its prescriptive force can be established" (Kratochwil 1984b: 706).

Norms and rules are "reason" for action, not "causes" of action in the strict positivistic sense. The counterfactual validity of norms, the fact that "norms are valid even if they fail to guide action in one of several specific cases" (Kratochwil 1984b: 705), and the counterfactual validity of rules—the fact that one individual may take the life of another does not invalidate a societal injunction against murder—illustrate this is so. Norms and rules "are problem solving devices for dealing with the recurrent issues of social life: conflict and cooperation" (Kratochwil 1989a: 69), they "are not only used to explain actions in the positivistic sense, but also to ascribe responsibility and assess praise or blame . . . [as] explaining an action is significantly shaped by the moral discourse and our pragmatic interest" (Kratochwil 1984b: 705). The reasons given for violating norms and rules in a specific instance must be adjudicated. And so we must also adjudicate the reasons given for abrogating a promise. We resort to norms to serve as a corpus of prior decisions to help us adjudicate the validity of the reasons given for abrogating a promise. In Kratochwil's words:

> Norms become the basis for validity claims, and conflicts among them can be decided by arguments that assign different weights to principles and norms in various circumstances.
>
> (1984b: 699)

The institutions of trust and reputation and the problem of order

Faithful and successful promisers can earn a reputation for keeping their promises, and the trust of other actors. Kratochwil has argued that the rational choice theoretic device of the prisoner's dilemma game, employed by rationalist IR scholarship to illustrate the difficulties of cooperation, relies upon the absence of mutual trust among actors as a fundamental premise of the structure of the game *qua* social setting. He has suggested that the utility of the game for analysis is less clear if promises are exchanged (a rogue's contract) between the thieves prior to their isolated encounters with the authorities.

> Trust between the two prisoners could have been strengthened . . . by advanced discussion of what to do in the case of their capture, and by their mutual promise to each other not to cooperate with "the law". The individual incentive of defection could have been weakened by "promising", i.e. by utilizing a social institution governed by rules and by trusting one another in accordance with the precept that one ought to keep one's promises.
>
> (Kratochwil 1989a: 90–1)

We need not rely in a naïve belief in "honor among thieves" to credit the assertion that the option of individuals engaged in illicit as well as licit professions, to the social institution of promising, would indeed obviate the structure of the generalized prisoner's dilemma game as presented to us by rationalist scholarship. We have established that the promiser surrenders both her/his moral as well as social agency by abrogating a promise. This is surely so with moral codes less savory than those to whom the denizens of "polite society" adhere (or at least profess to do). Should we doubt even this, we might at least assess the integrity of the payoff matrix of the generalized prisoner's dilemma game if the thieves should result to the twin social institution of mutual promising (or proto-contracts)—namely mutual threats. As Kratochwil suggests himself, so usefully in his application to the problem of nuclear deterrence,

> threatening [also] is a norm-governed activity . . . promises and threats . . . might actually have much more in common than is assumed in the conventional dichotomy. The effectiveness of both might depend upon certain common [intersubjectively shared] normative understandings . . . we seem to be able to add emphasis to our resolve by adding to a threat an additional "this I promise you". . . . When Vito, an enforcer for the Casa Nostra, "suggests" that "If you do 'x' I'll break your legs, this I promise you," it is quite clear what is meant.
>
> (1989a: 8–9)

If Vito will break your legs for doing "x" we can imagine how he might react if you "ratted on him" and got him locked up for 20 years. But for the sake of argument, let's accept Kratochwil's assertion that the thieves might have exchanged mutual promises prior to their co-commission of the crime that has them in hot water with the authorities. Matters are rather different if they have established mutual trust in whatever "promises" might have been exchanged. The authorities will face silent prisoners, who have constructed social institutions that eliminate the possibility of mutual defection. This is particularly so if the thieves have established "reputations" for keeping their "rogues bargains," whether constituted by "promises" of positive or negative inducements. Trust may be built on reputations for keeping promises. They are social institutions whose rules are a bit more complex than the practice-type rules that govern promising or threatening through performative speech acts. For example, their constitution is predicated on an actor's fidelity of performance in the ontologically prior social institution of promising (or threatening). As Kratochwil argues:

> Here Hume's argument about the importance of reputation becomes important. In potentially unlimited rounds of a PD situation an individual facing the same player not only trusts the others to follow a cooperative strategy but also chooses it himself, since the others will trust him to if he has the reputation of being a *bona fide* cooperative player. Thus generalised trust might resolve the information problem that otherwise inhibits coordination.
>
> (1984b: 695)

Thieves might resort to norms, and establish the trust of reputational effects, and more generalized systems of normative behavioral expectations in recurring social situations, quite as easily as those of us with more licit and less hazardous professions. Not only individual and collective reputations for promise keeping establish trust that helps us resolve the recurring problems of social order, but more generally, systems of intersubjectively shared social understandings regarding what we might normally expect in the behavior of others, as normatively proscribed. The Hobbesian problem of order, in Kratochwil's view, does not depend upon the threat of coercive enforcement by a sovereign to act as a third party with the power to resolve disputes among conflicting contracting (mutual promising) parties. Rather,

> order stems from the experience of trust, or assurance as Hobbes himself calls it . . . trust in the Hobbesian sense is no longer a simple human quality dependent upon personal acquaintance. Instead it is mediated through a social institution. It is trust in a general system of expectations, a system that continues to exist even in the face of occasional, perhaps even deeply felt and resented disappointments. Trust in the system is guaranteed by the intersubjectivity of the rules

> defining practices such as promising and contracting ... Hobbes invokes "reasonableness" as a standard for obligation. Thus the presence of the sovereign can for the most part remain residual, an implicit threat rather than an explicit third party to the transaction.
> (1984b: 698)

Money as a promise: Obligation and agency in the social relations of credit and debt

In our contemporary era of fiat monies, money itself is a social institution. It is a promise. Kratochwil's work on promising as a social institution, constituted by the "deontic component" of a performative speech act, is crucial to understanding the nature of the social relations of credit and debt in general, and of money in particular. Money is a claim on society. It represents a debt owed by society to its possessor that is not yet paid. Never mind that a lot of people with money made their money the old-fashioned way—they inherited it. In that case money still represents a claim by a forebear for services rendered to society but not yet redeemed. That this claim has passed to another—who continues to press it on behalf of the forebear by the mere possession of money's *promise* to redeem that claim—has no bearing on the validity of the claim, nor any bearing on the trust that the money's possessor places in the promise.

We may begin to find the social content of money in its acceptability and usage. These are the metrics of the trust and faith that people place in it, as "money is worthless unless everyone believes in it" (Greider 1987: 226). In purely economic terms trust is

> the binding cement of all contractual relationships. Whether unforeseen circumstances are likely to arise which could prevent the fulfilment of promises or obligations; through no fault of the parties concerned; is not a question of trust but of probability. This is the essential difference between a debt and an investment. The first involves a promise, the second only the expectation of a return. When we trust ... we are going beyond the mere assessment of probabilities.
> (Frankel 1977: 36)

When we trust in money, we are not actuaries calculating the probability that the promise that money represents will be redeemed. We are engaging in an act of faith. Recall in this context Kratochwil's development of the social and moral agency that the promiser acquires in invoking the institution of promising. What we can't understand, but has power over us, we have to trust. But when we lend, as we are incapable of ensuring repayment, we must also trust. A lot of money is created by precisely this highly social relationship between creditors and lenders. So "the fact that a debt represents a *promise* from the debtor to the creditor, or his successors in title, is crucial" (Frankel 1977: 46).

In this context, Kratochwil has explored the obligatory character of promises. It is important to recall that he has dismissed the suggestion that the reliance of the promissee's expectations that the promise will be fulfilled establishes this obligatory character from some first principle. Recall that drawing upon Hume, he notes the act of promising indeed generates expectations, but resolves the question of why expectations resulting from promises are so strong relative to expectations resulting from declarations of intent, or resolutions. Recall his explanation of why the illocutionary force of the promise generates obligation on the part of the promiser in view of her/his claim of moral agency. The theorist of money, S. Herbert Frankel puts it similarly in developing the social relations of credit and debt, also applicable to the issue of money by the central bank—and the promise implied that the money will retain its value:

> For not only do I signify my intention or resolution, my conviction that I can and shall perform the described action, I also present myself as a *moral agent* whose moral reputation and continuing moral relations with the person to whom I promise are at stake in the performance of the action. This I am able to do because I connect the performance of the action promised with my status as a *morally responsible agent*—to promise is to signify . . . that one has tied his status as a *moral agent* to the performance of the action in question.
> (Frankel 1977: 47)

These observations strongly and effectively emphasize not only that debt is a social, not just economic relationship, but also that it is a social relationship with an ethical basis by which the debtor must successfully represent herself to a creditor as not only an economically viable agent but as a moral agent.

Here, clearly, quite tangible benefits may result from the capacity to successfully represent oneself as a moral agent. The fact that the debtor may be an institution, such as a firm, or a government, rather than an individual, does not alter the social relations involved. Nor does the fact that the debt may be formalized by a contract that binds the debtor legally to discharge the terms of the debt contract alter the social relations involved. In contract, both parties promise. The development of the limited liability corporation may limit the exposure of its directors to the consequences of unfulfilled promises, but the rectitude of the fictitious personality of the firm as a moral agent capable of, and intent upon, fulfilling its obligations is advanced when the firm issues a debt instrument. The evaluation of the value of these promises by bond-rating agencies is a multibillion-dollar industry (Sinclair 2005). The failure of this industry to accurately evaluate the validity claims of the "promises" behind complex debt obligations might fairly be argued to be, contemporarily, of no small moment or consequence for the global economy, or to the stability of the global financial system.

A successful assertion of moral agency lies at the heart of any social relationship between debtor and creditor, when the relationship is entered into freely by both parties. Thus, as we have seen the manner in which credit functions as money, we have to consider the manner in which *not only social agency, but moral agency, is implicated in the process of money creation.* When money is instead created through the agency of the state, through the mechanism of its central bank, have the social characteristics of money-as-a-promise been lost? Contrary to nominalist critiques of the commodity theory of money, reference to Kratochwil's work suggest that this assertion of moral agency is not removed when money is created through the agency of the state. The state still "promises" when generating money. The state promises—for the neoclassically minded—that money will retain its functions as a "store of value" and remain a viable "medium of exchange" whose standard "unit of account" will not vary. As Frankel argues:

> Notwithstanding Keynes's frequent appeals to morality, his claim that all "civilized money" . . . is . . . "a creation of the State" is in effect a claim to place discussion of the nature, meaning and significance of money outside moral discourse and beyond the moral structure of a free community.
>
> (Frankel 1977: 47–8)

At the time of writing, governments around the globe are clearly issuing an awful lot of promises in the form of sovereign debt issues. They thereby hope to stimulate economies rendered moribund by the failure of performance of an uncountable number of prior "promises." Should participants in the global credit markets dismiss the illocutionary force of these promises, sovereign bond auctions will fail. Then states will engage in "quantitative easing" (e.g. print fresh money in order to buy distressed assets, without exchanging for them actual liabilities already on the balance sheet of the central bank), and thereby risk a new round of inflationary finance, thereby abrogating the promise that the money they have previously issued constitutes. A new round of inflationary finance of the order of the Great Inflation of the late 1960s to early 1980s will thereby wipe out the savings of a generation. It would appear they have rather a lot to learn from Kratochwil regarding the obligatory nature of promises, and the forfeiture of social and moral agency attending their abrogation.

5
What Do we Mean When we Say that Substance Matters?

Jörg Friedrichs

As disciplinary debates run their course, calling for a return to substance is a wildcard. It never fails as a discursive move. Commonsense opinion has it that substance matters more than rhetorical, formalistic, procedural, or other subtleties. Therefore, the call for a return to substance will go unchallenged. Interlocutors will nod their heads, and may even thank you for the reminder. After some embarrassment, however, the debate is likely to linger on unaltered. One reason for this is that you have failed to explain what you mean by "substance." This begs a more general question: What do we mean when we say that substance matters?

In various debates, Fritz Kratochwil has come down in the defense of substance. Not only when discussing legal theory, where he has emphasized that formal or procedural subtleties should never eclipse substantive considerations (Kratochwil 1989a: 9–10, 16–17, 143, 244–5, 2006d: 202–3), but also when engaging mainstream social science, where one of his mantras is that substantive problems should come first and methodological finesse second (Kratochwil 1998: 193, 196). In addition, Kratochwil has declared a predilection for substantive problems rather than trivial definitions, and a preference for a substantive over a power-based understanding of politics (1998: 198, 200).

Even when it comes to constructivism, Kratochwil has emphasized the irreducible importance of substance (2001a, see also Zehfuss 2001). This is somewhat surprising from a constructivist of the radical sort. The kind of constructivism Kratochwil espouses assumes that the social world is fundamentally "of our making" (Berger and Luckmann 1966; Onuf 1989; Kratochwil 1989a). It opposes the assumption of a social "world out there." Radical constructivists are therefore wont to dismiss "substantialism" (or essentialism, or realism) as an unwarranted obsession with ontological primitives (Abbott 1995; Rescher 1996; Jackson and Nexon 1999).

In fact, philosophers in the tradition of Aristotle have highlighted the unalterable qualities of substance. Here the fundamental idea is that phenomenal change could not take place, or not be understood, without a transcendental substratum (ὑποκείμενον) or substance (οὐσία), to which ephemeral change (γένεσις καὶ φθορά) can be related. Thus understood, substances can be both inanimate objects and organisms, or even human beings and God(s). Enduring substances are thus distinguished from accidental features such as properties, events, or actions (Jolivet 1929; Hoffmann and Rosenkrantz 1997; Wiggins 2001).

This is heavy metaphysical stuff, and it is clearly incompatible with the tenets of radical constructivism. But is it really what people like Kratochwil have in mind when they come down in the defense of substance? If not, what do they have in mind? Here is my response. The term substance is usually employed as a marker to indicate what should really matter to us. To call for a return to substance is simply another way of saying that we should return to whatever happens to be the fundamental point. Far from implying the assumption of an objective "world out there," it aims at bringing us back into focus. Whenever the fundamental point of something has been sidetracked, it is necessary and justified to call for a return to substance.[1]

Substance in discursive context

Following Wittgenstein's exhortation to look at language games rather than stipulating lexical definitions, let us examine contextual usages of the term substance. It quickly turns out that substance is one of those terms where a polar opposite is always intended, either explicitly or implicitly. Table 5.1 lists five discursive domains where substance is opposed to something else. The list is by no means exhaustive.

Table 5.1 Polar oppositions

	Substance	Nonsubstance
People	Personality	Public image
Food	Nutritional value	Taste
Poetics	Plot	Genre
Law	Substantive law	Procedural law
Politicies	Outcomes delivered	Popular appeal

In everyday life, we draw a distinction between who we are as personalities (substance) and our public image (nonsubstance). People are often more concerned with their image than with their personalities. For example, a model may be more worried about her public image than her mental stability. But this can backfire. The model may become anorexic and ultimately ruin not only herself but also her career. Somebody may therefore warn her not to forget that she is a human person after all.

Similarly, we discern the nutritional value (substance) and taste (nonsubstance) of our food. Wealthy consumers may have a tendency to prefer taste over nutritional value. For example, we enjoy chocolate truffles not for their nutritional value but for their delicious taste. But of course we know all too well that, no matter how it tastes, food sustains us physically by its nutritional value. Nutritional scientists remind us that we should concentrate our efforts on eating a balanced diet.

In poetics, the plot of a story is distinguished from the rules of the genre. The genre may be an important concern to the man of letters, but the public is moved to tears by the plot. Nobody experiences fear and pity when reading Aristotle's poetics, but some people do when following a tragedy in the theater. An author who fails to understand this will never touch his audience. He may be reminded by a critic or well-meaning friend that creative writing is all about substance and not art for art's sake.

Another familiar distinction is that between substantive and formal or procedural law. Legal professionals are often very concerned with formalities and procedural rules. Lawsuits are sometimes won or lost because of such machinations. Nevertheless all of this hardly touches the sense of equity and justice of the layman. Most people feel that for justice to be done it takes substantive prescriptions. If legal professionals fail to understand this, their jurisprudence is in danger of losing legitimacy.

Citizens are wont to differentiate between the popular appeal of certain policies on the one hand and outcomes delivered on the other. In the short run, the policy of subsidizing jobs is popular. However, this may backfire in the long run if the policy increases the public deficit and does not lead to higher employment. Elections are often won for reasons of popular appeal. But the next election may be lost for a failure to deliver outcomes. Politicians, one might argue, should therefore never take substance too lightly.

The bottom-line is that it is only by virtue of substance that things really matter. Nevertheless substantive issues are often pushed into the background. The tail sometimes does wag the dog. This is typically the case when a certain level of cultural sophistication has been reached (anorexic divas, chocolate truffles, art for art's sake, quirky lawyers, phony politicians). The result is a risk of a backlash against over-sophistication, at some point leading to the understandable call for a return to substance.

Substance in the social sciences

With that in mind, let us now turn to the social sciences. Here we can identify three ways by which substance is often lost to secondary aspects:

1. Problem-driven research is displaced by theoretically or methodologically driven scholarship.
2. The discussion of socially relevant problems is displaced by the discussion of problems relevant only to like-minded scholars.
3. The specificity of social life as the realm of intersubjective meaning is sacrificed on the altar of "scientific objectivity."

First is the drift from problem-driven research to theoretically or methodologically driven scholarship. In disciplinary science there is an unavoidable division of labor between those working on substantive problems on the one hand and those providing theoretical and methodological guidance on the other. Intellectual kudos tends to go to the latter, and rightly so. The availability of applicable theories and methods is invaluable to the scientific community at large. However, this intellectual imbalance bears a serious risk. Scholarship may become driven by theories and methods to such an extent that the available "lenses" and "tools" end up determining the research problems to be contemplated or fixed, and not vice versa (Shapiro 2002).[2] Theoretical and methodological sophistication may thus displace concern with substantive research problems. The remedy is to subordinate theories and methods pragmatically to more substantive concerns (Friedrichs and Kratochwil 2009c).

Second is the drift from socially relevant problems to esoteric scholarly debates. In disciplinary science it is unavoidable that peer recognition is an important yardstick for academic success. In specialized academic disciplines, "the requirements for entry become so elevated that producers have their rivals as their only possible consumers" (Bourdieu 1991: 15). Unfortunately, this drift leads to a serious danger that the discussion of socially relevant problems is displaced by the discussion of problems that are relevant only to like-minded scholars. Such scholarly self-encapsulation is particularly deleterious in scientific disciplines that claim to be about society. Fortunately, there is a remedy. There should be a continuous effort to make social scientific knowledge resonate with the human "objects" of analysis, with other academic disciplines, and with society at large. To the extent that scholarly consensus is meaningful and communicable to outsiders, we may be confident that substantive social relevance has not been lost in the process of esoteric scholarly debates.

Third is the drift from the intersubjective quality of social life to "scientific objectivity." Social facts have a specific quality that differentiates them from the brute facts of "nature," and a social science therefore requires a social ontology.[3] As Max Weber emphasized, the social world is constituted not by physical objects but by intersubjective meaning and "value relations" (*Wertbeziehungen*). This ontological distinctiveness of the social world has the epistemological implication that social scientific knowledge is based as much on *verstehen* as on *erklären* (Weber 1994, 2004a, 2004b). Weber was not opposed to causal explanation, but saw "explanatory understanding" as the comparative strength of social science.[4] Nevertheless the intellectual hegemony of "natural science" has made it tempting to reduce social facts to the status of brute facts. The price has once again been a loss of substance. Insofar as intersubjective meaning is the very stuff the social world is made of, it is unwise to sacrifice it on the altar of scientific objectivity. A renewed emphasis on the intersubjective quality of social life therefore means a return to what makes the social sciences substantively distinct.

Substance in Political Science

At the most general level, politics is about obligatory voluntarism in the conduct of common affairs (my claim). The idea is that after a moment of choice political decisions become binding on society. Since both "obligation" and "voluntarism" have negative connotations, my oxymoronic formula may not go down smoothly. However, a perusal of classical conceptions of politics shows that obligatory voluntarism is indeed the common denominator. We can take as a starting point the tough-minded views of conservative thinkers that the essence of politics is coercive decision-making (Schmitt 1932; Ritter 1947). We can pass from there to the more edifying views of liberal authors that politics amounts to the authoritative allocation of values in pluralistic societies (Easton 1971: 125–48). Or we may consider the republican view that politics takes place whenever free citizens meet in the public and struggle about the common fate (Pettit 1997). Whatever our specific understanding of politics—pluralism, elitism, class struggle, and so on—we will always find that politics is about obligatory voluntarism, that is, combines some form of voluntarism with the notion of binding decisions.

As any other social scientific discipline, political science has to struggle with the problems discussed in the last section. In addition, it has to struggle with the problem that obligatory voluntarism is constantly challenged in modern societies. The secular advance of formal-legal rationality, as well as the ascendancy of economic rationality, undermines the voluntarism of political decision making and the acceptance of communal obligations on the part of those subject to such decision making. Almost a century ago, Max Weber pinpointed the threat to politics posed by bureaucratization as part and parcel of modern rationalization processes (Weber 1994). In fact, the scope for political decision making is severely limited by the "dumb" power of bureaucracies, the decisions of which tend to be reached and followed not in a spirit of obligatory voluntarism but on the basis of formal-legal rationality.

Today, more than ever before, this is compounded by the ascendancy of economic rationality. The epitome is the now-familiar imagery of globalization and global governance. Regardless of whether globalization is understood in purely economic or in broader socioeconomic terms, it is usually represented as the hammer and politics as the anvil. The logic of the market, as it were, forces itself upon political actors. Political jurisdictions are seen as competing for vital investment. In addition to impersonal market forces, networks of nongovernmental associations are seen as imposing their will upon political decision makers. Thus powerful lobbies of economic stakeholders and societal activists set the agenda for the domestic, national, and international political process. If political elites struggle against these forces, they will be punished by the market and/or societal actors.

In other words, governance rather than government has become the name of the game. Politicians have no choice other than to undergo the imperatives of the market and to accommodate demands from civil society. While there may be some truth in this, obligatory voluntarism is almost entirely absent from "governance without government" (Rosenau and Czempiel 1992). As a corollary, the substance of politics is in jeopardy. Insofar as politics is about obligatory voluntarism, the possibility of swimming against the tide and/or setting in motion new chains of events is the whole point about engaging in politics. Real politicians are therefore committed to a professional ethos that upholds politics as an autonomous sphere of action and thus preserves the scope for obligatory voluntarism. For the same reason, real citizens are committed to an ethics of communal duty. As the 2008 financial crisis shows, at the end of the day societies and markets are the last to forgive politicians their failure to regulate socioeconomic intercourse.

If we recognize obligatory voluntarism as the substantive raison d'être of political practice, then this has moral implications for the discipline of political science (see Lynch, Bukovansky, and Rengger in this volume for further discussions of the moral implications of theorizing). Insofar as the idea of obligatory voluntarism that is enshrined in political practice represents, at the group level, the ideal of self-determination and freedom that make life worth living, political science has a responsibility for the provision of the conceptual tools and an adequate language to uphold politics as an autonomous sphere of action. To this end, political scientists should try to defend their discipline against colonization by other disciplines (especially economics), just as politicians should try to uphold their autonomy vis-à-vis the economy and society.[5] As political scientists we ought to elucidate where and how collective action is possible, even against all odds, lest our discipline lose its substance.

Substance in International Relations

As we have seen, politics understood as obligatory voluntarism risks losing its substance under the double strain of formal-legal and economic rationality. The academic discipline of International Relations (IR), by contrast, was originally defined by the absence of politics thus understood and has struggled ever since to find its proper substance. Unless one is ready to defend the hackneyed view that IR is defined by the state as the main international actor, and state power as the central analytical category, it is impossible to deny that the substance of the discipline is extremely evanescent. From IR's inception, scholars have therefore had serious difficulties in defining the substance of their study.

When IR was established after World War I, the dual credo was "peace through law" and "peace through commerce." After the "war to end all wars," liberal IR scholars advertised internationalism as a sort of politics to end all politics. Under liberal internationalism, the ultimate objective of international law and international organization was to get rid of state-based power politics and replace it by positive law and functional bureaucracy in the framework of the League of Nations. The hope was that formal-legal rationality and bureaucratization would put an end to the vagaries of international politics and particularly to the scourge of war.

When the liberal internationalist project came to naught in World War II, political realists such as Morgenthau redefined IR in a paradoxical way (Morgenthau 1948). On the one hand, they declared that war and power were fundamental facts of life and defined IR as "politics among nations" and thereby formally placed it within Political Science. On the other hand they insisted that, in the absence of world government, international relations were qualitatively different from domestic politics.[6] International anarchy was seen as reducing the scope for voluntarism, and the security dilemma was taken to imply that states could retract their obligations any time. IR was thus negatively defined by the absence of politics as conventionally understood.

As a consequence of this realist gambit, IR after World War II became a discipline in constant search of its substance. Because the substantive links with politics were so tenuous, it is understandable that beginning with the Cold War, IR scholars went shopping for substance in other places. Following are just a few examples.

Early in the Cold War, transnationalism harked back to sociology and emphasized the importance of cross-border transactions between societies (Deutsch 1954). Critical peace research relied on social psychology and stressed that peace is less the absence of hostilities between countries than the outgrowth of positive relationships between people (Burton 1962). Liberal scholars borrowed from economics and highlighted the direct and indirect effects of asymmetric interdependence (Keohane and Nye 1977). The search for substantive anchorage was accelerated after the end of the Cold War. Rules and regimes were rediscovered as the defining characteristic of international life (Kratochwil 1989a; Rittberger and Mayer 1993). Global governance was proposed as a paradigmatic alternative to international politics (Rosenau and Czempiel 1992). And the republican legacy of political thought was applied to the unlikely field of IR (Onuf 1998b; Deudney 2007).

The list could be continued ad infinitum, but the basic point is clear. IR is driven by a chronic lack of substance to constantly explore new avenues. Already during the Cold War, there were good empirical reasons to go beyond state-centrism and the realist obsession with power. Even more so, those who point to the obsolescence of traditional IR in the age of globalization and global governance do have a point. Economic and societal transactions are increasingly taking place in a transnational if not in a global context. For good and for ill, however, the effect is that the substantive delimitation of IR is completely up for grabs. Virtually anything happening across or beyond the boundaries of territorial states comes within the bailiwick of IR or, more broadly, "international studies." Leading IR scholars are now getting away with unsubstantial hobbyhorses such as *Harry Potter and International Relations*, or "Sovereignty and the UFO" (Nexon and Neumann 2006; Wendt and Duvall 2008).

Of course this is not to say that the traditional conundrums of IR, from the reasons of conflict to the prospects for cooperation, have suddenly become irrelevant. But calling for a return to substance is of little avail because the discipline has not been built around substance in the first place. In the absence of tangible substance it is hardly surprising that, as much as (or even more than) any other social scientific discipline, IR experiences the usual diversionary moves: a drift from problem-driven research to theoretically or methodologically driven scholarship, a drift from socially relevant problems to esoteric scholarly debates, and a drift from the intersubjective quality of social life to false pretenses of "scientific objectivity."

It has been said that IR is pursuing an elusive quest for its theoretical foundations (Ferguson and Mansbach 1988). However, the quest for substance has been at least as elusive as, and arguably a driving force behind, the elusive quests for theory and methods, academic standards of scholarship, and scientific objectivity. The problem is structural. For the foreseeable future, there is no definitive solution. Individual scholars may find their refuge in substantively defined subfields such as area studies or conflict research. But as a disciplinary endeavor IR is condemned to continue its desperate search for the Holy Grail.

Conclusion

So what do we mean when we say that substance matters? I have argued that the term substance is simply a marker to indicate that we should revert to whatever happens to be our fundamental point. My claim was substantiated by examples from various discursive domains, including the social sciences in general and political science in particular. Unfortunately it lead to a negative finding in IR's case, which has been constituted in a paradoxical way: as a subdiscipline of Political Science defined by the absence of politics understood in the conventional meaning of the term. The result is disappointing for IR scholars (like myself), but disillusionment is perhaps better than the continuation of self-delusion.

Leaving aside the ailments of our beloved academic discipline, I would like to end this chapter by pinpointing a general discursive pattern in intellectual life. There seems to be a sort of cycle that starts with substance, shifts to a progressive emphasis on nonsubstance, and finally places substance back into focus. The earliest known example of this cycle started with the concern of pre-Socratic philosophers with the substantive origin (ἀρχή) of the phenomenal world. In reaction to such crude materialism, Plato extolled transcendental ideas and saw them as prior to concrete manifestations. In reaction to Plato's philosophy, Aristotle saw matter (ὕλη) as prior to form, and form as accidental to substance (τὸ ὑποκείμενον).

The example shows that, in the long run, the drift away from substance can unleash a sequence of dialectical moves that may turn out to be progressive from the viewpoint of intellectual history. At least in the short run, however, this is far from automatic. Intellectual life can be stuck in formalism for intolerably long periods of time. It is in such periods when the call for a return to substance is the most important.

Notes

1. This view has emerged in amicable discussion with Rosalba Fratini.
2. Sometimes this tendency has achieved programmatic status: "The content of 'science' is primarily the methods and rules, not the subject matter, since we can use these methods to study virtually anything. . . . The unity of all science consists alone in its method, not its material" (King et al. 1994: 9, quoting Pearson 1892: 16).
3. This requirement was already evident to Durkheim (1982), and later reconfirmed by Wittgenstein (1958) and Searle (1995).
4. We can rise above the mere registration of functional relationships and rules ("laws") typical of all "natural science" (where causal laws are established for events and patterns, and individual events then "explained" on this basis) and achieve something quite inaccessible to natural science: namely an "understanding" of the behaviour of participating individuals.

   (Weber 2004b: 322)
5. Totalizing notions of governmentality à la Foucault or systemic self-organization à-la Luhmann are particularly unhelpful in this regard, as they obfuscate the scope for political agency.
6. The same realist adage was reformulated in structural terms by Waltz (1979).

6
On Norms, Communication and the Problem of Practice

Oliver Kessler

Constructivist thought has significantly changed the vocabulary and conceptual fabric of International Relations (IR). The previous focus on balance of power, warfare and military might has at least been augmented by now prominent concepts such as norms, ideas or institutions. At the same time, ongoing disputes and debates about the theoretical and methodological implications of these concepts, and thus on key tenets of constructivist thought, have probably created more heat than light for at least three different but certainly interrelated reasons: first, it is unclear how and what extent constructivism relates to postpositivist thought. Does constructivism *really* require a different epistemology or does it address ontology only? Do rationalists and constructivists *really* share a common "reality," or do they see completely different "things" (see Hollis and Smith 1994)? And what methodological consequences—if any—does constructivism actually imply? Although these questions certainly have no easy answer, the discussion became more complicated by what could be called the "fuzzy boundaries" of constructivist thought. The question of what constructivism "is," ignoring for a moment the performative contradiction of asking this question in the first place, and how it differs from critical realism, post-structuralism and rationalism still keeps us on our toes. Last but not least, constructivist thought is associated with different turns that augment, criticize, improve or outflank the concept of "constructivism" from various perspectives: the linguistic turn (Rorty 1967; Kratochwil 2001a; Kessler 2007), rhetorical turn (Simons 1990), aesthetic turn (Bleiker 2001), sociological turn (Guzzini 2000) and historiographical turn (Kratochwil 2001a; Bell 2001). All of these turns have left their mark in IR and yet it is unclear how they relate to each other. One can legitimately wonder whether the linguistic turn implies the sociological turn or how the historiographical turn relates to the aesthetic turn.

Now another turn has arisen in IR: for the last several years, the purported need for a "practice turn" has not only added another item to the long list of turns but has added fuel to the attempt to reconsider the entire arsenal of questions identified above (for general background see Schatzki et al. 2001). I am not sure whether the practice turn can already be regarded as the latest "development" of constructivist thought, but proponents of the practice turn do seem to distance themselves from the linguistic turn by arguing that "constructivism," however defined, cannot constrain itself to the study of discourses and texts but needs to take their embodiment in practices seriously. To study language, semantics and discourses is simply not good enough, one needs to look at how IR is "done," what its practices are and how they are reproduced.

At first sight, this call for going "back to the things themselves" to collect "empirical data" sounds awkwardly familiar. Yet proponents of the practice turn are eager to point out that their understanding of structure, time and science differs radically from positivist understandings and that their critique seeks to "radicalize" or "advance" postpositivist thought, not to trade it for positivism. Theirs is the world of "culture" and "assemblages," of performance, knowing-how and discourses that entangle the scientist in his/her material, and does not produce an objective point of view from nowhere. In a sense, the practice turn in IR mirrors Latour's critique of Foucault: while Foucault was interested in the micro-physics of power, disciplines and power/knowledge, he went to archives and read texts in order to trace them instead of going out and examining "real" practices (see in particular Latour and Woolgar 1986).

At first glance, there seems to be something to these claims and my contribution seeks to examine the relevance of the practice turn for constructivist theorizing. I argue that the practice turn, as it materializes in IR, is relevant only for those who have fallen prey to a misguided understanding of constructivist theorizing in the first place, that is, the infamous idea of constructivism as a "middle ground" between positivism and post-structuralism. Although it is still an open question whether two wrongs can make a right, I argue that the writings of Fritz Kratochwil serve as a healthy corrective. This is because the study of practical reason has been at the heart of his endeavors for the last 20 years and his work already answers some of the questions a "practice turn" unnecessarily reopens.

To develop my argument I proceed in two steps. The first part examines the practice turn in some detail and argues that it comes with two limitations: first, it introduces a binary distinction in the concept of knowledge (knowing-that vs. knowing-how) and thereby reintroduces principles of bivalent logic that positivists take for granted. Yet I argue that knowing-how becomes interesting because it requires the abandonment of bivalent principles. To conceptualize knowing-how as being something "inarticulate" through and through, as for example Pouliot argued (2008: 265), not only leads to a performative contradiction but actually leaves aside a third kind of knowledge: the knowledge of our nonknowledge. This kind of knowledge is located at the intersection of the known and the unknown and thus at the boundary of the horizon of possibilities and the continuous reproduction of potentialities and actualities. Second and related to the first point, the practice turn leaves the notion of intersubjectivity unspecified. As a consequence, it remains unclear how language and the physical world relate to each other and seems to reproduce—instead of transcending—the first vs. third person explanation. The second part turns to Kratochwil's work and argues that his work already provides a framework that is equally interested in practices, but circumvents these two limitations for two reasons: it takes the epistemological dimension of postpositivist thought seriously and it makes clear how language and the physical world relate to each other. He can thereby analyze practices by not looking "at" them but by reconstructing the conditions of their possibility.

The practice turn in International Relations

As a discipline, IR appears to be in the midst of a "practice turn." Concepts like "practices," praxis, practical reasoning and now the logic of practicality are increasingly highlighted in publications to mark another break from some existing dogma. Using diplomacy as prime example of a practice relevant for understanding international relations, Iver Neumann has recently argued that particular "narratives" could bridge the gap between discourses and practices and thereby allow us to get a better picture of knowledge relevant "on the ground." While the "linguistic turn" has led IR scholars to analyze speech acts, discourses and language games, Neumann contends that "the analysis of discourse understood as the study of preconditions for social action must include the analysis of practice as the study of social action itself" (2002: 627–8). In a way that is similar to Latour's critique of Foucault, Neumann criticizes "armchair analyses", by which he means "text-based analyses of global politics that are not complemented by different kinds of contextual data from the field" (2002: 268).

A different route is proposed by Emanuel Adler and Michael Barnett. Building on Adler's previous work on cognitive evolution and epistemic communities (Adler 1992: 101, also Adler and Haas 1992), the notion of practice is used to conceptualize the co-constitution of agents and structures.

> The key point to remember about the co-constitution of agents and structures, however, whether in the structuration or the cognitive-evolution version, is that it occurs in and through practice. Communities of practice, therefore, play a crucial role in the mutual constitution of agents and structures.
>
> (Adler and Barnett 1998: 15)

Communities of practice are defined as a group of like-minded people that learn together and engage in shared practices. They are neither stable nor fluid but constantly change with new knowledge, discourse and identities (Adler 2006:20). Adler focuses especially on the background knowledge prevalent in these communities. The knowledge shared in these communities is not simply the sum of each individual's knowledge, nor is it located in structures (2006: 21). This idea of some link between practice and background knowledge has been taken up by Pouliot (2008) when he emphasizes Polanyi's tacit knowledge and focuses on Bourdieu's discussion of the logic of practice, which are based on the notions of fields and *habitus*. *Habitus* is learnt not by "introspection" but rather the bodily engagement with the world. According to Bourdieu, a field can be understood as an arena of power relations, a "game" in which actors position themselves and struggle over scare resources (capital). Through these interactions, actors acquire practical knowledge of how to interact and play by the rules (see also Bigo 2002; Leander 2005; Abrahamsen and Williams 2008; for critical assessment, see Onuf's contribution to this volume). Pouliot is certainly right when he argues that much of what is widely perceived as "middle ground" constructivism is too focused on "motives," thereby building a theory of action defined in terms of beliefs and desires, and, as such, is open to a "thick" constructivist critique of the "new orthodoxy."

Although the arguments put forward have merits, I nevertheless think that there are two conceptual problems associated with the practice turn: it falls back on bivalent principles in the concept of knowledge, and it uses a rather ambiguous concept of intersubjectivity with further conceptual and methodological consequences.

Knowing-how and knowing-that

The proponents of the practice turn argue that IR has incorrectly paid too much attention to representational knowledge, or "knowing-that," and forgotten to highlight the importance of tacit knowledge, or "knowing-how." While positivists have long enough tortured us with a reductionist view of what knowledge "is"—a view that Russell's paradox shattered over a hundred years ago, and whose "force" and "unity" is simply a myth—the notion of practices allows us to give equal status to knowing-how. Pouliot, for example, argues that most constructivist approaches in IR focus only on "representational knowledge" and ignore knowing-how, which evades representation because it is "unreflective and inarticulate through and through" (Pouliot 2008: 265). As he explains:

> [W]hile representational knowledge is conscious, verbalizable, and intentional, practical knowledge is tacit, inarticulate and automatic. The former type of knowledge is acquired through formal schemes whereas the latter is learned experientially in and through practice, and remains bound up in it. . . . Representational knowledge is rational and abstract, practical knowledge is reasonable and contextual.
>
> (Pouliot 2008: 270)

I certainly concede that this distinction is crucial—but I think that the avenue proposed by "practice" theorists is part of the problem rather than part of the solution. Let me point out why I think this distinction is relevant before I turn to the problems.

The concept of knowledge as we usually define it is semantically linked to "truth." It is commonly thought that truth transcends the individual mind and differs from the belief in something to be true. Geometry, mathematical theorems or natural laws are true irrespective of our discovery of or belief in them. Likewise, knowledge of these facts is intersubjectively valid. On the other hand, we cannot acquire knowledge of these facts by observing the movement of objects alone, but need introspection and reason.

One of the most famous attempts to establish this view in modern times can be attributed to Descartes. Descartes based his thought on an ontological dualism where the mind and the body are conceived of as two distinct substances with each having its own properties. The mind (*res cogitans*) operates on thought while the body (*res extensa*) is essentially an extension in space. Descartes insists on our inability to be completely without consciousness while we can imagine our consciousness to exist without our body (Descartes [1637] 1996: 21). From this asymmetry Descartes contends that our knowledge of facts is based only on our thoughts (knowing-that) and not on our bodily movements (knowing-how): knowledge is a function of the mind and all knowledge derives from thought only. In this sense, for Descartes, knowing-that is prior to knowing-how. With this focus comes the primacy of *vita contemplativa* and reason over practical life or *vita activa*.

As a corollary, and leaving aside "the Matrix," it is pretty safe to say that we are not in the position to step outside of "discourse" in order to bend and break natural laws. What is true is true irrespective of space and time, and as long as truth is semantically endowed with references to invariant facts, our knowledge of those facts "should" show the same characteristics. Only the search itself, the gradual movement closer to the "truth" can see shifts and changes of our knowledge. Once we "know" that a fact is true, our knowledge of that fact can only change should we find out that the fact was not "true" after all. It comes as no surprise that most of the "evidence" for the scientific method and hence for the "reality" of knowledge consequently points to its success: if our knowledge was not "true" and objective, how come planes fly and pigs don't?

The question how and under what circumstances an individual mind can acquire knowledge and transcend the realm of "appearances" has bewildered epistemologists ever since Descartes and provides the rationale for scientific debates over criteria and processes by which we can be *certain* that something *is* true. The entire philosophy of science is full of stories and dead ends and incorporates illustrious incidents such as the *Positivismusstreit* between Popper and Adorno or the incommensurability debate between Popper and Kuhn. Although IR could certainly benefit substantially by a serious reengagement with these debates, I don't want to discuss their relevance at this point.

What is more important at this point is the ontological (in fact, metaphysical-logical) underpinning of this view. The primacy of knowing-that over knowing-how was established and legitimized on the basis of bivalent logic and associated ideas of knowledge and rationality. This idea of truth is firmly embedded in considerations about the "the being of being" (ontology) and its bivalent logic. Bivalent logic consists of the three principles of unity, noncontradiction and *tertium non datur*. The first principle postulates a unity between thought and being, that is, that thought and reality obey to the same rules of rationality. What "is" can only "be" or not be (noncontradiction), and there is nothing in between (*tertium non datur*). Something either is or is not and a sentence referring to something that "is" cannot be true and false at the same time. Most scientists adhere to this image almost all of the time.

However, as simple and convincing as these three principles are, they cannot be proven without either engaging in category mistakes or allowing for contradictions. As Bertrand Russell's paradox taught us, it is possible to construct contradiction in any sufficiently complex system. Logical paradoxes take on the form "A because non-A": the reason of possibility is at the same time the condition of impossibility. Consider the classic example "This sentence is false." If it is false, then it is true—and it if is true it is false. When we defer concepts onto themselves, we find ourselves circulating between these two alternatives and nature does not provide any answer. There is no proof of proof, no evidence of evidence, no set of all sets, no one language of all languages. As soon as we want to establish unity and force rationality onto the world, we are faced with cacophony. There is no reference between logic and reality by means of logic. In other words, we need a different logic that accounts for paradoxes, contradictions and the interplay between language and social reality. This is not an insight that we owe to "constructivism," nor is it particularly "postmodern" or particularly Kuhnian—but in fact put forward by logical positivists such as Carnap and Tarski, and later refined by analytic philosophers of mind such as Wittgenstein, Austin or Ryle.

The importance of the knowing-how/knowing-that distinction results from this inability to prove the foundations of bivalent logic. In particular Wittgenstein showed that Russell's paradox has far more radical implications than what logical positivists envisaged: it is simply not enough to introduce a plurality of worlds or different types of bivalent logic, as Russell, Carnap or Tarski suggested. If noncontradiction cannot be established fully from first principles, then bivalent logic and the idea of logical necessity a priori—and with it the primacy of knowing-that—must be abandoned.

While on the basis of bivalent logic, knowledge is associated only with knowing-that, a rehabilitation of knowing-how may lead the way to a different logic and thus a different "foundation" of scientific statements. For example, while bivalent logic is interested in the kind of knowledge we acquire when somebody responds to our question, with knowing-how we highlight what we already know and presuppose in the very process of questioning, promising, threatening etc. This is a corollary of Wittgenstein's insights that speaking is an activity and propositions have pre-predicative content. Whether it is the concept of "implicit or tacit knowledge" or "knowing how" (Polanyi 1958), life-world, cultural dependent categories (Goodman et al. 1992; Lakoff 1987), active cognition, metaphor (Lakoff and Johnson 1980) or social memory (Luhmann 1997), they are variations of this interest in the pre-predicative knowledge that provides meaning to propositions and that is relevant for understanding the social condition of cognition and perception.

While proponents of the practice turn are certainly correct in highlighting the importance of knowing-how, I think that they miss an important aspect—the abandonment of bivalent logic. Pouliot, for example, seems to suggest that knowing-how is ontologically prior to knowing-that (Pouliot 2008: 276) when he says that "the ontological priority of the logical of practicality means that it informs any and all conscious and reflective action, whether it stems from the logic of consequences, appropriateness, or arguing" (277). In effect, he puts bodily knowledge prior to the knowledge of the mind and hence treats the mind as derivative to the body.[1] What is sold as the practice turn then is based on a specific binary distinction of knowing-that and knowing-how as they are treated in substantive terms. Either something is known or it is not, either it is known that or known how.[2]

Now consider the following example: a diplomat has reacted a certain situation only intuitively and thereby solved a rather delicate situation. We might think that this is a classic example of knowing-how. Yet all diplomats are trained in their profession and they learn how to act appropriately. For example, the diplomat could have been trained to react in situations in certain ways. Even though he reacted intuitively, this reaction is the result of some instruction and knowing-that.

The same holds true for all instances of instructions, training or education: although some master mathematical problem intuitively by just looking at the equations, they were instructed in mathematics beforehand. Instructions precede the knowing-how even in "classic" cases to ride a bicycle or drive a car. In principle, even the most basic practices—such as questioning, promising, greeting, etc.—are not just natural givens but based on norms, learned and socially conditioned, as ethnomethodologists have pointed out long ago. This is not to say that knowing-that is prior to knowing-how but knowing-how is not ontologically prior to knowing-that either.

One could try to provide a typology of when one or the other comes first; but the more interesting question concerns the process-ontology underlying this distinction: knowing-how and knowing-that are not two different kinds of knowledge that require us to investigate how they relate to each other. Instead they jointly result from intersubjective and indeed constitutive social processes. Knowledge is an ascription, not a mental state. To claim otherwise would in fact produce a performative contradiction: if knowing-how is inarticulate through and through, how can we talk about it without engaging in ad hoc commentary?

Given that knowing-how is supposedly inarticulate, how can we speak about it?

Instead of dividing knowledge into two "camps," it is more productive to ask how knowledge is constructed by observing the processes by which nonknowledge is translated into knowledge. We are all aware that there are different schemes and systems by which this might occur, as Foucault has taught us. However it seems to me that we will find knowing-that and knowing-how intersubjectively related in every aspect of social reality. In particular, with a focus on this third kind of knowledge, it is possible to get a more process-oriented conceptualization of knowledge, as we can then ask how new nonknowledge gets produced. It is not the case—as bivalent logic would tell us—that either something is known or unknown (parallel to being/nonbeing). Nonknowledge exists, it has a history and we can observe the processes by which new nonknowledge is produced. Knowledge and nonknowledge—and I think the same holds true for knowing-that and knowing-how—are not simply opposites but stand in a relation of mutually reinforcing each other: the more we know, the more we do not know.

From this perspective, the main difference between practical and theoretical knowledge is that in the former categories like true and false are socially conditioned. Pursuing this line further would lead us to a host of new questions such as an examination of the very processes by which we decide whether something *is* or *is not*, whether something is true or false, an anomaly or a mistake, an interesting case or just nonsense. To observe these processes says nothing about being scientific or unscientific. Yet we could agree that science provides several avenues to derive to an answer while at the same time excluding others and that its boundaries have been altered over the last centuries.

Intersubjectivity

This brings me to the second problem in the practice turn: the problem of intersubjectivity. The literature on the practice turn—not only in IR—uses practices as located in-between given actors. Emanuel Adler argues that communities of practice can be conceived as a *group* of *individuals* and thereby uses a framework of part and whole that is in fact characteristic of English school and moderate versions of constructivism alike. Discussing the concept of practice, Neumann also argues that practices are "abstract accounts of incorporated and material patterns of action that are organized around the common implicit understandings of the actors" (Neumann 2002: 628) and he later summarizes his argument by confirming that "practices are integrative, inasmuch as they nudge human beings into relationships, be they of amity or enmity" (Neumann 2002: 637).

The question thus arises whether practices are conceived as located "in-between" human beings and not within them? Are they only regulative or also constitutive of social relations? If the latter is also included, the question arises how the transformation of "human beings" or "individuals" into social actors occurs? Where and how are the boundaries of inside/outside "practices" drawn? Who or what determines who has authority to act in certain ways to produce or reproduce some practice? Does the practice itself or some other constitutive rule determine who counts as diplomat, trader, statesman? The example of the fetiales given by Neumann is quite interesting in this respect. To quote Neumann:

> The fetiales had a particular function as ceremonial story-tellers when the Roman empire was about to take action towards another political unit, be that by going to war, by suggesting an alliance or the like. By physically moving from the inside of the empire, then to its frontier and then inside the other political unit, and by telling stories in each succeeding locus, the fetiales narrated a social field inside which acts of war, alliance and the like could then take place.
>
> (Neumann 2002: 635–6)

I am certainly not an expert on the Roman Empire, but I wonder whether it is really the practice of storytelling that is at the heart of this example? First, one could think that who counts as fetiales is part of a broader "discourse" and social role with certain rights, duties and directed expectations. Second, is not the storytelling an example for the importance of the linguistic turn that Neumann seeks to criticize? It is language in use that creates the social sphere and not simply the act of moving to the border. Clearly both are relevant. However, speech act theorists could here point out that the movement to the border is one of the necessary conditions for the speech act to be successful. This is not a critique of Neumann, but I do think that the notion of intersubjectivity implied in this example, and notion of "nestedness" he later introduces, remain puzzling. Critics could point out that in fact he—like Adler and Pouliot—thinks of intersubjectivity as a space in-between individuals, a notion that would fit uneasily with his concerns about discourse and governmentality. If in fact the "inter" is conceived of as in-between individuals, then the notion of practice would in fact simply replace the notion of "things" in bivalent logic.

In this sense, the quest for empirical data and the observation of "practice" itself seem to lose sight of the entire critique of metaphysics that gave rise to the linguistic turn in the first place. Metaphysicians always wondered what there "is" in the world, what really exists and out of what substances the world is made of. With the rise of relativity theory and complexity, it became clear that the focus on "is" has to shift to "becoming," that is, that becoming is an equal part of the conceptual framework necessary to understand social and natural phenomena alike. Meaning is not located in the things themselves but in between them. Both Husserl and Heidegger redefine the concept of meaning accordingly from the set of truth conditions to the boundary of actuality and potentiality. All that exists can only be understood within the context of the alternatives and of what does not exist. "Practices" exist only in a wider set of alternatives and within the horizon of the possible. With the actualization of potentiality, new possibilities emerge and, over time, the horizon of possibilities shifts. Taking up Pouliot's binary distinction of knowledge: only with the third kind of knowledge, the knowledge of our not-knowing, can we observe the processes by which the unknown and the realm of the possible are translated into knowledge. While practices in laboratories, universities, conferences and disciplines do have an impact on the way in which structure and meaning are imposed on an unstructured reality, the analysis of these practices escapes "direct" observation.

To highlight the methodological implications, let us reconsider the example from above: true to the focus on knowing-how, a diplomat solved a crisis during negotiations by following only his intuition. If asked, he cannot tell why or how he came up with his proposal or when and how he should speak and with what tone to bring the negotiations to a successful end. Now, an observer of this incident argues that in fact, the diplomat combined two well-established principles of diplomacy *a* and *b*, which he was taught in the school for diplomats. Confronted with this insight, the diplomat claims he was unaware of these principles and still doesn't know how he came up with them. So the actor does not know how to achieve the desired result, but the observer tells him that he applied, for example, "scheme *c*." Did the diplomat "apply" it or not?

In other words, is the ability to do something a necessary or even sufficient condition for knowing-how? If we answer yes, we have a case of knowing-that. If we answer no, we have to take everything "practitioners" say at face value—an apparently unsatisfactory state of affairs as there is certainly a difference between knowing-how and ability.

Unemployed people certainly know how to do their jobs, but cannot do them. The call for the observation of practices and the collection of data not only mirrors previous calls to the "things themselves," but buys into the same first vs. third person "explanation" we are trying to leave behind: if we start to interpret answers given to us, the knowing-how is the result of knowing-that—the knowing-that an observer-scientist formulates on behalf of the actor whose "intuitive" conduct is being observed.

Of course, this discussion was not intended to criticize or reject the claims that proponents of the practice turn make. Rather, I think that "radical" or "thick" constructivists have for a long time struggled with the same issues. They only differ in the route they take, not in the substantive interests. What I do think, however, is that in particular the work of Kratochwil helps us to circumvent the problems identified above.

Language, norms and practices

It is interesting to note what practice theorists seek to turn from: middle ground constructivism. Although their critique is certainly correct, it is strange that practice theorists seek to introduce a new turn instead of taking up the more radical versions of constructivist thought. In fact, Kratochwil's work is hardly mentioned and if it is, it is not taken up or seriously discussed but somehow taken as a precursor. Pointing to the concept of practice in Kratochwil's work, for example, Neumann concedes as much.

> When a new turn in knowledge production is heralded, it is always possible to go back and find precursors. Excavating the work of pioneers for the practice turn serves the function of giving it a history, and of reclaiming insights which may save one from reinventing the wheel.
>
> (Neumann 2002: 633)

Whether or not going back will save us from our prejudices, I do think that a more in-depth consideration with Kratochwil's work could be beneficial for at least two reasons: first, Kratochwil already pointed to the epistemological dimension of postpositivist thought, thereby circumventing the very problems the practice turn tries to address; second, he provides an account of how language and reality relate to each other, thereby providing a notion of practice that seems more promising than what a new "turn" can offer.

Epistemology and all that

That meaning is not reducible to the individual mind is a commonly shared insight of constructivist thought. Recourse to notions of convention or intersubjectivity themselves don't do the trick. Even the logical positivism of the Vienna Circle can be understood as a form of conventionalism that equated scientific statements with "intersubjective" validity. Carnap would have agreed immediately that there are various irreducible languages in which one could describe empirical phenomena and that the words, concepts and symbols in one language relate to the world by convention. However, the conventionalism of the Vienna Circle does not imply a conventionalist epistemology. If we want to make inferences, we need to observe the world. If we want to know whether swans are white, and that the name "white" is a convention, we nevertheless have to observe swans. Where constructivists and logical empiricists differ is exactly on this epistemological dimension: constructivists have abandoned the idea that words or concepts are like tags attached to things, but they refer to other concepts and words. Consequently, constructivists have abandoned the idea that meaning can be attached to "things." What something means depends on the semantic distinctions underlying the use of the concept. The epistemological question is not framed in terms of reference or adequate representation but in terms of the drawing of boundaries.

This epistemological dimension ultimately makes necessary a concept of intersubjectivity that is broad enough to analyze the *constitution* of subjects and objects through language instead of taking subjects as a given and then understand intersubjectivity as the space "in-between" those subjects. In other words, in its attempt to leave this subject–object distinction behind, the linguistic turn underlying constructivist thought also needs to (re)define intersubjectivity and disconnect meaning from the individual mind or the observation of things themselves. This is not the place to provide an overview of available alternatives. Rather, I would like to simply point out that a hook for "ontology" in human existence—and the idea of a layered ontology in general—appears to be problematic. And when we treat practices like things, then we buy into the same difficulties we actually want to leave behind.

To start from existing subjects and derive social categories as some higher form of "personality" already failed with Husserl's phenomenology. Consequently, constructivists have shifted the focus to processes: the world is the unmarked space of distinctions. But distinctions do not exist in the world, they are brought into the world. Epistemology is not the problem of representation but of drawing boundaries. This implies that the vocabulary and concepts by which we ascribe meaning are part of the world and hence that there is no subject–object distinction to start with.

In this context, Kratochwil differentiates the logic of subsumption from the logic of reconstruction. The logic of subsumption first develops a theoretical grid or topology and then examines in which box an empirical fact falls into. This is the world of technocratic science, objective "tests" and standard scientific procedures that we are all familiar with. The logic of reconstruction, on the other hand, as Kratochwil says, views a situation "from the perspective of the actor and impute[s] purposes and values based on evidence provided by the actor himself. This vantage point, in turn, provides us with an intelligible account of the reasons for acting" (Kratochwil 2000a: 65).

One could argue that Kratochwil proposes the ascription of motives to certain actions or treats actions "as if" they would fit a theoretical grid. But his argument has nothing to do with the imputation of motives. He simply points out that "explanations are not all of one and the same kind. What we accept as appropriate in a given case is thoroughly dependent on context and not reducible to some standard" (2000a: 67). Taking the "epistemological" aspect of postpositivist thought seriously thus highlights the boundaries by which something is constituted. It observes processes of inclusion and exclusion, the manifestation of the actual from the possible—and thereby the horizon of possibilities. We cannot simply look at an object to acquire its meaning but need to take the boundaries into account if we are to account for processes, change and "becoming." What constructivists do argue is that the constitutive rules are to be found in language and not the "external" world, a point to which I turn now.

Language and materiality

As Kratochwil often mentions, *Rules, Norms, and Decisions* (1989a) is often cited but seldom read. I certainly agree that that book is difficult, but it is worth the effort. Already on its first pages, Kratochwil's argument makes interesting twists and turns. Thus on the fifth page we find a remarkable sentence:

> In particular, I shall argue that our conventional understanding of social action and of the norms governing them is defective because of a fundamental misunderstanding of the function of language in social interaction, and because of a positivist epistemology that treats norms as "causes."

Interestingly enough, language is further analyzed not in terms of language per se (*langue*) but in terms of speech and communication (*parole*). Although the concept of communication is often referred to, it is hardly taken seriously in IR as a *theoretical* concept (Richmond et al. 2008, being an exception).

Within the norms literature, communication takes place between existing actors and describes the conveyance of meaning. In this sense, communication is reduced to the propositional content of an utterance and its reference. Communication takes place when the message of a sender is understood by the receiver. Almost inevitably, the question is then raised: under what conditions can effective communication take place and be considered an empirical and not a conceptual problem. This question leads down a path often pursued by "the new orthodoxy"—and that instantly falls back on questions of subsumption (that is, what is the case, what motives were relevant, what were the material interests, etc.). As the discussion above indicated, the examples proponents of the practice turn use similarly seem to point to such a sender-receiver model (which is based on the in-between concept of intersubjectivity): some given actors utter words. Maybe that is the reason why the boundary between language and material world somehow does not play a further role in the practice turn. Language somehow exists and Adler, Neumann and Pouliot certainly differ significantly on what role language and discourse play in "constructing" social reality, that is, they differ on how the materiality of language relates to the "materiality" of physical objects.

Kratochwil's discussion is illuminating in this respect. He takes up the common differentiation between the locutionary, illocutionary and perlocutionary effect and thereby departs from the common framework that captures only the conveyance of propositional content. Yet Kratochwil also departs from speech act theory, which locates meaning in the illocutionary force of the speech act and thereby produces a bias toward the logic of subsumption. That much of the literature on speech act theory (e.g. Onuf 1989) is rather taxonomical might be a case in point. For Kratochwil, it is not the illocutionary force but the perlocutionary effect, that is, the structure of the discursive interaction, which controls the meaning (Kratochwil 1989a: 30).

Locating the meaning "between" illocutionary force and perlocutionary effect, Kratochwil departs from monological social theories focused on syntax or semantics and embraces a plurality of different actors involved in communication. Orthodox constructivists will claim that they also recognize different actors. However, these actors are treated in terms of sender and receiver and not illocution and perlocution. The difference is that in the former model, communication is like a train running in between two cities and meaning like a parcel exchanged between individuals. In the latter model, meaning is a complex arrangement of selections and distinctions that consists of at least two different kinds of information: the illocutionary force and the perlocutionary effect. Language not only regulates communication between actors but constitutes actors. Kratochwil's discussions on generative grammar and constitutive rules all point to a broader concept of both intersubjectivity and communication than we can find in the new orthodoxy.

In this sense Kratochwil's discussion of Popper's three worlds is quite illuminating (Kratochwil 1989a: 21–5). Popper differentiates between observational facts, mental facts and institutional facts. There is a clear separation between mental and institutional facts and hence a distinction between the motives or interests actors may have, and any actual communication about them. As Kratochwil notes, the binding effects of a promise do not depend on individual beliefs. "Moves" have nothing to do with "some mysterious empathy or the private mind of the actor" (2000a: 66). Not the private feeling of pain but shared meanings make it possible to communicate even if we never consciously perceive the actual private sensation.

In this sense, the validity of norms cannot be attributed to some normative force or inner goodness but rather must be attributed to the role they play within communication: they allow for the creation and stabilization of expectations.

> Norms not only establish certain games and enable the players to pursue their goals within them, they also establish inter-subjective meanings that allow the actors to direct their actions towards each other, communicate with each other, appraise the quality of their actions, criticise claims and justify choices.
>
> (Kratochwil 1993a: 75)

Norms, in other words, do not causally determine some actions, and so it is simply useless to derive the validity of norms (and constitutive rules for that matter) by observing behavior. Taking up the distinction of being and becoming, norms provide the horizon of possible actions. They always allow for a plurality of actions and in fact violations without actually losing their validity. To reconstruct the meaning of norms and rules therefore requires one to identify the semantic distinctions giving rise to disparate set of practices, in order to place them in context of a wider set of alternative. This brings me to the last point: the concept of practices.

Again in *Rules, Norms, and Decisions,* Kratochwil identifies a certain unsatisfactory state of theorizing about the international system. He argues that there are in principle two ways of addressing this problem. We could

> start anew with certain assumptions concerning the role of norms and deductively trace their implications. The other approach is largely embedded in a historical recollection. It raises new issues by attempting to rid us of the amnesia of what usually we take for granted and by rearticulating the unstated assumptions of our practices and theoretical understandings.
>
> (Kratochwil 1989a: 2)

By implication, Kratochwil rejects the distinction between domestic and international politics (in contrast to orthodox constructivists), but then proceeds to examine the "practices" whereby this boundary is differentiated.

It is simply not the case that the concept of practice is entirely unknown to constructivists, as Neumann concedes. However, for constructivists the notion of practice is linked to the use of words and concepts. The reconstruction of practice is thus linked to the reconstruction of the grammar of concepts. From this perspective, the grammar of "practices" in the practice turn fuses several distinctions such as, for example, theoretical vs. practical knowledge on the one hand, and "text" or discourses vs. practices on the other (see Wittgenstein 1958: §90). Kratochwil and the more recent advocates of practice in IR theory build on different literatures based on different set of questions. What is now sold as a new turn is from this perspective old wine in new bottles. But whereas key distinctions like ideas/matter or questions of communication and language are somehow lumped into the concept of practices, the conceptual framework provided by Kratochwil avoids these pitfalls. In the end, the question is probably less what the practice turn can achieve, but why it is happening now.

Conclusion

Proponents of the practice turn are correct that the question of how norms matter has not been answered satisfactorily by the middle ground version of constructivist IR theory.[3] However, there are two limitations linked to the specific way that the practice turn is introduced in IR:

a binary opposition of knowing-how and knowing-that and an unclear concept of intersubjectivity. I think it is here that Kratochwil's work provides a valuable corrective. In particular, it seems to me that the critique by practice theorists presupposes that a specific "ontology" could somehow be associated with constructivist thought, with the consequence that Giddens is then considered the grandfather of constructivism. A reconsideration of Kratochwil's social theory might provide a healthy corrective to an emerging debate.

Notes

1. Ironically enough, this position is quite similar to that of Alexander Wendt's notion of supervenience. See Kessler (2007).
2. To hype the rediscovery of this distinction as a major break in the project of modernity (Pouliot 2008: 259) is problematic. The distinction goes at least back to Kant and his distinction between judgment and the capacity of making judgments and has been continuously used ever since, although predominantly in conservative social theory. What he misses is a third, more process-oriented kind of knowledge: the knowledge of our not knowing. I think the neglect of this third kind of knowledge highlights some limitations of the binary system.
3. Kratochwil 2000a. Certainly of interest in this context is Wiener (2008, and this volume) who emphasizes contestation and thereby formulates a valuable critique.

7

Social Science: A Social or Scientific Project?

Richard Ned Lebow

In the early years of the twentieth century, the Vienna Circle and its associates sought to devise logical foundations for science. Their project never had much appeal for physical scientists and key participants in this project, notably Carl Hempel and Karl Popper, ultimately developed quite different understandings of how science works and should work. The logical positivism of the Vienna Circle found its most receptive audience among American social scientists, who in the postwar era turned to it for scientific justification of their enterprise. Although logical positivism has been severely criticized by philosophers and largely ignored by scientists, it still strikes a responsive chord among political scientists. King, Keohane and Verba's *Designing Social Inquiry* (1994), perhaps the most widely used text in graduate methods seminars in the US, espouses a foundationalist epistemology based on arguments of Karl Popper that he himself subsequently disavowed (Popper 1972: 78–81). In addition to his many substantive contributions to the field of international relations, Fritz Kratochwil has sought to expose the scientific pretensions of American social science and by doing so, has raised and addressed important epistemological and ethical questions.

In several publications Fritz rightly argues against the possibility of a foundationalist epistemology and explores alternatives. In "Evidence, Inference, and Truth as Problems of Theory Building in the Social Sciences" (2007e), he addresses the problem of warrants in science by means of an imaginary scientific contest between Galileo and his Aristotelian opponents. Galileo maintained that air had weight—what we today we call mass—which Aristotelians, closely associated with the Roman Catholic Church, strenuously denied. In this counterfactual, the two sides agree to scour Europe for the best scales and pig bladders. On the day of the contest a large crowd assembles in St. Peter's Square and individuals trusted by both sides inflate a pig bladder and place it gently on a finely balanced scale. On the other scale they place an uninflated pig's bladder. Nothing happens and the Aristotelians are on the verge of proclaiming victory when Galileo says, "Do it again." For a second, and then a third, time inflated bladders are put on scales with no observable effect. Instrumental error is ruled out and the Aristotelians proclaim that the truth of their position is vindicated. A thoughtful and disappointed Galileo suddenly realizes why the scales have not moved and attempts to explain the principle of displacement to his interlocutors. Objects in air have buoyancy just as they do underwater. If we filled a bladder with water underwater the scale would not have moved either. The Aristotelians are puzzled and then infuriated by his attempt to discredit the experiment and its indisputable results. Science is science, they proclaim, and Galileo is being unscientific, if not a sore loser, by trying to change the rules of the game.

In this ironic tale, the Aristotelians, clearly on the wrong side of the debate substantively, nevertheless appear to have reasonable methodological grounds for their claim to be practicing good science. They agreed to an empirical test of the proposition in dispute, negotiated the nature of that test with their opponent, sought state-of-the-art technology, arranged for the experiment to be conducted openly by mutually trusted "technicians" and carried out several tests to minimize the possibility of experimental error. The reader is forced to go beyond the practices of so-called normal science to figure out what is wrong here. The problem, of course, is that it is difficult, if not downright impossible, to separate theoretical assumptions from propositions being tested and the methods used to test them.

Underlying assumptions about the world guide both our choice of propositions to test and the means used to do this. The Aristotelians in the story are insensitive to these connections and convinced that methods and warrants are derived independently of propositions. Galileo's appeal to displacement is not only an attempt to explain why the experiment did not produce the result he wanted but why that experiment was conceptually flawed and an inappropriate test of the proposition. The Aristotelians are unreceptive to his arguments because of the unquestioned assumptions they have brought to the experiment. They are neither stupid nor obtuse as the differences between their assumptions and Galileo's are subtle. Weight, they believe, is always measured by a scale. The failure of the scales to move means that air does not weigh anything. In practice, the scales did not move because they have the same weight of air above them (the column above them up to the top of the earth's atmosphere). The Aristotelians have limited themselves to visible objects and therefore count the air inside the bladder but do not consider the air outside.

The resistance of the Aristotelians to Galileo's argument cannot be attributed to close mindedness in the narrow sense. Consider the double counterfactual that they had lost the experiment. Many of them may have been willing to concede the point in this circumstance. What they were objecting to was Galileo's desire to change the experimental protocols, which they considered inappropriate and unscientific. In a deeper sense, of course, their opposition derived from what we now regard as an antiquated understanding of science. Experimental protocols are not graven in stone or somehow logically derived independent of the subject matter to which they pertain. Rather, they evolve in tandem with our understanding of the physical and social worlds and are therefore also open to criticism, refutation and reformulation. Galileo's move was the right one, but his audience, given their meta-understanding of science, was deaf to his appeals. It is on this level that Fritz intends an analogy between Aristotelians and many modern social scientists.

Modern philosophy and psychology have made it clear that neither the "order of being" nor categories of the mind can provide a universally valid Archimedean point from which to assess truth claims. Truth is not a property of the "world" out there waiting to be discovered but mediated by the concepts we bring to its study. These concepts, moreover, are inescapably "fuzzy" because they are built on and derived from still other concepts. There is an infinitude of questions, moreover, and no objective way of determining which are the important ones to ask. And if another nail in the coffin is needed, Fritz argues persuasively in "The Tartu Lecture" (2007a), that most of the answers to the questions we ask are neither "yes" nor "no" but something in-between. The standard binaries of social science that enable the coding of evidence in so many quantitative studies force researchers to make indefensible, even arbitrary choices. What are we to do in these circumstances?

Two indefensible responses, Kratochwil argues, are to deny the problem or offer indefensible warrants for truth claims. Truth claims must constantly be tested and defended. We must keep the notion of a "court," but one in which Kant already understood, scientists themselves are the claimants and judges. Kratochwil further asserts that we must become pragmatists in the sense of continuing our research despite uncertainties and unknowns and in the absence of logically defensible warrants. The rules governing research are best described as shared practices that evolve in response to the understandings of practitioners, emergence of newer methods and cumulative "wisdom" in the form of new and more sophisticated questions. A scientific community, as Popper came to realize, is a set of persons who share certain techniques, such as measurement procedures, methodological commitments and presumptions of what constitutes "good practice" in a given field (Kratochwil 2007e).

I fully support this approach to social science. Based on this understanding, Steven Bernstein, Janice Gross Stein, Steven Weber and I (2007) have argued for the reformulation of social science as a set of case-based diagnostic tools. Most of what moves human behavior is outside the theories that seek to account for it. As evolution is determined by random genetic mutation, mating patterns and changes in environmental niches—all outside the theory of evolution—evolutionary biologists direct their attention more to explanation than prediction. Social scientists should follow suit. We understand our theories as nothing more than starting points for forecasts. We should develop these forecasts as future narratives along other narratives might develop from the same starting point. The latter should be held in reserve while we focus on our preferred story line and seek information that enhances or diminishes our confidence that the future is unfolding s we expect. If not, we should switch to another story line, or develop a new one. We cannot predict the future by this means but can get early warning that our expectations are incorrect. More fundamentally, it teaches us that the world rarely coincides with our expectations about it, encouraging openness and humility.

Kratochwil does not elaborate what science as a practice entails beyond noting that all assertions must be backed by evidence and there must be some agreed-upon rules for collecting and weighing evidence. As he fully recognizes, these rules depend on shared understandings which risk becoming dogma, as they did for Aristotelians and arguably have for King, Keohane and Verba. Nowhere in *Designing Social Inquiry* is there even a hint that the rules and procedures they expound for research design, data collection and analysis are provisional, open to challenge and certainly likely to change over the course of time. Nor is their recognition that these rules are frequently violated to good effect by scientists. Research protocols are also open to the kind of distortion, exploitation and tautology that can make a mockery of science. The solution to this problem is social, not scientific. It does not depend on more elaborate description of research protocols and their communication to students—the focus of almost all North American and many European scope and methods courses—but on the commitment to open-minded inquiry and the acceptance of all methods and findings as at best provisional truths.

There is widespread agreement among philosophers and scientists that science is a set of shared practices within a professionally trained community (Kuhn 1970; Rouse 1987). The competent speaker, not the grammarian, is the model scientist, and each discipline, like speakers of a language, is the arbiter of its own practice. All insights and practices, no matter how well established, are to be considered provisional and certain to be superseded. Debates are expected to scrutinize tests and warrants as much as research designs and data. Consensus, not demonstration, determines what theories and propositions have standing. In his last decades, Popper himself spoke of relative working truths—"situational certainty" was the term he coined—and emphasized the critical role of debate and radical dissent among scientists (Popper 1972: 78–81).

In the physical and biological sciences, and in psychology, science as a practice works reasonably well. One reason for its success in these fields is a general consensus in these disciplines about the goals of science, appropriate research methods and rules for gathering and evaluating evidence. In psychology, where I have a quondam departmental affiliation, there is a sharp division between clinical and other fields, but universal regard for carefully constructed and implemented experimental studies. Disputes are frequent about the relative merit of particular experimental strategies, statistical tests used to evaluate data and the kind of inferences data will support. The allocation of resources among different branches of the field is also contested. One only infrequently hears discussions or reads articles (and never in peer-reviewed scholarly journals) about whether psychology or its subfields are sciences. In political science, by contrast, these conflicts rage, and articles about them appear in top professional journals. We differ from psychology and the hard sciences in at least two important ways. In psychology, there is not only an overall consensus about what qualifies as scientific method but a general willingness to let different fields work out their own more particular understandings. The newest field in psychology—neuroscience—has been successfully accommodated. Tensions exist, to be sure, but one finds few practitioners of neuroscience scoffing at other subfields and their research methods.

In political science, there is no consensus about fundamental issues in the discipline or within most subfields. Epistemological and methodological conflicts are often more acute within fields than between them, as researchers in the same field must compete for space in some of the same journals, jobs for their students and new positions or hires at their respective institutions. Intellectual controversies are the driving mechanism of scientific progress, but can destroy the practice of science when they get out of hand. There is often a fine line between progress and degeneration, and that line is more difficult to discern when there is no consensus about fundamental epistemological and methodological questions as in the case of political science. Ironically, the distinction Lakatos introduced between progressive and degenerate research paradigms is often used in rhetorical ways to excoriate opponents, which indicates degeneration of a social nature.

The obvious solution to dissensus is to allow space for each intellectual community to pursue its project and develop its own "court" for evaluating work within its tradition. Let me reflect on the situation in the US. To its credit, the *American Political Science Review* in recent years has made progress toward this goal. The *Review* now encourages work from all traditions and sends manuscripts out to review primarily to people who do the same kind of work. Some other prominent journals are less tolerant and less professional in their review procedures. Almost everyone I know—regardless of their methodological orientation—has a horror story to tell about a major journal. Having served on the editorial boards of many major journals in the field, I tend to believe most of these tales. At a board meeting of the *American Political Science Review* in the 1990s, I was stunned to hear a prominent comparative politics scholar condemn traditions other than rational choice as being in "the ash can of history" and undeserving of space in the *Review*. Differences encouraged a proliferation of journals, many with particular intellectual profiles. Neoliberals gravitate to *International Organization*, realists to *International Security*, quantitative researchers to the *International Studies Quarterly*, constructivists and critical theorists to *Millennium*.

Letting a hundred journals bloom is possible in a robust economy, but has its drawbacks when it is based on approach instead of subject. Intellectual fragmentation will almost certainly increase because people from one tradition will be less likely to read work of researchers from others. It encourages representatives of traditions with entrenched institutional positions to play the journal ranking game. At many US universities, chairs and deans assess publications less by their individual quality than by the alleged quality of the journals in which they are published. They rely on rankings, which privilege, of course, the dominant discourses in the discipline. British and European journals like the *European Journal of International Relations*, *International Relations*, *International Politics*, *Millennium* and *Review of International Studies* are ranked lower than their American counterparts, benefiting certain epistemological and methodological orientations over others in hiring, tenure and promotion decisions.

Consensus, or at least a "live-and-let live" approach, has been made difficult by successive waves of hegemonic projects in the postwar era. The first of these was the so-called behavioral revolution, whose leaders sought to advance their influence within the profession by wrapping themselves in the mantle of science and depicting their adversaries as fur-skin clad holdovers from the cave era. Once in authority, they purged many major departments of faculty in public administration, constitutional law and political theory, and reshaped the intellectual profile of the remaining fields. At more than one Middle Western "Big Ten" university where quantitative researchers have achieved institutional primacy, they have consistently excluded, and occasionally forced out, researchers from other traditions. In the 1990s, a former dean at one of these schools announced that there was no room at his institution for postmodernists—in which category he included constructivists. At certain coastal schools, rational choice scholars have behaved in a similar manner. Today, modelers are making a bid for hegemony. Students in a leading "Ivy League" political science department report being told in their introductory methods course that modeling is the future of the discipline and that they will find it difficult to get jobs at good schools unless they "tech up."

Prominent and influential professors—the kind of people Kurt Lewin called "gate keepers"—have a special responsibility for demonstrating leadership and tolerance. Many live up to this responsibility, but it takes only a few who do not to subvert or severely stress the kinds of practices that are essential to an open scholarly community. One scholar in the field is known to write unsolicited letters opposing the tenure of faculty members who work in traditions different from his. In one department in which I taught, the chair received and circulated a letter from the scholar in question, an intemperate attack on a constructivist up for tenure, noting that it was unsolicited. I suspected the letter was sent around in the expectation that it would backfire—as indeed it did—and help guarantee a positive vote from nonconstructivists not wanting to be dictated to by an outsider. I can readily imagine that some other, less distinguished and less self-confident departments might well be influenced by such a letter.

Epistemological and methodological disputes open space for another kind of abuse: the passing off of polemics as scholarship. On the one hand, scholars are not simply private citizens and expressing personal opinions, and their work may have an impact, sometimes directly, on the making of public policy. That they would like to have such an impact is to be applauded. On the other hand, it is tempting to simplify one's scholarly claims unduly or manipulate the factual record deliberately for partisan purposes. When self-restraint gives way to self-promotion at the price of scholarship, the public is misled and the profession as a whole suffers. It need not be this way. Over the last 70 years, the practice of foreign policy has been significantly influenced by the writings of E. H. Carr (historian), Thomas Schelling (economist) and Hans Morgenthau (political scientist), none of whom debased contemporary understandings of scholarship in their respective fields to better put their points of view before the public.

The two kinds of unprofessional behavior I have described encourage us to reflect further on the relationship between so-called facts and values. Because facts cannot be separated from values, social understanding is inherently subjective. Research agendas, theories and methods are conditioned by culture, beliefs and life experiences. So too is receptivity to research findings. Recognition of this truth has led some scholars to interpret social science as a political process and cloak for individual and group claims to privilege. Back in the 1960s, Hans Morgenthau (1966b: 71–2) warned that the government disposes of a wide range of professional rewards that help to determine the status of professors. As social science was responsive to the power structure, it was not surprising that its findings most often justified that structure and buttressed its legitimacy. "Truth itself," he warned, "becomes relative to social interests and emotions" (Morgenthau 1966b: 140–4). Morgenthau was not persuaded of the efficacy of the barriers the scientific method erects against theories and propositions that cannot be falsified or are demonstrably false. Neither, to his credit, is Fritz. When we compare their respective concerns, which span more than two generations, we see that not much has really changed.

This problem is real and continuing and attributable in large part to scientists themselves. Nineteenth century biological and anthropological studies of cranial capacity "proved" the superiority of the Caucasian "race." Some contemporary researchers (e.g. Herrnstein and Murray 1994) are still trying to do this with data from intelligence tests. Well-founded scientific claims also encounter resistance from the wider community. The theory of evolution continues to provoke widespread opposition from fundamentalist Christians with the tacit support of the Bush administration. Claims by medical researchers that smoking is harmful, and more recently, by environmental scientists that the waste products of industrial society threaten an irreversible transformation of the environment, have encountered predictable opposition from industries with profits at stake. The tobacco companies and some major polluters support scientists who dispute these claims.

Kratochwil makes it abundantly clear that there is no such thing as a "scientific method." Researchers and philosophers of science argue over what constitutes adequate specification and testing, the extent to which it is possible and, more fundamentally, about the nature and goals of science. Attempts to provide definitive answers to these questions, as Karl Popper recognized, inevitably fail and risk substituting dogma for the ongoing questioning, inquiry and debate that constitute the core commitment of science. These controversies render scientific truth uncertain, but working scientists, invoke the techniques and skills they have learned, for the most part have little difficulty in distinguishing good from bad science. Cases where there is no consensus are the critical ones. Disagreement among respected practitioners suggests that there is ambiguity or inadequacy in the rules we use to evaluate scholarship, or how they are being applied in a particular case. If the former, the controversy ought to welcomed as an opportunity to debate, rethink and further hone our procedures and practices. If the latter, it can provide an opportunity to foreground our commitment to appropriate norms. Both kinds of events, if handled professionally, can help socialize graduate students and junior faculty and increase the chances that future dissensus will be addressed with similar openness and introspection.

The scientific method in many ways resembles the Bill of Rights of the American Constitution. Its meaning is also interpreted through practice. Like the scientific method, it has not always been interpreted or applied fairly. The Bill of Rights has sometimes failed to protect political, religious and so-called racial minorities from the ravages of prejudice. In 1898, *Plessy* v. *Ferguson* paved the way for the principle of separate and equal education for African-Americans which endured until *Brown* v. *Board of Education* in 1954. De facto segregated education continues to this day in some locales. *Brown* v. *Board of Education* reflected changing attitudes toward African-Americans, the constitution and education more generally. Another impetus was extensive social science research that demonstrated that separate education was inherently unequal. Despite continuous controversy about the meaning of the constitution and periodic failures to apply its principles in practice, there is an overwhelming consensus that the Bill of Rights—and even more importantly, the American public's commitment to tolerance—remains the most important guarantee of individual freedoms. The scientific method is an imperfect but essential bulwark against many of the same kinds of passions. Like the Constitution, it ultimately depends on the ethical standards and commitments of the community it serves.

Kratochwil suggests that there is an important distinction to be made between the questions we ask and how we find answers to them. What distinguishes us from ideologues, is our commitment to finding and evaluating answers by means of a scientific method—a set of evolving procedures that we agree is appropriate to defining, collecting and evaluating relevant evidence. Social scientific research agendas are shaped by political beliefs, life experiences and desires for professional recognition. There is nothing wrong with these motives. Good social science should be motivated by deep personal involvement in the burning issues of the day. Research can clarify these issues, put new issues on the agenda and propose and evaluate the consequences of different responses. It can also influence the way people conceive of themselves, frame problems and relate to the social order.

As Max Weber (1994) recognized, the fact–value distinction and science conceived of as practice put a premium on the ethics of the scholarly community. The principles of ethics, not those of logic govern this process of knowledge production. According to Kratochwil (2007e: 98),

> [i]t brings to the fore the silent presuppositions and invites us to critically reflect upon them, establishing the importance of practical reason and judgment. In a way, these considerations also provide the strongest possible rationale for pluralism, not as the second best but as the most promising strategy for producing warranted knowledge.

Values not only enable facts but sustain our identities as scholars and enable the practice of science. In the absence of ethical commitments, we would become indistinct from polemicists and spin doctors. Ethics are in turn instantiated through practices. As graduate students we learn professional ethics the same way we learn other values and habits: by emulating those we respect. If we see that tolerance and pluralism routinely violated by our mentors we may calculate that it is in our professional interest to follow suit, if only because these values seemingly involve real professional costs.

In 1934, Hans Morgenthau published his third and final prewar book, *La réalité des normes*. It addressed the problem of sanctions, and its argument was deeply influenced by, but highly critical of, Hans Kelsen's abstract approach to international law. Morgenthau submitted it as his *Habilitationschrift* at the University of Geneva, where it was rejected by the first examination board. A second board accepted the manuscript primarily because the ever-magnanimous Kelsen made such a strong statement on Morgenthau's behalf (Frei 2001: 45–9). If Kelsen could act this way under the fast spreading penumbra of the Nazi regime, those of us who live in supportive political and economic environments should be ashamed to act any less honestly. To Fritz's credit he has always acted professionally in accord with the highest ethical principles and has taught his students to do the same. He is the living embodiment of a German intellectual tradition that was besieged and then suppressed in the first half of the twentieth century but due to people like him has made a notable and successful comeback.

Note

This is an revised version of Lebow (2007).

Part II

Arguing with Kratochwil: Rules, Norms and Ethics

8
Rules in Practice

Nicholas Onuf

Fritz Kratochwil has long talked about *practice*. In an early, important essay, he identified "the problem of praxis" as "the necessity of choice in situations where no logically compelling solution is possible" and thus a problem of "practical reasoning" (1983a: 40). In the shadow of Aristotle's *Nicomachean Ethics*, linking *praxis* and *phronesis* is plausible but, as I argue below, hardly sufficient. A later paper has a several-page section headed "Understanding Praxis" (Kratochwil 2000b: 59–63), which speaks of "practical matters" and "practical problems"—as if this were ordinarily understood ordinary language—in the context of theory building. Only recently, Kratochwil presented a paper at a conference on "The Practice Turn in International Relations" (see Pauliot 2008: 265–9). Since that paper (which he graciously sent me) is a preliminary, untitled draft, I will allude to it only in general terms.

In the field of International Relations, many of us use the term *practice* just as generally and loosely as Kratochwil did in his 2000 paper. In my own I case, I often refer to "rules and related practices" with no elaboration. No doubt Kratochwil and I are influenced by legal practice, where the sense of the term *practice* is taken for granted (see below). Some of us speak of practice, at least some of the time, to signal critical or postpositivist allegiances. Again, I do not doubt this is so for both of us, if not always as a conscious practice (again, see below). Insofar as recent discussion exhibits any coherence at all, it suggests a turn to pragmatism (a major concern in Kratochwil's unpublished paper; also see Bauer and Brighi 2008 and Kratochwil's paper therein; Kessler, this volume). If indeed a practice turn is underway, then Kratochwil will in some measure be responsible by virtue of adopting this turn of phrase.

Always concerned with use and meaning, Kratochwil strongly resists any effort to troll usage, discriminate senses of any abstract term and fix meanings by reference to ideal types or formal templates—practices he identifies with formal reasoning, rationalist theorizing and positivist science. On this we differ, perhaps more deeply than on any other issue. I prefer to identify categories and devise models (including taxonomies), and then refine them on the evidence. Here I will identify two general models of practice in circulation and then show that their terms are so poorly specified that the two models collapse into a single incoherent concept of practice.

In its place, I propose a pair of related but strictly differentiated models that offer complementary enticements for research. Next I consider Stephen Turner's telling critique of practice as generally conceptualized in social theory (1994, 2002: Chapters 1 and 8), to which, I might add, Kratochwil is exceedingly hostile. I affirm Turner's claim that the concept of practice results in bad theory, but only if the source of the concept is the mixed model in general use. Then I try to show how the concept of practice, once clarified, relates to the concept of *choice* (to which Kratochwil alluded in 1983a).

Choice is as central to positivists (not to mention the philosophical defense of free will, most conceptions of agency and intention, and liberal ideology) as practice is to critical and postpositivist thinkers. Here I suggest that there are two models of choice strikingly analogous to the two models of practice. I conclude with some very brief remarks on whether these two pairs of models complement each other.

Action and activity

In social theory, the term *practice* is a legacy of Marx. The young Marx defined *praxis* as "sensuous human activity (*menschliche sinnliche Tätigkeit*)" and further claimed that "social life is essentially practical" (1969a, b). He also invoked the distinction between theory and practice (specifically, revolutionary practice), thus seeming to suggest that theory is *not* one of the many practices making up social life. Ever since, Marxists have invested a great deal of effort in developing theory about the relation of theory to practice and distinguishing such a theory from theories that fail to take their own practical implications into account. I prefer to think that Marx's greater legacy was his emphasis on an inclusive conception of practice grounded in the material conditions of everyday life. Today, the best example of this way of thinking is perhaps Michel de Certeau's *The Practice of Everyday Life* (1984).

Writing in 1845, Marx may have read Kant's essay, "On the Common Saying: This May Be True in Theory, but It Does Not Apply in Practice"

(*Über den Gemeinspruch: Das Mag in der Theorie richtig sein, taugt aber nicht für die Praxis*, 1793). Here is how Kant began: "A collection of rules, even of practical rules, is termed a *theory* if the rules concerned are envisaged as principles of a fairly general nature. . . . Conversely, not all activities are called *practice*, but only those realisations of a particular purpose which are considered to comply with certain generally conceived principles" (Reiss 1991: 61, emphases in translation). Kant went on to say that this spare description of theory implies not just understanding—the ability to generalize from particulars—but also "an act of judgment whereby the practitioner distinguishes instances where the rule applies from those where it does not" (p. 61).

Understanding and judgment are two of the higher faculties, or powers, that human beings are said to possess. In the *Critique of Pure Reason*, Kant systematically reconsidered these faculties, to which Aristotle had given a privileged position as applied forms of reason. By contrast, Marx's emphasis on "sensuous activity" shifts attention to the lower, bodily faculties of motor activity, perception and emotions so pervasively affecting what we actually do from one moment to the next. Marx's view of practice includes the exercise of the higher powers. Yet it does seem to emphasize the importance of judgment, and not our knowledge of the rules, in how we carry on as sensuous beings.

If we look back beyond Marx, Kant and their early modern predecessors, all roads lead to Aristotle. Aristotle's *De anima* (*On the Soul* II, 414a29–415a13) considers the range of powers—"the nutritive, the appetitive, the sensory, the locomotive, and the power of thinking" (Aristotle 1984: 659)—that together make us what we are. *Nicomachean Ethics* considers theory in relation to practical reason (II, 1103b28–32; also see *Politics* VII, 1325b14–23). And yet Jürgen Habermas (1973: 2) has claimed that the "Aristotelian distinction between *praxis* and *techne* serves as the connecting thread" for a critical reconstruction of theory's relation to practice.

Something is amiss here. Aristotle never used *theōria*, as in looking at something carefully, and *technē*, or *craft*, as interchangeable terms. Quite the contrary: as "sensuous" activities they seem entirely different (see *Nicomachean Ethics* I, 1098a30–3, on the different way geometers and carpenters use right angles). Nor is it clear why "the skilled production of artifacts and the expert mastery of objectified tasks" (Habermas's definition of *technē*, 1973: 42) would not count as *praxis*, at least in a Marxian sense.

Reading Aristotle closely, we can see where Habermas has gone wrong. *Nicomachean Ethics* (1094a1–2) begins as follows: "Every craft and every line of inquiry, and likewise every action and decision, seem to seek some good" (Aristotle 1999: 1). *Action* here translates *praxis*, and *decision* is the translator's term for *prohairesis*, literally "choosing before." Aristotle's parallel construction suggests a distinction between action and craft too obvious to require comment.

The text continues: "But the ends appear to differ; some are activities, and others are products apart from activities" (1094a4–6, Aristotle 1999: 1). The term *activity* is not simply a variant of the term *action*. Instead it translates *energeia*. The translator, Terence Irwin, has argued that Aristotle used *action* as an inclusive term and *activity* as one kind of action (Glossary, p. 315). All human action has an end—a good end from the agent's point of view. Activity has as its end some result beyond the activity itself. To use two of Aristotle's examples of activities, shipbuilding has a ship as its end, and household management has the good of the household, or wealth, as its end (*Nicomachean Ethics* I, 1094a7–9).

By contrast, action construed in a more limited sense has no end or result beyond itself. In Irwin's interpretation, action in this sense "is not done exclusively for the sake of some end beyond it. It aims at doing well (or 'acting well', *eupraxia*) for itself" (Aristotle 1999: 315). Consider eating. If this is something we do because we are hungry, then it is an action that is its own end. Yet we all know that eating is never just for its own sake. Eating also constitutes an activity with our survival as its end. Immediate ends contribute to larger ends and, from Aristotle's teleological point of view, ultimately to nature's ends.

Rules and powers

For Aristotle, actions are merely an observer's incomplete characterization of some larger activity. If, however, we construe ends as intended results, and not instantiations of nature's purposes, then it may seem plausible to count actions and activities as generically separate categories. Some actions are intended to be nothing more than what they are. Much of what we do unreflectively and routinely fits here, and not just the accommodation of bodily needs and urges.

In our time, Pierre Bourdieu (1977, 1990) is particularly well known for adopting such a view.

> Practical sense is a quasi-bodily involvement in the world which presupposes no representation either of the body or of the world, still less of their relationship. It is an immanence in the world through

> which the world imposes its immanence, things to be done or said, which directly govern speech and action. It orients " choices" which, though not deliberate, are no less systematic, and which, without being ordered or organized in relation to an end, are none the less charged with a kind of retrospective finality.
>
> (1990: 66)

Actions of this kind result in "the orchestrated improvisation of common dispositions" (1977: 17). Such a claim makes practice both deep and fluid, and it emphasizes "practical mastery"—"tact, dexterity, or savoir-faire," as against "precepts, fomulae, and codified cues" (p. 10). Indeed Bourdieu insisted on the distinction between "savoir-faire" and "codified cues" as a formal opposition (as has Pouliot 2008: 269–78). "In contrast to logic, a mode of thought that works by making explicit the work of thought, practice excludes all formal concerns" (1990: 91; see Bourdieu 1984: 467–79, on how and why we turn distinctions of degree into categorical distinctions—just as he has done here).

Bourdieu's distinction between "savoir-faire" and "codified cues"—between norms and rules—in characterizing practical mastery does not stand up to scrutiny. *Savoir-faire* involves knowing (what the rules are, especially the informal ones) and doing (some activity within the rules' constraints). All norms are rules—informal, internalized rules—and all rules are normative—even instructions (Onuf 1989: 78–90; 2008: 243–51, 443–50). Nevertheless Bourdieu seems to have codified two views of practice: practice in accordance with shared norms *versus* practice in accordance with known rules, practice as doing *versus* practice as saying. Not least because saying *is* doing, this is a bogus distinction. Bourdieu's formulation also conflates what we do (practice) with how we do it (mastery). What we do accords with norms (internalized rules), while how we do it involves judgment, which is a faculty of mind, a cognitive power.

On Aristotle's account (*Nicomachean Ethics* II, 1103a27–8), powers come first, competence precedes performance: "if something arises in us by nature, we first have the capacity for it, and later perform the activity" (Aristotle 1999: 18). The Greek word for capacity is *dunamis*, which also means *power* or *potentiality*. In Aristotle's way of thinking, the actual is always the realization of some potential, whether in nature, of mind, or by design. Actions depend on the exercise of our various powers.

Repeated and imitated, these actions eventuate in normativized habits or routines (in Aristotle's Greek, *ethos*). We learn, and we are good at it. Activities also depend on our powers, in the process yielding goods, rules and skills. We use rules and skills to refine our powers—our own or others'—and to become good at what we do. This is craft, or *technē*, and it is the result of training.

It would seem that Aristotle developed the two models of practice that we found Bourdieu relying on. One highlights action, norms and habits, and the other highlights activities, skills and products. But I think we can read Aristotle to different effect. There are indeed two models of practice. One highlights rules and their internalization as tacit knowledge, and the other highlights powers and their externalization as skills and goods. One might call them the performance model and the competence model (*cf.* Certeau 1984: xiii). Given my own craft and associated discursive habits, I prefer calling them the rules model of practice and the powers model of practice.

I have already accused Bourdieu of conflating the rules model and the powers model. I would suggest that we keep the two models analytically separate—as Kant did—in order to show how they specify the terms of the agent–structure relation.

(1) Agents have powers, powers produce rules and rules enhance powers.
(2) Agents use powers, rules and skills to produce goods.
(3) Related rules, skills and goods constitute a field of objects, which an agent-observer could describe as a practice.
(4) Patterns of practice constitute social structure.
(5) Observing such patterns (the activity of theorizing) turns structures into institutions by giving them normative content (as per 1).
(6) Institutions are ensembles of rules that impose practical limits on agents and the exercise of their powers.

I would also suggest that the rules model of practice, in its several forms, dominates social theory, and it has done so ever since the rise of positivist science and its critique by Marxist thinkers. Early modern thought shows a definite tendency to favor the powers model—a tendency that reaches its epitome in Kant's philosophical program and endures in the liberal preoccupation with rights (see Onuf and Onuf 2006: Part I). While this is not the place to show how deeply and normatively the liberal mind has interpreted the primacy of our productive powers over society's confining rules, consider how thoroughly the liberal identification of practice with craft colors the sense of the term *practice* in ordinary language. The practice of law, medicine or scholarship offers pertinent examples.

Process and content

At this point it would be nice to thank Aristotle for his help and move on. Unfortunately, Aristotle complicated matters quite a bit when, later in the *Nicomachean Ethics* (Book VI 1139a18–19, b15–18), he claimed that our minds in action—our sensory abilities, reasoning powers and desires (wishes, urges and feelings)—produce different kinds of knowledge: technical knowledge (*technē*), scientific or systematic knowledge (*epistēmē*), prudence or, in most translations, practical reason (*phronēsis*), wisdom (*sophia*) and understanding (*nous, dianoia*) (1139b15–1144b1).

Aristotle's text is puzzling at best. It would seem, however, that technical knowledge involves theory (1140a11) while practical knowledge is more limited, since its concern is action as its own end (1140b1–4). Scientific knowledge starts with general principles (1140b30–1) and practical knowledge is necessarily concerned with particulars, as is understanding (1143a25–8). Wisdom is understanding plus science (1141a19); by implication it takes wisdom to move from general principles to particulars and back again. It also takes wisdom to use technical knowledge to its fullest potential (1141a10–11).

Taken together, these distinctions collapse into two categories—practical knowledge and understanding *versus* technical and scientific knowledge—with wisdom presiding over them as some sort of higher knowledge. By associating *praxis* and *phronēsis*, Habermas could oppose *praxis* and *technē*, and he is hardly alone in making this association. While this would seem to be a category mistake (for Aristotle, reasoning gives us reasons for acting), the bigger problem is that it ratifies the unhelpful distinction between action and activity.

Recall that Aristotle made this distinction only provisionally, and that his philosophical system does not sustain it. Nor does any contemporary philosophical treatment of action and intention. In other words, practice always involves wisdom. Or perhaps we can say, practice is the interplay of Kant's faculties of understanding and judgment, played out in normative settings.

Both models of practice I offer here—the rules model and the powers model—emphasize a different aspect of this process without forcing us to prejudge the content of a practice. By contrast, the action model and the activities model stipulate a different content to practice. If practice is action, then the relevant power is being adept with particulars, and the content of the practice comes to include shared knowledge, common habits and a fluid ensemble of norms. If practice is activity, then the relevant powers are being adept with generalities and being able to see the eventual consequences of immediate actions. The content of practice therefore includes the rules, skills and goods that activities end up producing.

Turner's question

To summarize, if we start with the idea that practice is a process, and that we can approach this process either by looking at rules or at powers, then we do not start on the same page, but we can see the possibility of ending up there. If we start with the idea that practice is either a matter of action or of activity, then we can end up on the same page only by running the two models together—just as Bourdieu did. Then the content of practice is shared ideational stuff, much of it immanently normative, and yet it takes the form of actual things—institutionalized routines and communicable skills to which we impute causal significance.

Let me use Stanley Fish's *Doing What Comes Naturally* (1989: Chapter 7) as an example. If we follow Fish and define practice by reference to an interpretive community, then the ensemble of interpretations constituting such a community is the shared ideational stuff of the action model. At the same time, those interpretations are the identifiable products of the skilled use of rules of interpretation. Actions fold into activities, and activities dissolve into actions; the two models merge. And this is the very point at which Turner has asked his troubling question (1994: 44–5, 2002: 33–4): Can we have practices in the sense of shared ideational stuff, and can we then impute to them the causal force that we take for granted when we think of practice as a craft?

The problem disappears if we limit practice to an ensemble of objects—things that some set of activities has produced and an observer can identify as such. The practice cannot be said to cause these objects to *do* anything, even if agents thereupon put these things to use in some other set of activities. Thus delimited, practice is no more than a state of affairs noted as such by an observer. Furthermore, when we impute structure to this state of affairs, we have smuggled in a causal claim that we cannot sustain.

The problem also disappears if we simply assume that we actually do share ideas, in the sense that we come to have the same ideas in our minds by virtue of the way our minds work. The implicit claim here is that our powers are so powerful—so causally efficacious in the same way—that they swamp differences in experience and situation. Turner has no patience with this kind of argument, which is absurd as soon as it is made explicit. To say that we share in a practice, and to say in the same breath that this practice has an effect on the world, is an unreflective excursion into ordinary language, or a rhetorical move perhaps, but not a philosophically defensible claim. And this is what we—as scholars—all too often *do* say.

Now, it should be clear that I think Turner's problem is an artifact of giving too much attention to the contents of a practice. Even then, the problem only arises when we treat the contents of a practice as a whole—a thing in itself possessing causal powers of its own. If, however, we think of practice as a process, then we can go on to ask how powers and rules constitute the causal mechanism we call agency, and we can ask how the interplay of empowered agents creates the illusion of shared ideational stuff. When we encounter collective fictions that seem to have causal effects, we should go on to ask what rules authorize agents to act on behalf of the fictive whole.

It might seem from what I have just been saying that I am a methodological individualist and thus a conventional positivist. I expect this is what Kratochwil will say (judging from what he has said, for example, in Kratochwil 2007). With positivists (and against philosophical realists: see further Onuf 2009), I resist the attribution of causal powers to entities that cannot be observed. Instead I would direct attention to the specific statuses, offices and roles that turn us (and derivatively, our institutions) into the social agents we do see in action (Onuf 1998: 71–2).

These conditions of agency result from the application of rules and speak to the pervasive presence of what I earlier called a normative setting and here call an institutional context. In my opinion, norm talk puts too much emphasis on internalization and too little on institutionalization. (For more on both processes, see Onuf 2008: 453–5.) Whether we emphasize rules or powers, the related practices must be processes. Beyond those just mentioned, constitution and structuration come to mind in relation to rules, and imitation, argument and training in relation to powers. Above all is production (*poiēsis*): this is Aristotle's most powerful, if implicit claim. As the most general of processes, making and doing depend on the interplay of rules and powers.

Production and consumption

If production is a process of the most general order for social beings, we might want to ask what this makes the process of consumption. Obviously, production depends on the availability and then the consumption, or utilization, of resources, but these resources have themselves been produced as such. It would seem then that using resources are actions embedded in more general productive processes, and Aristotle's claim stands unchallenged. There is, however, a conceptual advantage to treating production and consumption as different, if complementary, kinds of activities: we can highlight *choice* as a distinguishing property of agency.

Aristotle himself assigned an important place to choice, or decision. We need only recall the first words of the *Nicomachean Ethics*, as quoted above: "Every craft and every line of inquiry, and likewise every action and decision, seem to seek some good." The Greek term for decision, *prohairesis*, suggests that one deliberates and then chooses before acting. Another recent translation renders *prohairesis* "rational choice" (Aristotle, 2000: 1). We should recall, however, Bourdieu's remark, quoted above, that our sense of having deliberated before choosing is often enough a retrospective invention.

We make rational choices—at least some of them deliberate—in the process making things. As Aristotle suggested, each choice is itself an action (or is necessarily followed by an action; I am not sure Aristotle thought deciding not to act would be an action in itself). Many such choices involve the consumption of a good, or resource, that ongoing activity makes available for use. More than this, every action depends on a choice about the use of resources broadly defined; any general conception of production as activity depends on an equally general conception of consumption as rational action.

Aristotle offered no such general conception of consumption. It remained for early modern thinkers such as Grotius, Pufendorf and Locke to situate productive individuals, as sensuous beings, in a grid of rights and duties enabling them to make choices, consume resources and exercise their powers. The gradual emergence of a general theory of unconstrained consumption and unintended consequences is, of course, a hallmark of liberal practice and duly eventuated in the conceptual edifice of microeconomic theory.

Nor did Aristotle have a general conception of *strategic choice*—choice that takes into consideration its effect on someone else's actions. In other words, he had no worked-out view of that class of activities we call games, and thus of those actions that we think of as moves in a game. While he thought of process as movement (*kinēsis*, *metabolē*), his metaphors are physical, not social. Strategic interaction is a pervasive kind of social activity, but one whose indeterminacy is difficult to reconcile with Aristotle's teleological worldview.

The conceptual developments necessary for theorizing about strategic interaction are one of the most impressive achievements of modern thought. (See Hardin 2003 for an accessible treatment.) In my view, microeconomic theory only became possible with these same developments, beginning with abstract ideas of utility and ordinal scaling, as against subjective conceptions of worth and worthiness. These same developments have produced two models of rational action.

One model emphasizes the goals, tastes or preferences that rational agents are equipped with. Thus microeconomics starts with a general view of consumption. Individuals make choices in accordance with their tastes, and their tastes are stable enough to be taken as given. The other model of rational action emphasizes rules and institutions. Rules narrow choices and form institutions within which agents act on their preferences; in turn the choices that agents make have an impact on rules and institutions.

These two models are strictly differentiated. Yet they call on each other for satisfactory assessment of individual conduct and collective consequences. Agents have tastes, they makes choices in situations for which rules are always relevant. Consequences follow for agents' welfare, their tastes and the rules affecting subsequent choices.

Obviously the rational choice model oriented to goals or tastes parallels the practice model oriented to human powers: both start with the individual agents. Just as obviously, the rational choice model oriented to rules and the practice model also oriented to rules are closely related. Indeed these two models converge if we conceptualize rules as deontic propositions which, as a class, have relatively stable institutional implications. I have undertaken to show this elsewhere (in discussions of means, ends and interests: Onuf 1989: 270–83; policy statements and their relation to rules: Onuf 2001; and consistency, proportionality and reciprocity as master rules of social construction: Onuf 2008: 458–66).

Scholars show little interest in bringing the two rules models together. I suspect that at least some of them are deterred from doing so because, in their view, rules are either as exogenously fixed algorithms having direct causal effects or shared beliefs making the world intersubjectively meaningful, but not both. In other words, bringing the models together would effectively relocate Turner's problem from practice to the rules guiding practice. Yet moving the problem from practice to rules *could* make the problem go away by giving due attention to the deontic, and thus normative, properties of rules as such.

To make a larger point, choice is integral to action; action always involves consumption of resources; at the same time, action contributes to productive activity. Agents have goals and powers, and they act in ruled settings. Goals and games are nested. Every assessment of action depends on a theoretical or explanatory model of consumption, and every assessment of activity depends on a model of production (even if both kinds of models are folk theories).

In the most general terms, neither set of models can do without the other. If rational choice achieves its logical coherence by dissociation from larger context of productive processes, this achievement is only provisional. If students of practice disregard rational choice, this exclusion undermines the empirical richness that an inclusive point of view makes so attractive. Ontological differences and methodological preferences always affect scholarly practices and limit choices. Nevertheless we should never lose sight of the productive processes situating choices, rules and practices and eventuating in social construction.

Note

I presented earlier versions of this chapter in 2004 to the Miami International Relations Group and to the Department of Political Science, University of California, Irvine. I am grateful to Vendulka Kubálková for her support and enthusiasm on this and many other occasions in Miami, and to Cecelia Lynch for her advice and encouragement in Irvine. Aside from the opening, revised on Oliver Kessler's advice, somewhat greater attention to Pierre Bourdieu, which Stefano Guzzini suggested, and a few clarifications, the version published here is the one presented in New York, February 14, 2009.

9

Constructivist Historicism in the Light of Thucydides' Aesthetics of Power

Michael Loriaux

International Relations (IR) theory freezes history. "Neoliberalism" freezes the horror of world war. "Neorealism" freezes the frustration of Munich. Theory freezes history in the hope of mastering it. The leap of faith that precedes freezing is the wager that history will, in the future, serve up the "same dish" that sits, inactive, awaiting consumption, in the quiet cold of theory's freezer. The most characteristic feature of Friedrich Kratochwil's scholarship is its refusal to leap. Its unstated but foundational premise is that history never serves up the same dish twice. In the place of theoretical hope, Kratochwil, from an avowedly Humean posture, advocates greater awareness of humanity's dependence on historically constituted (and perpetually *re*constituted) practices and habits of speech, of normative judgment, and of conceptualization of the political world. Absent such practices and habits there is simply no way to debate or even discern the challenges or opportunities that world politics thrusts at us. Kratochwil is critical of abstract theorizing because the effort to freeze history obscures the *living* practices and habits of speech that make reasoned argument possible.

It is not surprising that Kratochwil's scholarship has sparked controversy. His skepticism regarding the promise of behavioral theory in IR has triggered defensive polemics about method. The alleged but inaccurate contention that "mere words" matter more than "real things" (weapons, armies, money) has provoked incredulity. But it is Kratochwil's historicism that readers—not merely those who labor in the confines of behavioralist theory, but even those who participate in constructivist scholarship—have found most challenging. According to that historicism, the norms and practices on which humanity relies evolve. They are not fixed. Actors, Kratochwil writes, "reproduce and they change by their practice the normative structures by which they are able to act, share meanings, communicate intentions, and justify choices" (Kratochwil 1989a: 61). Many of the words we use to discern and signify elements of such structures—"interests," "rights," "nations," "states," "regimes," "systems," etc.—do not refer to transcendental, transhistorical things. Their meaning is historically situated and always provisional. The only constant is humanity's dependence on words like these (but not necessarily these words) for the very capacity to think.

Discomfort with this kind of historicism has caused even self-identifying constructivists to retreat to emotionally more reassuring (yet philosophically less stable) ground. Alexander Wendt has shown a fascination for progressive teleologies (Wendt 2003). Many constructivists seek refuge in behavioralism, that is, in the detection and description of causal patterns that establish the "role of norms" in a transhistorical manner.[1] One of the conceptual narcotics that enables such flights from an unnerving, antifoundational historicism is the "thing" power. The concept of power has remained largely untouched by constructivist historicism, left behind in the realm of things that are assumed to exist as real things or as ideal forms of real things, independently of historically situated and culturally local discernment.[2] It is this abandonment that has conditioned debate regarding the "power" of "mere words" to oppose the "real power" of armed governments. Constructivism's interpretive, historicist, and hermeneutical impact has been blunted by the drive to prove the *transhistorical power* of *historically* situated norms within the antihistoricist, antihermeneutical methodological framework of behavioralism.

The reluctance to historicize power may reflect the commonsense that power is a "material" thing that cannot be located in culture or discourse. Power, commonsense tells us, is made up of weapons and the armies that use the weapons, or by money and the authorities that bestow or withhold the money. And yet commonsense is easily refuted. The thing power has never been discerned "in its essence" (the choice of this turn of phrase is explained below), or even as a theory-dependent, instrumental fiction. Power is not like a stone or a tree, visible and tangible, nor is it like an atom or a quark, discernible, perhaps as conceptual fiction, through the lens of a theory that works.[3] Theories that rely on power to explain things generally do not work very well. The quantitative accumulation of the components of power—weaponry, money—is at best a mediocre predictor of outcomes. The "powerful," as identified by such accumulations, are frequently frustrated in their undertakings. On reflection, this is not surprising. Weapons and money, as tools, must be mobilized by someone and must be suffered by someone. Both mobilization and tolerance are historically located, and therefore dependent on local conditions and cultural understandings that inform beliefs regarding such things as "identity," "justice," "fate," the "afterlife," etc. History—recall, for example, Marc Bloch's classic *The Royal Touch* (1990)—abounds with evidence of the cultural construction of the thing "power."

Power's obscurity "in its essence" or even as a theoretical convenience, manifesting itself in history and yet "existing" outside of history, may explain why it is common, in the behavioral spirit in which IR theorizing occurs, to seek power in its effects rather than in its essence or in some instrumental productivity. Power, accordingly, is "defined" as "that" which induces people to do something they would not normally do. (The quotation marks point to the fact that power is actually not being defined.) Behaviorally oriented constructivists themselves construe "the power of norms" in this way. But power, by this "definition" is relational, not transcendental, not transhistorical. As a relation, it invites historical treatment.

If one could point to the thing power in its transhistorical essence, then Kratochwil's historicism would have met its master. The soft glove of norms would fall, revealing the iron hand of power within. Discerning power in its essence is what I seek to do in this chapter. The vehicle for this search for power is the "phenomenological" reading of Thucydides *History of the Peloponnesian War*. The choice of the *History* is due not only to its canonical importance (three contributors to this volume have written on it: Friedrichs 2000; Lebow 2003; Monoson and Loriaux 2006) but more importantly to the attention it pays to the hard, apparently *transhistorical* realities of power politics: "The real cause of the war," Thucydides writes, "I consider to be the one which was formally most kept out of sight. The growth of power of Athens, and the alarm which it inspired in Sparta, made war inevitable" (1.23).[4]

But the chief reason to take up Thucydides' classic text once again is its amenability to a "phenomenological" reading. Phenomenology is about discerning essences. In order to discern essences, the phenomenologist assumes an attitude of *epochê*, of hesitation to conclude, postponing the moment of theoretical judgment so as to accumulate a kind of thick description of the "thing" (in this case, power) from all possible angles so as to bring it to light in its unchanging, transcendental truth. The thing in its essence is never simply, unproblematically given to discernment. On the contrary, "the natural thing . . . is given to me in and by a ceaseless flood (*flot*, flow) of sketches, of silhouettes [translating *Abschattungen*, the outlines cast by shadow]. . . . The thing can never be given to me as an *absolute*" (Lyotard 1954: 21–2). *Epochê*, as contemplative attitude or posture, positions the observer to sift through the phenomenal appearances of the thing so as to discern its unchanging essence, which lurks, enveloped, within the myriad of fleeting manifestations.

Thucydides' *History*, though written 2400 years before Husserl first put pen to paper, exhibits features that suit it for a phenomenological reading. His hesitation to judge, thematize, and conclude—his perpetual suspension of the reader between antithetical claims—mimics the *epochê*. He chronicles the "ceaseless flood" and postpones the theoretical conclusion. He does not shy away from theoretical statements, but neither does he allow them to structure his narrative. Rather, such statements enter into a kind of resonance with the narrative and induce the reader to view the "ceaseless flood" from unfamiliar angles. Thucydides offers a narrative of "power," moreover, that was written before our customary categories of political analysis were thematized. He provides the reader with a "naïve" "first" encounter, freed from—because anterior to—the sedimentation of discursive habit. One of phenomenology's ambitions is to achieve this kind of freedom.[5]

The word that Thucydides uses to signify "power" is *dynamis*. He uses it in a way that is, at first blush, familiar and unproblematic. It signifies strength, as assessed visually and quantitatively by counting ships, troops, and tax revenues. And, like the word "power" in English (as, for example, in the phrase "the great powers"), Thucydides also uses *dynamis* to signify the cities that possess ships, troops, and money in quantity. But the *History* as a whole questions the importance of this signification. "Power" is supposed to condition success. But "power" as visual, measurable strength has little explanatory weight in Thucydides. The narrative is a succession of surprises and reversals, as illustrated most dramatically by the campaigns at Pylos and Syracuse. More than *dynamis*, it is chance, or *tychê*—Machiavelli's *Fortuna*—that governs the fates of the warring cities. Indeed, the narrative, as it progresses, suggests that *dynamis* is a product, an effect, a "dependent variable" of a prior mobilization. It is itself, we surmise, a shadow, outline, or *Abschattung* of some deeper lying immanence.

Thucydides refers to this immanence with startling effect in the very first lines of the *History*. He characterizes the war as "a great war . . . indeed . . . the greatest *movement* yet known in history." The unusual (in this context) term "movement" translates *kinêsis*, a noun fashioned from the verb *kineô*, to move, to set in motion, to remove, to rouse, to disturb. For W. Robert Connor, "*kinêsis* is an unusual word at this point in the development of Greek, clear enough in general meaning but obscure and surprising in this context. It has a neutral, perhaps even technical or scientific tone, as do many of the *-sis* coinages of the late fifth century" (Connor 1984: 21, fn. 1). But the term makes only this one appearance. *Kineô*, as verb, is used on only a half dozen occasions. Thucydides, in other words, does not belabor the reference, nor does he offer a definition or theoretical discussion. He prefers historical description to convey, throughout the book, the image or feeling of movement, of dislodgment, of disturbance. The fact that the term *kinêsis* makes a dramatic appearance in the first paragraph suggests that Thucydides wants, but then hesitates (in a posture of *epochê*), to advance an ontological claim about some entity or immanence, about some transhistorical thing *kinêsis*, which is somehow related to war and the *mobilization* of military power. Despite his hesitation, Thucydides' use of this uncommon term authorizes suspicion that he adopts or perhaps even fashions it to advance his analytical and narrative purpose, in much the same way that twentieth century phenomenologists—Husserl, Heidegger, Levinas, Derrida—strained and contorted language to "remove" readers from the comfort of linguistic and ontological habit.

Whatever Thucydides' intentions, the reader is effectively alerted to a succession of outlines, shadows, *Abschattungen* that point toward some thing that "moves." The word *kinêsis* points not only toward the thing that is the condition of possibility of military "mobilization"—"mobilization" is a species of "movement"—but toward a more general movement that reveals itself in occurrences such as the earthquakes and eclipses that punctuate the *History* at periods of high tension, affect actions, and move the narrative. In the "archeology" (1.2–1.15), Thucydides describes the early history of Greece as one of migrations, of experiments with sea crossings, and of efforts to "secure movement," that is, to embrace the attractions of movement while defending against its perils, by surrounding ports with walls and by building navies to "secure" passage by sea. But, as the oxymoron suggests, "movement" cannot be "secured." It escapes its confines in ways that are unanticipated. The plague, after coursing around the eastern Mediterranean, invades Athens through the fortified walls of its port. *Stasis* or uprising (from *histêmi*, to stand up, to make rise) disregards city walls, shatters political order, exiles, colonizes and foments military expeditions. "Later on, one may say, the whole Hellenic world was convulsed" (*ekinêthê*—a past passive of *kineô* and one of the rare appearances of the verb). Language itself, Kratochwil's central concern, falls victim to movement.

> Words had to change their ordinary meaning and to take that which was now given them. Reckless audacity came to be considered the courage of a loyal supporter; prudent hesitation, specious cowardice; moderation was held to be a cloak for unmanliness; ability to see all sides of a question incapacity to act on any. Frantic violence became the attribute of manliness; cautious plotting a justifiable means of self-defense. The advocate of extreme measures was always trustworthy; his opponent a man to be suspected. To succeed in a plot was to have a shrewd head, to divine a plot a still shrewder; but to try to provide against having to do either was to break up your party and to be afraid of your adversaries.
>
> (3.82)

The narrative unfolding of *kinêsis* aims to disclose the power that convulses language, of which military mobilization is itself mere instantiation. To this end Thucydides indicts the adventurism of youth. Youth's strength and excitability (today one might say its "hormones," from *hormaô*—to set in motion, to urge, spur on, to rush headlong—Thucydides employs the verb often) emerge as a shadow, outline, or *Abschattung* of the yet undiscerned thing that is power. Young men run faster, hit harder, and are more aroused by the prospect of military adventure than their elders. Archidamus cautions: "I have not lived so long, Spartans, without having had the experience of many wars, and I see those among you of the same age as myself, who will not fall into the common misfortune of longing for war from inexperience" (1.80). But as war looms, young men grow restless:

> Zeal is always at its height at the commencement of an undertaking; and on this particular occasion the Peloponnesus and Athens were both full of young men whose inexperience made them eager to take up arms. . . . Further, some time before this there was an earthquake at Delos (*Dêlos ekinêthê*, from *kineô*), for the first time in the memory of the Hellenes.
>
> (2.8)

The energy and inexperience of youth disturb—*kinoûsi*—the attempt to discern or foresee dangers, to oppose or control the unfolding *kinêsis*. Young men have no more patience for cautious military strategizing than they do for consulting oracles. Youth rumbles. The earth quakes and threatens Delos, birthplace of Apollo, god of divination. Thucydides makes the reader feel the movement, the instability.

Thucydides observes with characteristic irony that peace with Sparta, concluded in the tenth year of the conflict, made possible the culminating calamity of the *kinêsis*, the Sicilian expedition. "As [Athens] had just recovered from the plague and the long war, and a number of *young men* had grown up and capital had accumulated by reason of the peace, everything was the more easily provided" (6.26). In the "move" to win approval for the expedition to Sicily, youth finds its voice in Alcibiades, a committed imperialist and adversary of peace with Sparta, "a man still young in years for any other Hellenic city, but distinguished by the splendor of his ancestry." Alcibiades opposed the peace because he had been barred from the negotiations and thus denied "the respect due to the ancient connection of his family with [the Spartans] as their *proxenii* [representatives at Athens]." Despite his youth, Alcibiades was an effective leader of the war party, which "wished to cancel the treaty immediately [and] put themselves in motion" (5.43). Nicias, Alcibiades' adversary, exclaims:

> [T]his is a matter of importance, and not for a young man to decide or hastily to take in hand. When I see such persons now sitting here at the side of that same individual [Alcibiades] and summoned by him, alarm seizes me; and I, in my turn, summon any of the older men that may have such a person sitting next to him, not to let himself be checked by shame, for fear of being thought a coward if he does not vote for war, but remembering how rarely success is gained by wishing (*epithumia*) and how often by forecast, to leave to them the mad dream of conquest.
>
> (6.12–13)

Memory, the privilege of elders, is opposed to the wishing—or more accurately, to the *epithumia*, zealous excitement—that is characteristic of youth.

Thucydides' "politics of youth" has not attracted the same scholarly attention as his enigmatic use of the term *kinêsis*. The theme of youth is no less important, however, because it sheds light on the historian's understanding of another term, *physis* (generally translated as "nature"), that is so philosophically charged that one cannot but examine its use and relation to "movement" and "power." Thucydides makes a half dozen references to *anthropeia physis*, "human nature." It explains the refusal of domination by others (1.76). It causes revolution to recur (3.82). It is "always rebelling against the law" (3.84). It is, say the Athenians at Melos, "a necessary law of nature [that people] rule wherever they can" (5.105). IR scholars have read a kind of *animus dominandi* into these observations. But Thucydides' theoretical scruples, his posture of *epochê*, cautions against perfunctory conclusions. Other terms are sometimes preferred to "nature," as, for example, the "common practice of mankind," where the Greek *tropos*, rather than point to a transcendental truth, suggests something akin to habit, or to Kratochwil's "practice." In a frequently cited passage, Athenians argue in their defense that it was "not a very remarkable action, or contrary to the common practice of mankind (*apo toû anthropeioû tropoû*), if we did accept an empire that was offered to us, and refused to give it up under the pressure of three of the strongest motives, fear, honor, and interest (*hypo tôn megistôn nikêthentes, timês kai deous kai ôphelias*)" (1.76). Despite the preference for *tropos* over *physis*, the passage, in translation, would appear to posit "human nature" in its psychological essence. But the original undermines this reading. "Practices," like habits, can be changed—*tropos* is derived from *trepein*, to turn, turn about, to alter. It is, so to speak, a "historicist" rather than an "essentialist" word like "nature." Nor does Thucydides suggest that the "three motives" somehow reflect some essential feature of human nature. There is no noun in the clause "three of the strongest motives," but only the adjective *tôn megistôn* "the greatest." "Under the pressure" translates *nikêthentes*, which means, literally, "overcome by." It is the passive form of *nikeô*, which means to overcome, defeat, vanquish, conquer. The word therefore suggests resistance to "pressure" that has been vanquished rather than some natural inclination. *Timê* is honor, social authority, or material acknowledgment of valuation. *Ôphelias* means "interest" only to readers trapped in the ontological cage of modern economics. For Thucydides' readers, it meant "help, aid, succor, use, advantage, benefit, spoil, booty." *Deous*, fear, can also mean alarm and awe, and, in certain contexts, a *means* of inspiring fear. An alternative translation might read: "not a very remarkable action, or contrary to common practice, if we did accept an empire that was offered to us, and refused to give it up because overcome by three of the greatest temptations, the power to strike fear, to be seen with awe and dominance, and to amass spoils and resources with which to defend ourselves." "Temptation" and common practice, in sum, overcome scruple. There is no essential *animus dominandi* in this passage.

One must therefore handle the term *physis* with care. Although it would come to mean "nature" in later philosophical literature, it is far from evident that Thucydides' readers would have understood it in this sense. *Physis*, like *kinêsis*, is a verbal noun in *-sis*. It comes from the verb *phyô*: "to bring forth, produce, put forth, make grow, beget."[6] As we contemplate *physis*, like *kinêsis*, or youthful restlessness, as an outline, shadow, or *Abschattung* of power, we discern, not a *thing* that can be grasped transcendentally, but rather a *mode of being*, bringing forth, producing, putting forth, making grow, begetting. This mode of being is not imaginable outside of time. Moreover, it is manifested by life in general and is not specific to humanity. Indeed, *physis* as mode of being participates in *kinêsis*, which relates living "movement" to the "movement" of the inanimate world that heaves as earthquake or ocean swell.[7] *Physis*, as living *kinêsis*, can emerge to discernment as military mobilization and expedition, but only as local instantiation of a more general mode of being, *physis*, or living *kinêsis*. For this reason, Hermocrates, the Syracusan leader responsible for Athens' final defeat, refuses to lay blame on the Athenians for being imperialistic, observing that "it is just as much in man's nature to rule those who submit to them, as it is to resist those who molest them" (4.61). Hermocrates expresses "nature" as a verb: *pephyke to anthrôpeion*: "the way of humanity has brought forth, produced, put forth, made grow, begotten, just as much through ruling those who submit as through resisting those who molest." *Physis* moves and makes move. It is a manifestation of *kinêsis* specific to life and a manifestation, an *Abschattung* of power as *mode of being*, "power-ing," rather than as a thing in its essence.

Through Thucydides' narrative and narrative style, power emerges to discernment not as *dynamis*, the visible, quantifiable elements that are amassed through "mobilization," but as *kinêsis*, and as *physis* as living *kinêsis*. Power resists discernment as a "phenomenon," that is, as something that *phainetai*, that "comes to light, is seen, appears."[8] It resists appearance because it comes to discernment not as a thing *but as a verb*: moving, bringing forth, making grow, colonizing, rising up, exiling, fighting. Power is "to move." One cannot contemplate "to move" visually, as metaphysical "form." We can see things moving, but not the "thing" power, "to move," in its essence.

Visual discernment of the thing in its essence is nevertheless a basic metaphysical ambition. The thing seen is extracted from time. It becomes eternal, unchanging, and immediately, accurately recognizable. But power is not a thing that has an eternal essence, but rather a mode of being in time and in the world: "power-ing." As mode of being, "power-ing" is more easily heard than seen. Hearing occurs in time and presupposes movement, verbs. We can hear the sound of "to move," for example, as "to mobilize," in the blows of axes, the felling of trees, the hammering on anvils, the shouting of orders and instructions, the feet of hoplites marching in rhythm. We can hear the excitement and bravado of youth as it disrupts the murmured skepticism of old men. We can hear the flutes and *paeans* that keep the armed ranks in formation, and the clash of metal on metal as phalanges meet. We can hear it at Syracuse as the Athenians watch, transfixed, the last desperate sally of their fleet: "there was every sound to be heard at once, shrieks, cheers, 'We win', 'We lose', and all the other manifold exclamations that a great host would necessarily utter in great peril" (7.71). Power as mode of being, "to move," *kinêsis*, comes to discernment as the sound made by a verb, and not, like *dynamis*, as a thing that can be extracted visually from time and quantified as *visible* timeless truth. Power, "to move," *kinêsis*, is "felt," "heard," "experienced" in time. But the noise is not immediately and accurately discernible as "power-ing." The attachment of the signifier "power" to the sound of "to move" requires an act of interpretation. The *History* is famous for replicating debates, the principal purpose of which is to interpret the sound of *physis*, of *kinêsis* as sign of "power-ing."

If power, as mode of being, emerges to discernment as a verb rather than as a noun, rather than as a thing in its essence, what are we to make of *dynamis*—power as visible, measurable phenomenon? The Athenians at Melos famously proclaim, "the strong do what they can and the weak suffer what they must" (5.89). "The strong" is translating *dynata prouchontes*, "those who *hold forth,* or *display* powers," *dynamis*. Alternatively, "Those who *hold forth*, or *display* powers act (translating *prassousi*, 'act', or perhaps in this context, 'negotiate'); those who lack strength concede." The Athenians are "displaying powers." The thing "power" they are "displaying" is the fleet that lies, visibly, menacingly, off Melos' coast. But the fleet as visible thing is inert. It does not yet perform except as a stage prop. The floating boats participate in the projection of meaning, but the meaning is being conveyed by the *noise* produced by the Athenians' thuggish speech. Without that noise, the thing, "floating boats," is meaningless. The thuggish speech itself only signifies power to the extent that it echoes a deeper rumbling—the rumbling of the verbs *phyô* and *kineô*. Without that echo, thuggish speech is merely offensive. But the Athenians speak like lions.[9] They roar, luxuriating in their *physiological* vigor, in the force with which they *move*. It is the deeper rumbling, not the visible *dynamis* in and of itself, that alarms the Melians. It is this same deeper rumbling that spurs the Corinthians to denounce the Athenians as

> addicted to innovation . . . their designs are characterized by swiftness alike in conception and execution; . . . *they are adventurous beyond their power* [*dynamin*] . . . they are never at home . . . they are swift . . . their bodies they spend ungrudgingly . . . ever engaged in getting . . . they were born into the world to take no rest themselves and to give none to others.
>
> (1.70)

In the paragraphs immediately preceding the Melian dialogue (the proximity is no accident), Thucydides complains of the difficulties of assessing power as a "quantity," as *dynamis*: "as to putting down the numbers of either host, or of the contingents composing it, I could not do so with any accuracy . . . men are so apt to brag about the forces of their country" (5.68). "Men are so apt to brag" translates *to anthrôpeion kompôdês,* human boastfulness. The expression echoes *hê anthrôpeia physis,* human "nature." The root of *kompôdês* is *kompos*: noise, din, or clash. Homer uses *kompos* to convey the sound of boars whetting their tusks, or the stamping of dancers' feet. It is the sound of Dionysian intoxication that Nietzsche signifies by the word *Rausch*: drunken fit, drunkenness, intoxication, frenzy, transport, ecstasy; or as verb, *rauschen*: rush, rustle, murmur, roar, thunder. *Kompôdês* is the indulgence in *physis,* the living instantiation of power as mode of being, as "power-ing," as "to move." It is the celebration of *physis,* the vocalizing that expresses and communicates, like a roar or a howl, humanity's indulgence in its *physiology*. Power as mode of being rumbles, shouts, clamors, even as it refuses to "come to light, to be seen."

The Greek verb that indicates discernment of the unseen *kinêsis* is *aiô,* to hear, to listen. From *aiô* is derived the verb *aisthanomai,* to perceive, apprehend by the senses, to hear, to feel. From *aisthanomai,* in turn, is derived the noun *aisthêsis,* yet another verbal noun in *-sis,* which means perception by the senses (as in Euripides' *aisthêsis pêmatôn,* the perception or discernment of suffering or misery). *Aesthêsis* is, of course, the root of our "aesthetics." Thucydides' *History* is an *aisthêsis*—an *aesthetics*—of power. When Thucydides grumbles that *kompôdês* complicates the evaluation of *dynamis,* he is, therefore, not saying that the *aisthêsis* of power masks, dissimulates, or drowns in noise the "phenomenon" or appearance of the thing power. The noise made by the verb does not disturb the effort to discern the thing power visually in its transcendence. It is rather *in noise* that one discerns—*aisthanetai*—power. But one discerns power not as thing—no thing power has emerged to discernment—but as mode of being. And it is in expression of that discernment, *aisthêsis,* that one utters the noun "power."

By this reading, *dynamis* is the human fabrication that seeks to engender the *aesthêsis* of power by visually signifying, through artful, "aesthetic" production, the mode of being power. It provides visible, phenomenal representation of the *kompos*—the *Rausch*—of *kinêsis* so as to stimulate the *aesthêsis* of power. Witness Thucydides' narrative of the Sicilian expeditionary fleet's departure from Athens:

> Indeed this armament that first sailed out was by far the most costly and splendid Hellenic force (*dynamei*) that had ever been sent out by a single city up to that time. . . . The fleet had been elaborately equipped at great cost to the captains and the state . . . [who spent] lavishly on figureheads and equipments, and one and all making the utmost exertions to enable their own ships to excel in beauty and fast sailing. . . . From this resulted not only a rivalry among themselves in their different departments, but an idea among the rest of the Hellenes that it was more a *display of power* and resources (*epideixin . . . tês dynameôs kai exousias*) than an armament against an enemy. . . . Indeed the expedition became not less famous for its wonderful boldness and for the splendor of its appearance, than for its overwhelming strength as compared with the peoples against whom it was directed. . . . The hymn sung and the libations finished, they put out to sea, and first sailing out in column then raced each other as far as Aegina.
>
> (6.30–2)

This passage challenges the modern reader not because of its descriptive language but because of the temptation to skip over it so as to learn "what really happened." Such is the prestige of "material" practicality in our age that we recognize in this description nothing more than incidental details that have no bearing on the "functional logic" of the expedition. But Thucydides has little respect for the "logic" of the "function" of *dynamis*. The drama of the Sicilian expedition is one of *artistic* exertion and tragedy. An *epideixis* is a show or an exhibit, like the Athenians boastful "display" of power at Melos. The fleet's success as "display" is clear. But the fleet's adequacy to the practical task that the modern reader wants to assign to it—to subdue Sicily and annex it to Athens' empire—is hotly debated, philosophically unknowable, and even of secondary importance. *Dynamis* as thing—as a visible, generally quantifiable, and functional "tool," as understood by IR theorizing—never proves its mettle in Thucydides. In the *History*, as in history generally, the outcomes of battle startle and shock. *Dynamis* as visible thing seems to excel primarily at inviting or hastening *tychê* (chance, luck, *Fortuna*). *Dynamis*, as functional "tool," is far from reliable. Nor, Thucydides suggests, should it be relied upon. It is "effect" rather than "cause." It is a "dependent" rather than an "independent variable." It is the *expression*, like Athenian bullying at Melos, of a "youthful" indulgence in, and even arrogance regarding one's "physiological" vigor, discerned not as a timeless noun but experienced, indulged in, delighted in, as a verb, as a historically local mode of being, revealing itself primarily as noise, but only in time. *Dynamis* is the aesthetic exertion that seeks to stimulate the *aesthêsis* commonly produced by the noise, the *Rausch*, that is signified by the word "power."

Humanity fashions *dynamis* as the visible, *artful* representation of the unseen thing power. But the noun "power" signifies in fact a verb, a mode of being: *phyô, kineô*. Measurement is of little use in assessing the significance of the visible thing *dynamis*. Measurement is misleading. The meaning of *dynamis* must be sought in the interpretation of the "noise" that accompanies its fabrication, that accompanies the effort to engender the *aesthêsis* of *kinêsis*. The common sense of IR theory has reversed the order of things. It is not the putatively timeless *thing* power, *dynamis*, discernible as quantity, that makes things move in time. *Dynamis* is not originary. Rather *kinêsis*, "to move," as mode of being, discernible (necessarily in time) as noise, as *Rausch*, as *kompos*, precedes *dynamis*. Humanity brings *kinêsis* to light—represents visibly the noise of power as mode of being—as *dynamis*, as the *artful illusion of a timeless phenomenon*. *Dynamis* is artwork. It represents power, "to move," as a timeless ontology. As such it is an illusion.

Empire participates in the artful illusion. Pericles and Cleon, imperial leaders, both call their empire a "tyranny" (2.63, 3.37).[10] Pericles goes so far as to concede that its acquisition may have been wrong (2.63). But Pericles also proclaims, in a kind of lion's roar: "We have forced every sea and land to be the highway of our daring, and everywhere, whether for evil or for good, have left *imperishable monuments* behind us" (2.41).[11] The *phenomenon* of empire, unlike the lion's roar that it seeks to embody, is visible and timeless. The *phenomenon* continues to shine even after the empire falls. Empire in this light does not serve a functional goal. Functionality at best provides only rhetorical justification. Empire is about forging a narrative that stands the test of time as a work of art. The work of art bestows a kind of immortality—timelessness—on the artist. It preserves the *aesthêsis* engendered by the *kompos* that is expressing indulgence in physiological vigor. Pericles continues:

> [E]ven if now, in obedience to the general law of decay, we should ever be forced to yield, still it will be *remembered* that we held rule

> over more Hellenes than any other Hellenic state . . . and inhabited a city unrivaled by any other in resources or magnitude [the display of *dynamis* as measure]. These glories may incur the censure of the slow and unambitious; but in the breast of the energetic they will awake emulation. . . . That which makes the *splendor* of the present and the *glory* of the future remains forever unforgotten.
>
> (2.64)

Empire is about "splendor," "glory," "remembrance," and—the ultimate validation—"emulation." Empire is, *eo ipso*, artwork. Unfortunately, the English translation obfuscates the aesthetic enterprise that is empire. The clause "general law of decay" is not Greek, but high modernism. There is no reference in the original to a "law." The original has *physis* in verb form: *panta gar pephyke kai elassoûsthai*—"all things have brought forth (produced, put forth, made grow, begotten) and are to diminish." Empire is not a thing, discernible in its timeless essence, that is liable to corruption. It is rather the aesthetic representation of a mode of being, *kinêsis*, that is necessarily located, as *kompos*, *Rausch*, or noise, in time. As artful representation it seeks to engender the illusion of timelessness. The question of "functional utility" as it relates to the "thing" empire loses all meaning when posed in the context of a world, a *physis*, in which all things bring forth, grow, and then diminish. Empire as tyranny, like power as *dynamis*, is the artful representation of *physis* as living *kinêsis*, of power as verb "to move," as mode of being. It is, in Heidegger's terms, the *Entwurf* or sketch of *physis*. It is the artistic representation that humanity, "thrown" into the maelstrom of *physis*, "throws back" at *physis* as its monument, so as to bring *physis* to light in its truth.[12] Nor is the aesthetic representation of power as mode of being, as "to move," limited to the visual arts. It can assume the guise of a kind of "play," like the race to Aegina, a *Darstellung*—representation or performance—that brings *physis* to discernment (Gadamer 2004: 114–16). The rhythmic *kompos* of the phalange, by this understanding, is not mere tactic, but the echo, the imitation, the choreographic performance of power as noise, the deep-lying, imperfectly discerned *kompos*, which in turn is the perfectly unnerving immanence—the "beat" of *physis*—in whose maul humanity is "thrown." What is specific to the "visual" representation of power as mode of being is the *illusory* gesture toward a transcendental, visually discernible thing power.

The idea of power as artful indulgence in *physis*, as performance of *physis*, could not be more alien to the "objectified" world of IR theorizing and its behavioralist "operationalization" of power. It challenges the truth of that world by casting suspicion on the measurable ontology that is foundational to it. It submits that power is not discernible as transcendental, transhistorical thing, but is a mode of being that reveals itself in time (as noise) and in history (as empire as aesthetic fabrication). It is not a noun that can be extracted from history, but a verb that can only be discerned, described, and understood in history. As mode of being, power is akin to other modes of being typically signified by a noun, such as "play" (Gadamer 2004: 101–21). Kratochwil's own notion of "practice" should probably also be characterized as a mode of being. Doing so would clarify the ontological nature of the thing "norm," which term, like "power," is a substantive that is being used to signify a verb: "judging," "arguing."[13] Characterizing practice as a mode of being dispels the confusion caused by use of the noun "norm." Modern linguistic habit tends to equate nouns with transcendental, transhistorical things. That confusion, in turn, invites the behavioral, antihermeneutic deviations that have plagued constructivist scholarship in recent years.

The mode of being is not like the transcendental thing, which lends itself conceptually to analysis as "object" by a scientific "subject." Gadamer (2004) reminds us that aesthetic judgment once pertained not only to artistic but to moral and even political matters, and was therefore essential to participating in the mode of being "practice." The cultivation of aesthetic discernment was the goal of a humanist education. But under the influence of Kantian philosophy, which introduced a radical subject–object binary into everyday speech, aesthetic discernment was relegated to arenas of activity that science and reason could not master, notably the "fine arts." This radical subjectivization of aesthetic judgment was "truly epoch-making" (Gadamer 2004: 41).[14] Although Kratochwil comes from a different philosophical tradition (Humean customary morality and Austinian speech act theory), he shares Gadamer's suspicion that we are not merely "subjects" examining, theorizing about, and attempting to master "objects" (like "power," "war," "the enemy," "security," "order," etc.). Constructivism's definitional claim that subject and object—"agent" and "norm," "state" and "anarchy," "strategy" and "structure"—are mutually constituted reflects that suspicion, however uncomfortable many self-identifying constructivists have been with this foundational insight.

Analysis of a world in which the opposition between subject and object is put in question requires "interpretation." It requires discerning and establishing "meaning" rather than assessing mechanical effect. The characteristic activity is not mastering things through science but expressing and understanding *aesthêsis* and the artistic and discursive expression of *aesthêsis*. This is the task of hermeneutics, which is Gadamer's central concern. Kratochwil's scholarship is deeply hermeneutical. It is about meaning—the projection and the assimilation of meaning—in international politics. Having thus set out to read Thucydides so as to discern the thing power in its transcendental essence, and in so doing to place "objective" boundaries around Kratochwil's historicism, it becomes apparent that Thucydides' text itself requires a historicist interpretation of power as verb, "power-ing," as mode of being. Thucydides ratifies rather than resists Kratochwil's historicism. But a hermeneutics of power as artful indulgence, representation, and performance, rather than fall passively under the "dominion" of historicism, can make a significant contribution to our understanding of historicism by emphasizing its critical possibilities. Despite the fact that advocates and critics alike often equate constructivism with internationalist, "progressive" politics, even with "liberalism," the emphasis on humanity's dependence on "norms" can just as readily culminate in an Oakeshottian, even Burkean conservatism. But the hermeneutics of power as artful representation and performance of a mode of being invigorates constructivism's critical potential. For Gadamer, hermeneutics by nature inclines toward critique. It is engagement with a "polarity of familiarity and strangeness"(2004: 295). The familiarity is that of our historically local commonsense, or what Gadamer prefers to call "prejudice." The strangeness is that of the discursive world of the text or artwork which we seek to understand. The strangeness is disorienting. But equally disorienting is the discernment of the strangeness of the discursive world one inhabits when seen *from the perspective of the historical text*. That discernment enables critical engagement with one's own prejudices. Hermeneutics "foregrounds" prejudice. It opens up new worlds of possibility. The tension between prejudice and text becomes a "positive and productive condition." "It is impossible to make ourselves aware of a prejudice while it is constantly operating unnoticed, but only when it is, so to speak, provoked. The encounter with a traditionary text can provide this provocation" (Gadamer 2004: 297). Thucydides' *History* works in this way. Indeed, all texts that record discursive constructions of another time or place can work this way. The encounter with power as mode of being, as verb, which destabilizes our contemporary assurance that power is a thing that can be acquired and scientifically applied, is an example of the efficacy of the historical text.

The disclosure of *dynamis* as artful representation or performance of power as mode of being invites scrutiny of contemporary *stagings* of power. Artful representation brings the rumbling of *physis* as living *kinêsis* to discernment in the pageant and performance of *dynamis*. The strangeness of Thucydides' aesthetics "foregrounds" the strangeness of our prejudices. We read NSC 68 and begin to discern the rumblings of Pericles' funeral oration. The splendor of the Athenian fleet's departure for Sicily sheds an arresting light on "Shock and Awe." The flags and banners, the uniforms and decorations, the drums, the goose-step, the arcs and somersaults and roar of fighter jets are doing something more, philosophically, and even something other than pursuing a functional end. Scholars have struggled with such suspicions. George Mosse (1966, 1981) has tried to show the centrality of art to the mobilization of power in Nazi Germany, and described Nazi ideology itself as a kind of artwork. Murray Edelman (1988, 1995) has labored to expose the artfulness of America's "pragmatic" politics. The analysis of the aesthetics of power is, of necessity, historicist, hermeneutical, and critical in its posture toward contemporary practice. It is also, it follows, critical of scholarship that has the effect of legitimating "prejudice" by searching for truth outside of history, where nothing *is*.

Notes

1. See discussions on the variety that characterizes constructivist scholarship in Klotz and Lynch (2006), Hurd (2008).
2. Stefano Guzzini, who contributes to this volume, is a notable exception. See, among other publications, Guzzini (1993), a critical analysis of the conceptualization of structural power in neorealist theory.
3. By the term "theory that works," I am assuming a pragmatic criterion. See Laudan (1986) and (1996). On the inapplicability of the pragmatic criterion to the social sciences and the need to conceptualize social science in the framework of political, normative, or moral debate, see Hesse (1978).
4. Note, however, in a preview of things to come, that the word "power" does not actually appear in the original. The Greek text states that the Athenians had "become great"—*megalous gignomenous*. The translator's need to make Thucydides accessible to our modern(ist) idiom is the source of much theoretically laden misinterpretation. Quotes from the *History*, unless otherwise indicated, are from Strassler (1998).
5. In this regard, phenomenology is in tension with Kratochwil's historicism. "The rootlessness of Western thought begins with the appropriation of Greek words by Roman-Latin thought" (Heidegger 1993: 149). Nevertheless Heidegger and Gadamer, discussed later, moved Husserl's phenomenology decisively in a historicist direction.
6. "Nature," derived from *nascor*, to be born, denotes features acquired genetically and, perhaps, developed through some *teleiosis*. *Physis* in Greek, while participating in that sense, deviates from it by emphasizing "movement" as growth. It retains this connotation in Aristotle. Heidegger dwells on the term

in his *Introduction to Metaphysics*, and will relate it, by its root, to *phainomai*, to appear (David 2004: 854). Aristotle associates *physis* with *kinesis* (Cassin 2004: 458).

7. Nietzsche, who called the *History* his bedside book, labored to identify the mode of being with an ontological "will to power."
8. *Phainôn*, as a substantive, can refer to planets, notably Saturn, as expression of their brightness against the night sky.
9. Nietzsche's blond beast!
10. One might ask over whom the tyranny is exercised. One presumes the answer is Athens' allies. But Athens itself may be the designated victim of this tyranny. Indeed humanity as a whole, or the "human condition," might be indicated as the victim of the tyranny of empire as artful representation of *kinêsis*.
11. Pericles' confession resonates with the Nietzschean "beyond good and evil." See Nietzsche (1997: I.1). Nietzsche discerns in Pericles' imperialism the manifestation of the "good" barbarian (Nietzsche 1995: 241–3).
12. Heidegger develops his thought with the help of a series of German words that build on *werfen*, to throw: *Entwurf* as sketch, *Geworfenheit*, "thrownness," as description of humanity's condition, *Gegenwurf* as humanity's representational, intellectual or artistic reaction to that condition. See, for example, Heidegger (1993: 241): "Being is illuminated for man in the ecstatic projection (*Entwurf*)." On The *Gegenwurf*, see Heidegger (1993: 245). Heidegger likens political creation to artwork: "Another way truth occurs is in the act that founds a political state" (1993: 186).
13. See Huizinga (1950: Chapter 4) for a presentation of law as a form of play, and Chapter 5 for a presentation of war as play.
14. Gadamer (2004: 41) adds: "In discrediting any kind of theoretical knowledge except that of natural science, [the subject–object binary] compelled the human sciences to rely on the natural sciences in conceptualizing themselves." From a different disciplinary perspective, historians of science Daston and Gallison (2007: 33) make the same observation:

    > Post-Kantian subjectivity . . . presumes an individualized, unified self organized around the will, an entity equivalent to neither the rational soul as conceived by seventeenth-century philosophers nor the associationist mind posited by their eighteenth-century successors. Those who deployed post-Kantian notions of objectivity and subjectivity had discovered a new kind of epistemological malady and, consequently, a new remedy for it. To prescribe this post-Kantian remedy—objectivity—for a Baconian ailment—the idols of the cave—is rather like taking an antibiotic for a sprained ankle.

10

Debating Moral Agency and International Law in an NGO World

Cecelia Lynch

In this chapter I address a cluster of interconnected issues regarding the relationship between norms and morality, the role of people as the primary actors in promoting them through the means of international law, and (as a result) the constitutive nature of political practice. While not the main focus of his own research, Friedrich Kratochwil's work opened new paths for legitimizing studies of the relationship between norms and agency. It also inspired me when I began dissertation work on interwar peace movements under his direction (see the Introduction to this volume). Yet, I assert in this chapter, some styles of conceptualization and especially classification of moral action—employed by Kratochwil and others—can also, paradoxically, discourage further inquiry at the very point at which intentional agency becomes most interesting. This is also the point at which the 'constitutive' nature of norms is exposed. As a result, I pay homage to Kratochwil's insights while attempting to keep them in play, so that the tensions and contradictions in moral action can be better analyzed and understood.

One of the numerous virtues of Kratochwil's work is that it allows a space for "morality"—and contestation over what should be done, how, and why—to exist. The space for morality, in turn, lies in the "reasons" actors employ to engage in arguments and attempts at persuasion, based on norms that are intersubjectively shared and understood, but often still contested. Kratochwil's conceptualization of norms is interesting in that it denies a foundational morality for norm-based law and action, yet it also stops short of a positivist view of international law (e.g. Nardin 1983; also noted by Bukovansky in Chapter 11 of this volume). Kratochwil's elaboration of norms and their place in law also avoids being rooted in an essentialized ideology of either the liberal or the Marxist varieties. In this construct, legal and moral norms are not isolated from agency but depend on actors to produce, reproduce, or challenge them.

I begin with an overview of Kratochwil's opening toward law and moral action and its relationship to agency and structure more broadly construed. This task also engages current debates about "normativity" and the conceptual relationship between morality, legality, and norms that connect to other contributions in this volume, including those of Antje Wiener, Nick Rengger, and Mlada Bukovansky. I then review work on nineteenth, twentieth, and twenty-first century uses of law by social movements concerned with humanitarianism and peace to suggest that the content of norms promoted during these periods emanates from constitutive processes that contain significant moral tensions and contradictions for the movements and actors involved. Both drawing from and taking issue with Kratochwil (in the best Socratic sense!), I discuss some of these tensions and contradictions to highlight not only the moral and agentic limitations of these actors but also the boundaries of contemporary conceptual debates about norms for understanding NGO intentionality and processes of co-constitution. I argue that the Foucauldian concept of governmentality helps expand these boundaries to enable a better understanding of the constitutive processes at issue in the construction of agency, although it does not answer the conceptual and substantive questions that arise in analyzing intentionality.

Norms and morality in Kratochwil's work

Kratochwil's insights about norms elucidate foundational constructivist tenets regarding the relationship between agents and structures. It is agents who employ reasons necessary for persuasion, and structures are not given or unchangeable. On the other hand, as I have learned from Kratochwil, NGOs, social movements, and other civil society organizations are shaped by their political and historical contexts, begging the question of 'to what degree agents can transcend or change given sets of practices, rather than merely reproduce them' (Lynch 1999: 16; for a statist approach to the question of agency and change, see Chapter 15 of this volume).

Despite this critical opening to questions of agency, much of Kratochwil's work on norms through the 1980s appears intent on demonstrating the importance and role of norms without reference to ethics or morality. Such an approach was necessary in that decade, an era in which morality and ethics were *persona non grata* in international relations theory. This approach was also appropriate for Kratochwil's arguments about the importance of norms. For example, in *Rules, Norms, and Decisions*, Kratochwil emphasizes the distinction between legal and nonlegal norms, in part to question any necessary relationship between "values" and "law": "Since actors normally *do* make distinctions between the prescriptive force of legal norms and imperatives of 'comity' or 'morality', the distinction between legal and non-legal norms is important for practical as well as theoretical reasons" (1989a: 36). Later in his book, he states,

> [m]y discussion rejects the conventional dichotomy explaining social interactions either in terms of communitarian attitudes or in terms of individual "rights." An analysis of the two societal models allows then for a characterization of international relations as a "practical association", in Nardin's terms, based on the mutual recognition of rights and shared practices but not on a vision of the good life.
>
> (1989a: 46)

NGO and social movement agents do make distinctions between the prescriptive force of law and the imperatives of morality, but their actions to advance particular legal norms are very much based on their desires to advance their vision of the good life. In his advising and mentoring, Kratochwil was quick to acknowledge that such a role was played by nonstate actors in areas of peace and security, racial equality, and other domains (Lynch 1999; Klotz 1995), even while in his writing he maintained a healthy skepticism regarding the intentions and actions of liberal utopians. For example, in "The Limits of Contract" (Kratochwil [1994b] 2000), he returned to the realist/idealist debate to criticize utopians for moral rigidity, asserting that they lacked the flexibility necessary for endogenous bargaining in situations of incomplete contracts. For these actors, "the uncompromising character of justice made it impossible to subject the role of unprincipled adjustments that depended on bargaining, or even coercion, to critical appraisal" (Kratochwil [1994b] 2000: 47).

I argue that the nonstate actors who attempt to promote justice-through-law do in fact bargain quite consistently, and they often sit incompletely (and uncomfortably) within the ideal-typical Kantian moral paradigm that keeps them in a deontological straightjacket.[1] This uncomfortable position is illustrated by the struggle over the moral content of norms and law exhibited by social movements and "private voluntary organizations" in the past, as well as by the explosion of NGOs working in areas of conflict-resolution, development, and humanitarianism today. It is possible and even necessary, therefore, if we accept the burden of Kratochwil's arguments about norms, law, and persuasion, to reject the communitarian/cosmopolitan dichotomy while retaining and analyzing the notion of moral contestation. Such a focus is in line with others who question this dichotomy (e.g. Calhoun 2007) and requires loosening the assumption that contemporary debates about justice lack either pragmatism (in the sense of ability and willingness to bargain) or moral content (in the sense of devolving into amoral forms of practical association).

I want to make clear that I take Kratochwil's point that moral action often falls far short of providing useful solutions to legal problems. Agents' as well as states' actions can coalesce into legal solutions for political problems that are questionable conceptually as well as pragmatically. In several recent articles, the burden of my argument is that humanitarian NGOs have by-and-large become caught in a neoliberal morass, constraining their ethical significance and making them sometimes willing, sometimes uneasy abettors of illusionary goals of progress, efficiency, and bootstrap development (Lynch 2009). Nevertheless I want to use the opening of a space for moral action to suggest that it is the constitutive *process*—shaped by states as well as nonstate actors in the context of liberal forms of governance and knowledge—that gives rise to the problematic solutions to legal problems that trouble Kratochwil and others, including myself. In this construct, the content of moral values and the goals and practices of NGOs (as well as states) can and should be critiqued. But the struggle over moral content is often obscured by the disciplining functions of liberal governance, including legal norms, and the ways in which states themselves adopt and act upon liberal identities. The term "governmentality," introduced by Foucault and currently in high vogue among critical scholars, captures the mechanisms and techniques of these types of liberal power (Foucault, 1978, in Burchell et al. 1991). While this concept has perhaps become overused in contemporary critical international relations, I find it helpful in describing an important dynamic component of the constitutive nature of law and moral action. I suggest that Kratochwil's conceptual work requires us to investigate these constitutive processes and the role of moral agency more fully.

Moral actors, international law, and nineteenth century realpolitik

The work of Kratochwil as well as others contrasts the legal nature of liberal norms with the practices of realpolitik, highlighting conceptual problems in defining both. This project entails a reconceptualization of power as constitutive rather than essentially material; consequently, international relations theory's previous emphasis on the brute nature of power became a primary target of Kratochwil's work.

Given these conceptual priorities, it was perhaps necessary or at least tempting to subsume the intentionality of actors—and their struggles over moral meaning—as relatively easy to classify into categories. Once we have labeled motives as liberal or utopian, we can simply move on to focus on their normative and legal limitations, as E. H. Carr did in his seminal work (Carr 1964). Instead, I argue that Kantian ethics—in their conceptual, deontological form rather than the practical form described by Kant in "Perpetual Peace" (Lynch 1994)—provide an extremely limited understanding of constitutive processes as well as state and nonstate moral action. To elucidate this argument, I look below at attempts to understand nineteenth century humanitarian actors' motivations and intentions, in order to compare and contrast the understandings that result with an analysis of the moral dilemmas confronted by nongovernmental organizations today.

Nicholas Onuf provides a masterful account of nineteenth-century humanitarianism in "Humanitarian Intervention: The Early Years" (2004). In Onuf's narrative, nineteenth century humanitarian intervention represented a progressive solution to problems of social reform: "Progressive movements in liberal society learned how to construct longstanding but despised social conditions into humanitarian emergencies warranting intervention within the law" (p. 757). But the categorization of humanitarian impulses does not end with progressivism for Onuf. Religious and secular fundamentalisms, Romanticism, and utilitarianism that eventually fed into Darwinism all played major roles in crafting the nineteenth-century humanitarian legacy.

As Onuf also explains, nineteenth-century liberalism did not preclude considerations of power; in fact, "The Monroe Doctrine makes explicit the necessary relationship between recognition and intervention, and it makes this relationship a constitutive feature of the liberal world" (p. 765). As a result of this intersection of state and nonstate agency, "humanitarian sentiments drew their sustenance from a potent combination of evangelical and utilitarian beliefs and practices—a Protestant ethic, as it were. They also combined with Romantic tendencies so much in evidence at that time to reinforce imperialist, nationalist and orientalist beliefs and practices. In turn, all of these beliefs fed a sense that humanitarian concerns demanded action, whether by governments or against them" (pp. 778–9).

Nevertheless these reformist sensibilities gave way in the latter part of the century to social Darwinism. According to Onuf, "[l]iberalism has never recovered from the split between positivist science and social reform on the one hand and the cultural smugness of Darwinist materialism on the other. Indeed, this split marks the boundary between left and right among liberals in our own day" (p. 780). It was in this context of "an international relations increasingly conducted on Darwinist premises," that modern humanitarianism in the form of the Red Cross was born. "Inspired by the example of the International Committee of the Red Cross (ICRC), national red cross societies and many other organizations throughout the liberal world join governments in treating natural disasters as humanitarian emergencies warranting concerted intervention" (p. 781). Onuf also points out that this type of "emergency intervention" required a legal framework, first outlined by Henri Dunant's successful efforts to bring governments together to negotiate a treaty in 1864 (p. 782).

Placing actors into ideal-typical categories based on assigned intentionality still undergirds Onuf's analysis. Actors reflect dominant trends and ideologies, including progressivism, romanticism, and Darwinism. Yet Onuf is also sensitive to the interplay and mutual conditioning of ideological tendencies, though he locates the motivations for action within historical circumstances and the creation of new ideational tendencies rather than actors' ethical struggles over meaning and intentions. Nevertheless Onuf captures some of the constitutive nature of law and moral action by weaving together material and ideational elements to show how humanitarianism emerged out of—and despite—the legal protections of state sovereignty. The result is not deontological moral action but contextualized ethical contestation.

Classificatory tendencies also partially characterize my own earlier work on peace movements, in which I conceptualized British and US movements as including pacifist, feminist, liberal internationalist, progressive, and socialist categories, among others. What I tried to capture as well, however, was the *movement in peace groups' intentionality*—how their goals and actions evolved with changing circumstances, and how they had to rethink their motivations and legal strategies and link these to the ethical importance of anticipated outcomes. Deontological and consequentialist logics meshed and resituated themselves uneasily in this story, with neither winning out in the end.

Of course, some groups and individuals, in hindsight, negotiated moral concerns better than others within this context of rapidly evolving political circumstances. But my archival research demonstrates that the upshot of moral agency by nonstate actors encompassed constant bargaining and negotiation internally as well as with official government representatives (Lynch 1999). Moral and pragmatic struggles over content, procedure, law, and policy merged together in these negotiations. If principles and norms, such as the equality of sovereign states, the reduction of arms, and the peaceful resolution of disputes, guided this moral agency, the process was very much like that enacted by government officials, whose internal debates as well as negotiations with other governments and nonstate actors were guided by principles of "national interest," which included promoting British moral as well as material superiority. Both types of principles had moral consequence, but both were also equally ambiguous in terms of the actions they might instantiate. In other words, if the national interest was a moving target, so were principles of peace and justice. The legal "solutions" embraced by both government and nonstate actors were shaped by the norms and practices of sovereignty as well as considerations of moral value.

The implications of living in an NGO world

The examples of nineteenth and early twentieth-century nonstate moral action discussed above emanate from liberal (primarily Anglophone) society, and were shaped by liberal principles and legal norms, in both the democratic theory and economic senses of the term. Nonstate actors have since become adept at using moral reasoning and existing legal norms to push for a variety of actions, including an expansion of legal institutions, mechanisms, and procedures (the League of Nations, the UN, the World Court, the ICC) and the extension of norms, charters, and treaties to cover new areas from human rights to humanitarian relief, from Just War principles to war crimes and genocide charges. Nonstate actors have also expanded their reach into other facets of global governance—humanitarian relief, peacebuilding, development, health, education—with the result that we now live, arguably, in an "NGO world" (Lynch 2009). These developments pose the question of whether the moral agency of nonstate actors has become symbiotically and inescapably tied to the disciplining mechanisms of neoliberal procedures, norms, and laws. In such a construct, human rights norms provide the dominant legal discourse for redressing humanitarian problems of suffering and conflict.

In other work, I compare the Foucauldian conceptualization of civil society actors—as part and parcel of the resulting governmentality—with conceptualizations articulated by Gramsci and Hegel (Lynch 2009;

see also Lynch 1998). Whereas the Hegelian construct views the moral agency of civil society as a necessary and proper support for the social unity and cohesion of the state and economy, the governmentality approach focuses on the construction of subjectivity that results from such disciplining power, and implies that any resulting moral harmony comes at the cost of emancipation. Gramsci holds out the possibility of subjects' emancipation through enlightened agency (i.e. the concept of a "counter-hegemonic bloc"), a prospect that the Foucauldian conception cannot fathom (despite always looking for "ruptures" and "discontinuities" in modes of governance) and that the Hegelian model would find immoral. Even the "freedom" of the subject that Nikolas Rose finds in the governmentality framework is constrained, if not by structures, then by techniques and processes: such freedom is "not to be defined as the absence of constraint, but as a rather diverse array of invented technologies of the self" (Rose et al. 2006: 100). Nevertheless all three types of social theory move away from rigid models of conceptualizing the principles underlying moral agency.

The concept of governmentality captures some of the features of state and humanitarian NGO action in contemporary politics. Governments rely on NGOs to fulfill functions from health, education, and shelter to emergency relief and conflict resolution, while trying to preserve their own freedom of action. States also require their NGO "partners" to abide by neoliberal logics (e.g. Sending and Neumann 2006), promoting techniques that are supposed to further norms of efficiency and achieve results. Consequently, states encourage the expansion of human rights law to humanitarian issues even while they resist their application in particular circumstances.

The contemporary focus on human rights as the solution to humanitarian problems has been noted (with concern) by a variety of commentators and scholars. Onuf, for example, points out that emphasizing human rights violations in situations of "complex emergency" paradoxically refocuses attention away from the immediacy of human suffering (Onuf 2004: 784–5; see also Debrix 1999). But the push toward a human rights view of humanitarianism remains strong on the part of states and IGOs as well as NGOs. As Brent Steele points out, this is not necessarily due to states' altruism but rather due to their need to preserve their "ontological security," or sense of self-identity (Steele 2008). As a result, it is not so much that humanitarian legal norms are imposed on states by international society or nonstate actors but rather that these norms become part of the very conditions of possibility of state and nonstate interaction.

State and NGO processes of debate and negotiation, in turn, reproduce liberal international legal norms. One recent example encountered in my research concerns the UNHCR annual consultations with humanitarian NGOs. These consultations, which I attended in 2008,[2] were organized around the question, "How UNHCR and its NGO partners can increase the use of human rights mechanisms as tools for the protection of persons of concern." In this section, I analyze portions of the 2008 printed program as well as notes and observations made at the consultations.[3]

The Rapporteur's Report on these consultations listed numerous ways to apply human rights strategies to resolve the problems of humanitarianism. The report states, for example, that "Fully utilising Human Rights mechanisms will require more knowledge and understanding of the opportunities that they offer and UNHCR and NGOs should seek to extend their collaboration in this context." Nevertheless the report also notes the types of tensions that inevitably result:

> While UNHCR has increasingly provided confidential reports to human rights mechanisms, this reporting must maintain its non-political and non-partisan humanitarian profile. UNHCR may not be able to comment on a State's practices as it would jeopardise its funding and/or its ability to provide protection. As such, NGOs must increase efforts to work more strategically with UNHCR to ensure that human rights mechanisms are being fully utilised.

Moreover, human rights mechanisms should be "strengthened" to address the "special protection needs of women and children" (Thompson 2008), especially regarding rape prevention and gender empowerment. NGOs, then, are placed in the unenviable position of having to confront or at least name state violations while also providing assistance to those violated.

These and other statements point to the recurring struggle between state practices and NGO principles noted by the first generation of constructivist work on nonstate actors and the agent-structure debate. They also point to the belief that recurs in each period reviewed in this chapter that technocratic solutions provide the answer to human suffering, and that legal mechanisms simply need to be fully enacted to resolve political problems. As the report states, "whilst sound instruments and standards now exist, more efforts must be made to ensure they are implemented and their effectiveness is measured." The technocratic push for "sound instruments and standards," however, emanates primarily from the UNHCR (Thompson 2008).

Nevertheless the struggle between state and nonstate exemptions to moral and legal norms, and the imperative to promote technocratic solutions, are perhaps not the most important constitutive features of contemporary humanitarianism. In particular, the neoliberal focus on efficiency and results channels humanitarian action into paths designed to meet donor requirements. These paths often emphasize rights-based strategies; for example, the current move toward funding women's rights has resulted in increasing numbers of groups including a gender component in their programs to accord with donor RFPs. But, as the discussions during the annual meeting panels as well as separate interviews demonstrate, NGOs are by no means united on how to conceptualize rights or which ones to prioritize; they also recognize the problematic nature of showing "results."

In the UNHCR/NGO annual consultations, for example, NGO representatives gave numerous examples about those left out of assistance, in particular the disabled, urban IDPs, and those likely to fall behind the media spotlight. The annual consultations noted a number of shortcomings by both the UNHCR and NGOs, including "the tendency to assist IDPs in the media spotlight more than those hidden from view," the lack of including "host communities" in planning for assistance, "which has serious ramifications, including the tendency to deliver assistance according to the status of a group rather than on the basis of equality of need," and "the tendency for UNHCR to overlook urban IDPs in finding durable solutions" to suffering and conflict. Donors respond well to demonstrations of assistance to refugees in media-heavy areas, and conversely neglect "to properly fund early recovery" in favor of more dramatic forms of assistance (Thompson 2008).

Moreover, the moral content of rights-based approaches for NGOs is affected by neoliberal pressures. The move from "charity" to "rights" promoted by many NGOs can be seen as attaching strings to aid and neglecting immediate suffering in favor of addressing less urgent longer-term issues. Onuf, for example, questions whether the "visceral commitment to charity" displayed by both religious and secular "humanitarian fundamentalists" is eviscerated by "the (mis)management of relief by progressive liberal reformers" (p. 786; see also Lynch 2000 on the move from charity to rights-based dignity). But *both* "fundamentalists" *and* "liberals" take on board the techniques and mechanisms of neoliberal governance—all worry about showing "accountability" and "results" in exchange for donor investments, and they avoid the image of giving something for nothing whenever possible.

Yet the same moral content is also in a constant process of articulation and revision. Using the discourse of rights, for example, connotes bootstrap assistance for many groups and donors. Yet NGOs also debate how to employ the notion of accountability and responsibility to shift "the symmetry of power . . . ensuring consultations with refugee and IDP women and children, shifting from seeing refugees and IDPs as 'objects of charity', and recognition that we do not necessarily know what is best for those we seek to assist." The moral dilemma includes how "to ensure that refugees are seen and considered as rights holders with aspirations and dreams, skills and experience, not just 'illegals' or 'victims'" (Thompson 2008). This debate about the moral responsibility of those who try to ensure rights is important for the problem of conceptualizing moral agency. Visceral charity might theoretically be given without strings attached (although, according to my interviews, this is rarely the case), but it also avoids responsibility for what happens after aid is handed out. The acknowledgment that NGOs do not know what is best for aid recipients reflects an ongoing moral struggle that too often escapes even constructivist understandings of agency.

NGOs also struggle with their incorporation into "humanitarian governmentality," including the fact that they have become extensions of government bureaucracies in some cases and must cope with funding trends and pressures for results by all donors. Since the early 1990s, First World, transnational NGOs have often become an arm of government foreign aid programs, and many First- and Third-World NGOs are funded by Western government donors such as US AID, the EU, and the Danish, Irish, and Norwegian governments, among others. It is simply more cost effective to run humanitarian assistance through NGOs already on the ground than it is to devise and implement government-run aid programs. Nevertheless NGOs chafe at the regulatory, practical, and moral burdens placed on them by US AID and other government and IGO agencies, even as they work to comply with donor requirements.

Finally, the larger and wealthier Western NGOs are becoming donors in their own right; they act at times as virtual extensions of government bureaucracies. Oxfam and other prominent groups that receive funding from official sources pass on part of these resources to local NGOs in the Third World, acting as another bureaucratic layer in the process of deciding who is worthy to receive assistance and who is not. Rights-based discourses tend to guide programs not only because nonstate actors are liberal idealists but also because providing "rights"—to food, shelter, education, health care—is promoted by state donor agencies, ostensibly giving them a measurable standard by which to evaluate their success in helping others. The quest to find technical solutions to the problem of helping people *elsewhere*, then, becomes an integral component of neoliberal governance on the part of all actors, state and nonstate.

Governments, of course, often chafe at legalizing human rights protections for refugees and internally displaced persons at home (Budz 2009). Yet they have also found it advantageous to advance their own foreign policy goals by charging others with human rights violations (the US in Iraq is only one of the most obvious examples). In other words, in their attempts to cast problems of human suffering in both technical and national interest terms, state governments as well as nonstate NGO actors have played an important role in consolidating human rights norms within humanitarian law in contemporary global politics.

Conclusions

A first generation of work on norms was instrumental in demonstrating the simple "fact" (if it is possible to use such a term in a volume like this one) of nonstate actors' role in promoting normative change. Work on recent legal innovations such as the International Criminal Court (e.g. Struett 2004) continues in this vein, expanding our knowledge of the relationship between nonstate actors and legal norms to new areas.

As Kratochwil argued, norms are "the means which allow people to pursue goals, share meanings, communicate with each other, criticize assertions, and justify action" (1989a: 11). All of this work demonstrated the malleability of social structures, encouraging scholars to conceptualize them as sets of rules and practices in need of production and reproduction to exist.

I argue, however, that the constructivist conceptualization of agency too often remains problematic, characterizing actors' moral intentionality as static. Ironically, this is especially the case for nonstate actors who negotiate the boundaries of sovereignty and liberalism vis-à-vis states and IGOs. The conceptual problem resides in the failure to account for the constant struggle over moral content that is diverse in its manifestations, both among and within given actors, and produces tensions that are rarely resolved by resort to unchanging principles.

In this regard, the first generation of constructivist work on agency probably overstated the effectiveness of nonstate actors in articulating and promoting legal solutions to problems of conflict and human suffering. Some norms (and not others) became salient not simply because principled social movements and NGOs willed them and refused to compromise but rather because they became possible in the very act of bargaining and negotiation with states and IGOs, or to buttress states' and IGOs' own "ontological security." Today, we can see similar mechanisms at work in the way in which humanitarian NGOs both wrestle with and reflect neoliberal forms of governance, as well as with the human rights norms that have become the common foundation for bargaining among NGOs, IGOs, and governments. Thanks to the work of Kratochwil, scholars no longer carry the burden of "proving" that NGOs and other nonstate actors wield power and that structures are not immutable. But perhaps we still need to incorporate the full force of his argument to account for the possibilities and movement in the moral intentionality of agents.

This chapter also examines, however, the ethical upshot of this NGO world. When we look at the disciplining functions of economic and security practices, it becomes clear that NGOs have made a considerable difference to which norms are promoted, and how they are expanded to encompass new realms. Nevertheless even with (and perhaps because of) the enormous proliferation of NGO activity, it remains unclear that these groups have made much difference to the overall content of liberal norms *writ large* or their translation into new modes of global governance. Indeed, their attempts to advance moral paradigms of justice, equality, and human rights often display internal tensions and contradictions, and sometimes enhance liberal market practices and "human" security dilemmas. As a result, while law-based "moral action" has become a prime target and educational tool of NGO practices, its power to advance ethical paradigms that transcend neoliberal (and realpolitik) frameworks is uneven and haphazard. Attention to the techniques and mechanisms of state and nonstate governance together thus allows us to transcend overly limiting philosophical appellations and move toward a more complete understanding of constitutive processes and their results. But only sustained attention to the debates about the intentionality of these nonstate actors can help us understand the degree to which they transcend both philosophical appellations and the techniques of governance in which they themselves collaborate.

Notes

1. I made this argument at length in Lynch (1999).
2. I wish to thank the Andrew W. Mellon New Directions Fellowship for enabling me to attend this consultation and conduct additional interviews of humanitarian NGOs in Geneva.
3. I attended about two-third of the sessions of this program.

11

Cynical Rascals or Conscientious Objectors? Interpreting Noncompliance with International Norms

Mlada Bukovansky

> Noncompliance is usually conceived as a transgression in which an actor works for his/her advantage by violating the prescriptions in the hope of not being discovered. Even in the domestic arena, however, there are cases of noncompliance in defense of a valued position and with the explicit purpose of changing an objectionable rule. Cynical acts of rascality, therefore, are different from actions of civil disobedience.
>
> (Kratochwil, 1989a: 256)

> [T]he concept of an intelligible action is a more fundamental concept than that of an action as such.
>
> (MacIntyre, 1981: 209)

On what basis do we judge whether failure to comply with a rule is the act of a cynical rascal or a conscientious objector or, for that matter, an act of an enlightened statesman departing from the letter in order to sustain the spirit of the laws? This is a particularly difficult problem for international relations. Should India's refusal to join the Nuclear Non-Proliferation Treaty (NPT) be read as an act of civil disobedience, or cynical rascality? Is resisting liberalization for certain "vital" economic sectors consistent with the spirit of the trade liberalization regime, or is it a short-sighted evasion of the principle of free trade? In order to interpret noncompliance without remaining confined within the parameters of supposedly value-free explanation, scholars must ultimately resort to some sort of moral vocabulary. What are the sources of such a vocabulary?

In this chapter I critically explore three different standards by which we may interpret noncompliance with a rule: the legalistic standard, the cosmopolitan standard, and the identity standard. I use examples primarily, though not exclusively, from the nuclear proliferation issue to illustrate problems with these different standards. I develop a theoretical critique of the legalistic and cosmopolitan standards based on the work of the moral philosopher Alasdair MacIntyre, and of the identity standard based on recent analyses of US policy toward India's nuclear program. The specter of moral incommensurability haunts all attempts to draw distinctions between cynical rascals and conscientious objectors. I articulate an alternative way of interpreting noncompliance, which attempts to confront and contain, rather than to evade, the problem of moral incommensurability. This alternative makes *the practice of governance* the touchstone for developing criteria for evaluating noncompliance. I derive my notion of practice from MacIntyre's virtue ethics. A key feature of this notion is that it challenges the distinction between practical and purposive association, a distinction articulated by Michael Oakeshott (1975), reiterated by Terry Nardin (1983), and taken up by Kratochwil (1989a) in his first book. The distinction has become less central to Kratochwil's work as he has increasingly focused on theorizing the practical (Kratochwil 2006b).

Noncompliance is not merely a problem of bringing deviants into line, because the legitimacy of rules cannot always be taken for granted. There are different qualities to different forms of rule breaking. Kratochwil's distinction between the characters "cynical rascal" and "conscientious objector" evokes these different qualities. A cynical rascal is an actor who breaks rules out of crass self-interest; her failure to comply has the potential to damage the institution constituted by the rules she is breaking. A conscientious objector, in contrast, breaks the rules to challenge their legitimacy, in the interests of some higher good. Whether this is done in the spirit of revolution or reform is an interesting question that would take me beyond the scope of this chapter, though I come back to this question in the conclusion. In either case, whether reformist or revolutionary, the conscientious objector has a higher moral purpose, while the cynical rascal does not.

To distinguish between these two characters requires not only practical but moral reasoning. But if we accept the claim that international relations should be characterized as a practical rather than a purposive association, where "association is united by the recognition of rights and practices but is not organized for the pursuit of a common vision of the good life" (Kratochwil 1989a: 256), then the option of using moral criteria to interpret noncompliance with international rules appears off limits, since the distinction between practical and purposive presupposes the absence of such shared criteria. Or at least the use of moral criteria to make such judgments immediately raises the specters of relativism, arbitrariness, and incommensurability.

To illustrate the difficulty of interpreting noncompliance from the point of view of the "rights and practices" of a specific regime when these are separated from a sense of common purpose, consider the nuclear nonproliferation regime. In its later years the Bush administration became willing to "read" India's nonparticipation in the Nuclear Non-Proliferation treaty as acceptable, while Iran's and North Korea's noncompliance with treaty norms remained unacceptable. As William Walker (2007: 448) has noted with respect to the turn in US policy toward India, "[a]lthough the Indo-US Joint Statement of June 2005 contained some pledges to support non-proliferation goals, the Unites States neither secured nor even sought constraints on India's military ambitions." Moreover, "[w]hile further delegitimizing and stigmatizing, often with good reason, the acquisition of nuclear weapons by selected actors, the United States therefore appeared to emphasize simultaneously the legitimacy of the general existence of nuclear weapons and their possession by the primary holders of nuclear technology."[1] According to Walker's interpretation, the US abandoned the multilateral and mutually restraining practices and norms of the nuclear nonproliferation regime, choosing instead to determine whose violations are legitimate and whose are illegitimate based on hegemonic assertiveness or, put another way, on the power of arbitrary will.

According to Walker, this is a case where an actor in a regime (the US) interpreted noncompliance in terms of a friend/foe distinction. Walker then overlays this assessment with an interpretation of the appropriateness and consequences not only of India's, North Korea's, and others' noncompliance with the regime but also of the US's decisions on how to interpret that noncompliance. In his view, the US has undermined the nonproliferation rules and practices of the regime by acting according to a purpose other than regime sustenance. On this reading, how the US interprets noncompliance with the NPT may have enormous political significance. Some rule violators are to be tolerated while others are not, and this affects the viability of the regime. But we should look more closely at the available standards of interpretation.

The legalistic standard

A legalistic standard would simply hold that the law, expressed in legal texts, constitutes the definitive criterion by which we should judge the legality of actions. If legality is equated with legitimacy, then any act of noncompliance is illegitimate. There can be no conscientious objector as I have defined him, because there is no standard outside the law by which to judge an action's legitimacy.

Certainly there are good semantic reasons to equate *leg*ality and *leg*itimacy! But problems arise when there is disagreement as to what the law actually is, a frequent enough occurrence in international law. In the nuclear proliferation case, the rules of the regime alone cannot tell us how to "read" noncompliance. How seriously should the agreement by the nuclear haves to eventually disarm be taken, in contrast to the injunction against proliferation? Whose bending of the rules should we tolerate, and whose not?

Similarly, the codified rules of United Nations peacekeeping alone cannot tell us how to interpret the humanitarian NATO intervention in Kosovo in 1999. Was the latter intervention a violation of the letter of the law in keeping with the spirit, or was it merely a violation that set a precedent for the less palatable debacle in Iraq? Legal texts, and especially international treaties, are often ambiguous enough to permit multiple and competing interpretations. They may contain contradictory imperatives, as evidenced by the UN Charter's enshrinement of sovereignty as exclusive jurisdiction while simultaneously the status of human rights within a sovereign state is treated as a legitimate concern of the UN. Such ambiguities are often necessary to secure agreement among parties with diverse and conflicting interests (Bukovansky 2010).

Even if one is fully committed to the letter of the law, interpretation of noncompliance becomes a problem in any case whose circumstances the law does not anticipate. And since we lack an authoritative international court to engage in the interpretation of any but a very narrow range of cases, the task falls to policymakers, commentators and also, I believe, to academics.

The cosmopolitan standard

Liberal internationalists, the English School, and many mainstream constructivists share at least a tacit, and often an explicit, acceptance of a specific moral fabric, that of enlightened liberal modernity. By this I mean a commitment to the liberal democratic state as the pillar of an international order reflecting and reinforcing the values of representative democracy, individual human rights, freedom of exchange of goods, services, and people, and peaceful resolution of conflicts between states. This commitment is both practical (this is the best way to secure peace and prosperity) and moral (this is the best way to secure the good life). No matter how much we might disagree on its contours, some form of liberalism is the touchstone by which many—perhaps the majority—of those who study international regimes evaluate those regimes, their rules, and their legitimacy (see Price 2009).

To further elaborate the moral content of the liberal internationalist vision would be no easy task, since volumes of material could be brought to bear on it, and it is unlikely that a coherent picture would emerge from even a thorough review of the literature. But it is reasonable to propose that at the core of the liberal vision stands a commitment to the rights and freedoms of the individual human being. Thus the standard by which we judge whether or not an act of noncompliance is justified may well boil down to the question of whether that act can be seen to further the cause of human rights, freedoms, and flourishing. This is surely the argument the conscientious objector would use to defend herself against legalistic condemnation. And it is often the argument that is made to defend the NATO intervention in Kosovo from accusations about its illegality.

But in international relations, the cosmopolitan standard leaves a good deal of room for argument and uncertainty. Can this standard help us to interpret the main example I have been using to illustrate our problem? Is it possible to "read" India's noncompliance with the nuclear nonproliferation regime in terms of whether or not such noncompliance furthers or hinders the cause of human rights, freedoms, and flourishing? I do not see how it can, unless we stretch the concept of human rights to include the right to bear nuclear arms, which is surely outside the scope of reasonable liberal interpretations of rights. What we are left with is a resort to legalism itself, or we must find some other basis for interpreting noncompliance.

The cosmopolitan standard may have problems beyond the question of practical applicability in certain cases. It is obviously possible to conscientiously object to certain aspects and interpretations of liberalism, producing the pluralistic discourse that is vital to liberalism itself (Shklar 1984: Chapter 6). But it is also possible (and it seems increasingly common) to conscientiously object to *liberal modernity as such*—and this sort of objection does not merely generate a debate within liberalism but rather constitutes a challenge to the whole liberal enterprise. Surely this was the gist of the ideological challenges to liberalism posed by both national socialism and communism after the First World War (Mazower 2000). The victories of the Allies in World War II, and of the "West" in Cold War, have not eradicated the possibility of another such challenge, which we now face not only from some parts of the Islamic world but arguably from within many liberal democracies themselves. This brings us face to face with the problem of moral incommensurability.

What does a defender of cosmopolitan liberal internationalism have to say to one who rejects it as an ideology imposed by arbitrary power? Moral incommensurability does not figure as a major problem for those who are committed to a cosmopolitan ethic in international affairs, even when they attempt, as Richard Price (2009) has recently done, to address the issue of moral relativism. Price articulates a commitment to a Kantian standard and focuses on problems of evaluating progress toward that standard in the face, not of competing moral standards but of practical and situational limitations.

But what if the moral roots of the liberal project cannot be publicly articulated without exposing that they are rooted in a specific configuration of power? For opponents of liberalism, the claim that the liberal project is rooted in a specific configuration of power is an admission of its arbitrary status. Since the coming of the unipolar moment, it has become far too common and far too easy to make the claim that liberal modernity is merely the product of hegemonic power, and therefore illegitimate. This is especially common in discourses wherein the vague identity of "the West" has been replaced by the far more particular identity of the United States of America.

In this context it is appropriate to confront the argument of the moral philosopher Alasdair MacIntyre that the moral discourse of liberal modernity is incoherent, as this elaborates on the problem of arbitrariness. MacIntyre (1981: ix–x) contends that the "dominant moral culture of advanced modernity" is incoherent because its moral utterances "were once at home in, and intelligible in terms of, a context of practical beliefs and supporting habits of thought, feeling, and action, a context that has since been lost, a context in which moral judgments were understood as governed by impersonal standards justified by a shared conception of the human good." Once the traditional context grounding morality was lost, Enlightenment philosophers provided,

> several rival and incompatible accounts, utilitarians competing with Kantians and both with contractarians, so that moral judgments, as they had now come to be understood, became essentially contestable, expressive of attitudes and feelings of those who uttered them, yet still uttered *as if* there were some impersonal standard by which moral disagreements might be rationally resolved.
>
> (MacIntyre 1981: ix–x)

MacIntyre calls this tendency to utter contestable moral attitudes as though they were impersonal standards "emotivism."

While this is not the place to fully engage MacIntyre's argument, his insights are relevant to the problem of how to interpret noncompliance in that they undercut complacency about the universality of liberal norms, meeting the problem of moral incommensurability head-on.

Some of MacIntyre's most powerful and challenging points derive from his overall argument about the moral incoherence of liberal modernity. In the course of his analysis, he explicitly rejects the concept of human rights as a foundation for a moral standard in our society, arguing that, like the concept of utility, the idea of human rights is a moral fiction for which there is no rational defense in a contest with other standards (MacIntyre 1981: 70). In my view, such a critique helps us to better understand the potential power (however disturbing) of those arguments rejecting liberal human rights standards, and liberal modernity itself, as products of arbitrary power. According to MacIntyre,

> when claims invoking rights are matched against claims appealing to utility or when either or both are matched against claims based on some traditional concept of justice, it is not surprising that there is no rational way of deciding which type of claim is to be given priority or how one is to be weighed against the other. Moral incommensurability is itself the product of a particular historical conjunction.
> (1981: 70)

He goes on to state that in the politics of modern societies dominated by a culture of bureaucratic individualism, political debates end up being

> between an individualism which makes its claims in terms of rights and forms of bureaucratic organization which make their claims in terms of utility. But if the concept of rights and that of utility are a matching pair of incommensurable fictions, it will be the case that the moral idiom employed can at best provide a semblance of rationality for the modern political process, but not its reality. The mock rationality of the debate conceals the arbitrariness of the will and power at work in its resolution.
> (MacIntyre 1981: 71)

Though it would be comforting to be able to reject it out of hand, developments in international politics lend this argument a special resonance. The virtues of liberal internationalism, globalization, and modernity itself are being contested in public discourse, and it is increasingly common to find noncompliance with key liberal internationalist norms such as nuclear nonproliferation, democratization, free trade, and even human rights being justified by reference to the notion that such norms are grounded in the arbitrary will of a hegemon.

MacIntyre argues that such an attitude of protest is itself one of the products of late modernity. "Unmasking the unacknowledged motives of arbitrary will and desire which sustain the moral masks of modernity is itself one of the most characteristically modern of activities" (MacIntyre 1981: 72). Judith Shklar (1984: Chapter 2) has also observed that this process of mutual unmasking is a characteristically liberal activity which may just as easily reveal moral incommensurability as common ground. Turning a blind eye to the problem of moral incommensurability in international relations, even if one believes in the virtues of the liberal internationalist order, will not help to render intelligible the practices of those who contest that order.

MacIntyre explores two possible solutions to the moral incoherence of late liberal modernity: the Nietzschean embrace of the arbitrary will in its unvarnished self-assertion, or the recovery of Aristotelian teleology, minus Aristotle's metaphysics and biology. Where Aristotle develops an account of human virtues grounded in a metaphysical biology, MacIntyre (1981: 197 and Chapter 14) offers a "socially teleological" account of virtues, grounded in a carefully crafted notion of *practice* (see also Onuf's chapter in this volume). He develops a fuller alternative in a later book, based on the Thomist tradition (MacIntyre 1990). MacIntyre's Thomist turn is less useful for the problems addressed here, but I want to use his notion of practice as a starting point for developing an alternative framework for evaluating noncompliance with international norms. Before developing this alternative, I review the identity-based standard for judging noncompliance; it has emerged both in real practice (as the nuclear nonproliferation regime example shows), and in constructivist theory as a way of drawing the distinction between the cynical rascal and the conscientious objector.

The identity standard

It is becoming more common to evaluate noncompliance with international norms on the basis of a judgment of whether a state is a "good" or a "bad" state, a friend or a foe. This has not only been true of the Bush administration, with its axis of evil rhetoric. Kant's qualitative distinction between republics and nonrepublics, and the whole democratic peace discourse it has spawned, can be used in this way. Alexander Wendt's application of his own constructivist apparatus very much depends on making identity-based distinctions; friends generate different anarchies than enemies (Wendt 1999). When it comes to noncompliance with norms, are we not more tolerant of the legal and procedural failings of states which have embraced democracy than the deviations of those which have not?

Clearly the identity standard has moral connotations, though these are not always made explicit. One may presume that the moral weight an actor attributes to a certain identity comes from the actor's assessment of historical patterns of behavior associated with that type of identity, and the prediction that such patterns are likely to continue into the future.[2] Alternatively, some authors assign moral weight to a certain type of political constitution, regardless of actual behavior. In either case, if identities are not "shared" in a deep sense, then the judgment of one "type" of state by a different "type" of state will appear to the other "emotive" and arbitrary simply because of the lack of shared identity which is the basis of moral judgment.

The character of the identity standard and the issues it raises comes into very clear relief when considering nonproliferation policy. The NPT itself asks less of the nuclear "haves" than of the have-nots—at least of those "haves" who are liberal democracies. The have-nots are supposed to renounce aspirations to gaining nuclear weapons technology, while the haves are merely supposed to some day work toward limiting and eventually eliminating their nuclear arsenals. Although civil society organizations aiming for a nuclear-free world may protest the limitations of the treaty, it hardly bears mentioning that North Korea's possession of nuclear weapons generates far greater alarm than does France's or Britain's.

But the most interesting recent case is that of India. According to nonproliferation analysts, the July 18, 2005, India-US Joint Statement "represents and especially significant shift in policy" (Potter 2005: 343; Walker 2007). The Bush administration explicitly articulated the identity standard in explaining the change of policy that would "enable full civilian nuclear energy cooperation and trade with India," despite India's refusal to accede to the NPT, and despite its 1974 "peaceful nuclear explosion" (Potter 2005: 344). As William Potter sees it:

> By promising that the United States will work to achieve full civil nuclear cooperation with India, President Bush has announced, for all practical purposes, that technology control is no longer

> the cornerstone of US nuclear export and nonproliferation policy. Instead, it has given way to a strategy in which politics has primacy and regional security and international economic objectives trump those of nonproliferation.
>
> (2005: 344)

A significant aspect of Potter's criticism of this shift is his judgment that the US has behaved irrationally. "A rational decision would have required input from all of the major governmental players with nonproliferation responsibilities. . . . In fact, however, the new policy appears to have been formulated without a comprehensive high-level review of its potential impact on nonproliferation, the significant engagement of many of the government's most senior nonproliferation experts, or a clear plan for achieving its implementation" (Potter 2005: 343). Potter's logic here presents a strikingly apt example of MacIntyre's bureaucratic rationality standard as discussed above, but that is of course its weakness. Someone committed to a principle other than utility and bureaucratic efficiency will not buy Potter's argument.

Potter's review of the US willingness to loosen nuclear export controls for India presents clear evidence that the US was using an identity standard in justifying its decision to ignore India's noncompliance with the nuclear nonproliferation regime. Moreover, the US is applying an identity standard to its own violation of the principles and practices of the regime: it is a good state, and leader of the free world besides, and so its noncompliance with the letter of the law is not threatening to the spirit (a similar rationale is used when the US bypasses UN norms). But Potter's argument that politics has trumped a rational commitment to nonproliferation obscures things. It is not politics that has trumped (utilitarian) rationality, but rather an alternative rationality is being deployed—what William Walker (2007) aptly calls "counter-enlightenment." And we have no clear way of rationally adjudicating between these alternative rationalities—between the rationality of global nuclear restraint on the one hand and the rationality of US realpolitik statecraft on the other.

If the character of a state's constitution (democratic or nondemocratic) determines its "goodness," then presumably any behavior can be rationalized so long as it does not alter that constitution. Do we really want to argue that democracies can do no wrong because they are democracies? If on the other hand the distinction is made in terms of an evaluation of past behavior, then identity is merely the accretion of past behaviors. In this case, is the identity standard really an identity standard, or is it a (reified) behavioral standard? And if it is a behavioral standard, then have we not simply pushed the question of how to interpret noncompliant behavior backward in time? How did we decide that the earlier acts of rule breaking were morally wrong, so that now the state can no longer be trusted because of past actions? The turn to shared identity as a basis for moral judgment amplifies rather than contains the problem of moral incommensurability.

Toward a practical-teleological standard

I propose the following alternative to the legalistic, cosmopolitan, and identity standards for interpreting noncompliance. Global governance conceptualized as a practice of mutual restraint and respect should be the basis for a criterion by which we judge whether an act of noncompliance is that of a cynical rascal or a conscientious objector. We need refer to no purpose or end outside of *the practice of governance itself*; the purpose is the practice and the practice embodies the purpose. We judge failure to comply with rules in terms of whether the act sustains or corrodes the practice of governance in a specific issue area. To make such a judgment, we assess not only the act itself but also the character (but not simply the identity) of the actor. I develop and defend this position in the following paragraphs.

Alasdair MacIntyre's attempt in *After Virtue* to articulate the grounds for intelligible moral action involves recovering a meaningful concept of virtue, grounded in a deep notion of practice. This effort serves as my starting point in attempting to transcend the distinction between practice and purpose. Further, MacIntyre's critique of liberal modernity has resonance for international relations scholarship. Retaining the distinction between practical and purposive association in international relations makes it possible for us to evade the problem of moral incommensurability, and we need to stop evading this problem in order to address the attacks on liberal modernity which are grounded in the observation that it is based on arbitrary power. But since I do not embrace the moral relativism of the postmodern turn, I argue that a reconfigured conception of practice, a conception where practice embodies within itself, rather than cordons itself off from, a sense of common purpose and vision of the good life (*telos*), can begin to lead us in a promising alternative direction.

The first step in my argument involves tackling the distinction between practical and purposive association, derived from Oakeshott (1971) and imported into IR by Nardin (1983). I want to begin with

MacIntyre's reading of Max Weber's distinction between an ethic of consequences and an ethic of ultimate ends. This reading shows that the problem of incommensurability cannot be avoided in the ethic of ultimate ends. "Questions of ends are questions of values, and on values reason is silent; conflict between rival values cannot be rationally settled. Instead one must simply choose—between parties, classes, nations, causes, ideals" (MacIntyre 1981: 26).

When teleology (or an ethic of ends) comes into play in politics, we face the problem of the impossibility of rationally adjudicating between rival ends. Legitimacy is also a value among rival values, and so rival claims to legitimacy cannot be rationally adjudicated. Only power can make one legitimacy claim beat out another.

Although Weber claims to draw a distinction between power and legitimate authority, MacIntyre isn't buying, and his critique affirms the intuitions of many IR scholars who claim Weber as a realist despite Weber's own efforts to articulate criteria for legitimacy that cannot be reduced to arbitrary power.

> For on Weber's view no type of authority can appeal to rational criteria to vindicate itself except that type of bureaucratic authority which appeals precisely to its own effectiveness. And what this appeal reveals is that bureaucratic authority is nothing other than successful power.
>
> (MacIntyre 1981: 26)

Despite Weber's faith in the progressive character of utilitarian bureaucratic rationality, such rationality is itself an ultimate end or value, and thus does not allow us to evade the problem of how we should weigh it against other values. Managerial effectiveness is no more self-legitimating than any other form of power, on this reading.

How does this apply to the problem of interpreting noncompliance? If we adopt a Weberian logic whereby international institutions are bastions of bureaucratic rationality and expertise (think European Commission), this will still not be enough to legitimate them and defend them from the accusation that they ultimately rest on arbitrary power. From this perspective, to decide when a sovereign state (or any other actor) is right or wrong in denying the legitimacy of international institutions and rules, one must simply make a choice, and that choice itself is not justifiable by reference to any rational moral standard.

Because of these types of problems, students of international relations have often retreated into an anemic pluralism where conflict over values is cordoned off, and instead we see international relations as an arena governed not by shared values but by practical "rules of the game"—rules that may not bind us in common purpose, but might nevertheless stand between us and total disaster, or unrestrained war. In the process, we tend to sidestep the conclusion that such pluralism and practicality is itself a value.

The story I absorbed unreflectively from the moment I first heard it as a Teaching Assistant for Professor Kratochwil runs roughly as follows: the project, beginning with the Peace of Westphalia, of removing religious conflict from the sphere of international relations was a worthy one, since conflict over spiritual and moral beliefs is much more likely to be unsolvable than conflict over more concrete things like territory. Since there is no central power in international relations capable of authoritatively resolving disputes, and since sovereignty entails an exclusive claim to rule authoritatively in a given territory, the best order we can hope for is for these sovereigns to come to agreement on practical rules for managing their relations. We cannot hope for agreement about religion, morality, common purpose, or a vision of the good life, and indeed, any attempt to inject such issues into international relations is risky because of the potentially limitless conflict such questions may trigger. To this story may be added the insight, nicely developed by Chris Reus-Smit, but traceable to Hegel, that the sovereign state claims for itself a moral status and purpose. Seen in this light, international anarchy is also moral anarchy—an anarchy of potentially incommensurable moral perspectives.

This is a precarious situation to be in during an age of weapons of mass destruction. As Dan Deudney puts it:

> One awesome fact about the new nuclear world is beyond controversy: science and technology has empowered human beings to wreak violence of unprecedented scale and speed. For the foreseeable future, and perhaps forever, the physical survival of vast numbers of human beings, and much of the nonhuman life on earth, rests upon the adequacy of the system to restrain the large-scale use of nuclear weapons.
>
> (Deudney 2007: 245)

The reason the cosmopolitan standard fails to adequately confront the problem of global nuclear governance is that the liberal internationalist strand of thought and its apparent realist alternative are each incomplete fragments of a republican tradition which Deudney (2007) calls republican security theory or security-restraint republicanism. Only by recovering knowledge of the historical and material context of this tradition can we begin to construct a structural-material security theory capable of grappling with the issues we now face, including nuclear annihilation and ecological disaster.

I am struck by the parallels between Deudney's and MacIntyre's attempts to recover and build on *a neglected tradition* in order to overcome the obstacles posed by the incoherence of IR theory and liberal modernity, respectively. While Deudney (2007: 258) has been developing a "distinctive federal-republican contextual-materialist answer to the nuclear political question," my own aim here is to explore the problem of moral incommensurability that is raised by trying to answer the question of how we distinguish between various forms of noncompliance with an international governance institution, rule, or standard. This is especially urgent when considering the question of nuclear proliferation, but the problem is not exclusive to that question. Many institutions of the liberal international order appear today to be increasingly shaky (Bukovansky 2007). When a compliance problem becomes a full-blown legitimacy crisis, something more is needed than the exhortation to bring deviants into line.

There have of course been other attempts to confront the foundational incoherence of IR theory as it faces the problem of moral incommensurability. Very much worth noting in this context are English School discussions of pluralism, nicely summed up in an article by Chris Brown (2000). Brown draws on the concept of virtue ethics to address the problem of moral judgment in a context of moral pluralism. Like MacIntyre, Brown turns to classical, and especially Aristotelian, thought to flesh out the contours of virtue ethics. "Moral philosophy on this count is not a matter of teaching us directly how to take difficult moral decisions but of teaching us how to develop the capacities (virtues) which will enable us to know how to take such decisions when we are required to do so" (Brown 2000: 210). I would add that such learning cannot simply happen in school, or in abstract contemplation. The notion of practice has to be central to the formulation of the capacity for moral judgment.

What would constitute a reconceptualization of the processes of generating global governance as *practices*, in the sense suggested by MacIntyre and other proponents of virtue ethics? MacIntyre grounds his notion of virtue in an account of practice. By practice, he means

> any coherent and complex form of socially established cooperative human activity through which goods internal to that form of

> activity are realized in the course of trying to achieve those standards of excellence which are appropriate to, and partially definitive of, that form of activity, with the result that human powers to achieve excellence, and human conceptions of the ends and goods involved, are systematically extended. Tic-tac-toe is not an example of a practice in this sense, nor is throwing a football with skill; but the game of football is, and so is chess.
>
> (MacIntyre 1981: 187)

And so, he goes on to add, is the formation and sustenance of human communities. As Edward Slingerland (2001: 100) summarizes and elaborates:

> For MacIntyre, virtues cannot be understood except in the context of socially constituted, cooperative practices that contain their own internal goods and standards of excellence. The virtues themselves are acquired through systematic training in these practices, which produces in individuals stable dispositions to act and to perceive the world in certain ways. These dispositions have been compared to a kind of know-how, or skill, and as such go beyond anything that can be adequately characterized by rules.

If a global governance project were to be conceived not primarily as a problem of how to sustain *institutions* and engender *compliance with rules* but rather as how to *sustain the goods internal to the varied practices of governance and constitution of communities of governance,* then we would find the standards for evaluation—whether an action is virtuous or vicious—in thinking about those practices as constituting their own purpose. Walker's assessment of the US corruption of the nonproliferation regime can be read in this way. An attitude toward governance that is excessively focused on rule-compliance cannot provide a sustained defense of the legitimacy of the rules themselves. Nor can an attitude that depends on labeling whether an actor is good or bad, friend or foe. A proper defense of the legitimacy of a regime must come from an evocation of the good that the regime generates, and that good is (in the present example) collective governance of weapons of mass destruction.

In the case of the nuclear nonproliferation regime, both Walker and Deudney argue that a revitalized approach to governance is desperately needed. Their prescriptions are well worth reading in full. My contribution here is one of shifting the emphasis away from institutions and norms alone, and toward practices. Walker (2007: 452) points out that confronting the nuclear proliferation issue today will require the "recovery of an exceptional politics and statecraft." This exhortation implies the concept of practice as I have sketched it out here. It implies that human beings of good judgment born of experience working in this area of governance, attuned to the histories and traditions that have evolved along with this governance practice, should remain engaged in the sorts of diplomacy and negotiation that are needed to generate or regenerate nuclear governance (as a practice) itself.

Walker's indictment of US nuclear policy under the Bush administration can be defended in terms of a practical-teleological standard. He writes:

> After its long struggle to establish international order, Washington appeared to indicate that the national interest might now best be served by reducing its ambitions to the optimization of the US's competitive position in a disorderly international system in which nuclear proliferation would accelerate.
>
> (Walker 2007: 449)

On this reading, the US essentially pulled its personnel out of the practice of nuclear governance. Its claims to be doing good were defensible only in terms of an identity standard. But in terms of a practical-teleological standard, the actions cannot be defended. This is because the virtue or character of the actor is judged in terms of the practices he, she, or in this case, it (the state) engages in to sustain the governance regime. Commitment to and experience with the process of nuclear governance is what renders states, international organizations, and the policymakers who represent them capable of the types of good judgment needed to sustain the governance regime when new problems and crises arise.

An interpretation of India's noncompliance would require a more complex assessment because India has long worked outside the NPT, but at the same time has claimed to be doing so because of the failure of the NPT to stress disarmament. So if we are to take its declarations at face value, India has been trying to contribute to nuclear governance, and support the spirit of the nonproliferation regime, from outside the regime. But it is not enough to make a judgment based on declaratory policy. An historical assessment of India's nuclear governance practices would be needed in order to assess whether its noncompliance with the NPT has been the act of a virtuous conscientious objector (i.e. sustaining of the practice of nuclear governance), or a vicious cynical rascal (corrosive of the practice of nuclear governance). That task is outside the scope of this chapter, though hopefully I have offered a framework for making the attempt.

This line of thought does not deny the fact that a given regime may achieve a variety of goods, and serve a variety of different interests, besides the practice of governance itself. It only stresses that the practice of governance is itself prior to the achievement of other goods and interests, and that sustaining the practice of governance can be defended in moral terms. One may further object that there are a multitude of practices in the world, so if different communities of practice make incommensurable claims to the same resources, and about the moral worth of actions designed to sustain one domain of governance while they simultaneously undermine another, have I just evaded the problem of incommensurability in a new and tedious manner?

Slingerland (2001: 111) notes that for MacIntyre, practices must be "ranked in terms of some overall *telos*—the good of a whole human life." But this is not the same as saying practices should be ranked in terms of their contribution to human *rights*, since the concepts being developed by MacIntyre and Slingerland are not grounded in a rights-based tradition but rather a virtue-based one. I believe it is possible to further articulate such a *telos* in terms of the republican tradition being both recovered and transformed by Deudney and others. Both the cosmopolitan liberal and the republican traditions are committed to human dignity and flourishing. But as noted above the concept of human rights may provide too shaky a ground for assessing the legitimacy of global governance regimes. Civic virtue was once central to the republican tradition, and this makes republican thought a natural place to turn in laying out a concept of practice that embodies rather than distinguishes itself from purpose.

Contemporary proponents of republicanism have been rather circumspect in their use of the concept of virtue, perhaps because the idea of civic virtue is thought to be one of those aspects of republican thought which cannot be recovered. Perhaps the concept has little resonance in the modern, let alone postmodern, era, not to mention its associations with conservatism (anathema to many academics) and an aggressive nationalism. In addition to reviewing the centrality of military virtue to republican thought, Deudney (2007: 171) notes the relevance of the concept of republican civic virtue to the American founding: "Liberty was understood to be sustained by virtue, a mixture of self-restraint and compromise norms, and a skilled knowledge of procedures and mechanisms." But the concept of virtue does not figure at all into his discussion of the contemporary world.

A central reason for the relative neglect of virtue is that modern liberal thought seems to have evolved in such a way as to render it unnecessary. Moreover, liberal anxieties about authenticity and sincerity of virtuous motives, reflected in an abhorrence of hypocrisy, heighten the desire to avoid relying on virtue. But as Judith Shklar has so subtly observed, liberal societies cannot abandon character or virtue entirely.

> It is a mark of the ethical radicalism of Montesquieu and *The Federalist* that neither worried in the least about the consciences of rulers. They assumed that this was a moral relic that would cease to mean anything once absolute rulers and their confessors were replaced by an institutional "system" that demanded only justice from public officials. That, in effect, was too limited a vision of leadership. Whether it be a psychological necessity or only the effect of electoral politics, personal leadership appears to be inescapable, and this is especially so in circumstances of danger.
>
> (Shklar 1984: 244)

For Shklar, liberal institutions, no matter how perfect, cannot render political leadership unnecessary, and leadership requires virtue. The development of good judgment and character in a liberal society involves exercising choice, something which would not be possible in a purely tradition-bound social and religious context. Whereas MacIntyre despairs at the possibility of rationally defending one choice over another, Shklar places on the individual in a liberal society the ethical burden of making a good choice.

> No one has ever promised us an effortless moral life. . . . Given that as liberals we have abandoned certainty and agreement as goals worthy of free people, we have no need for simple lists of vices and virtues. On the contrary, it seems to me that liberalism imposes extraordinary ethical difficulties on us: to live with contradictions, unresolvable conflicts, and a balancing between public and private imperatives which are neither opposed to nor at one with each other.
>
> (Shklar 1984: 249)

When it comes to questions of international governance, we cannot take liberalism for granted, as Shklar does. But I read Shklar to be suggesting that political life in a liberal, pluralistic society does prepare people for making choices in a morally complex world, provided we are conscious of the ethical content of such choices. Thus, to return to Aristotle, such a life can prepare us for both governing and being governed. These are important character traits to nurture if we as a society are to be fully engaged in the practices of global governance that are needed not only to ward off nuclear catastrophe but to sustain economic life and global ecosystems.

Conclusion

The above articulation of a teleological-practical standard for evaluating noncompliance with international norms may appear both idealistic and conservative. Idealistic, in that it refuses to cede ground to the realist insistence that only power and self-interest motivate the statesman. Conservative in that it values tradition. Are practices of governance not hobbled by tradition? Indeed they are. But this does not mean that they are static and unchanging; reform is possible within any given tradition and without it traditions are less likely to survive. Earlier I side stepped the question of whether a revolutionary conscientious objector should be treated differently from a reforming one, but it is an important question. It is debatable whether the framework I have sketched here would accommodate a revolutionary change in global institutions, because such a framework constrains our ability to judge rule breaking and binds it to existing traditions and practices of governance—and thus to some extent to existing institutions. A revolutionary actor who wholly rejects the standards of the institutions she is trying to overthrow would not accept any judgment of her rule breaking other than affirmation by her fellow revolutionaries (a variation of the identity standard). That is a limitation of my argument; perhaps it cannot be applied to revolutionaries at all. But it is also possible to counter that no revolution is so revolutionary that it does not embrace some aspect of the order it sought to overthrow.

The challenge for reformers, then, is to engage in those practices of global governance which will cultivate the types of virtues human beings need in order to make good judgments about when an act of noncompliance, or a deviation from a rule or legal norm, entails a corruption rather than an enhancement of that domain of governance, and whether that domain of governance is legitimate in light of the broader purpose of human dignity and flourishing. The acts of interpretation, judgment, and choice cannot be eliminated from this process. The law alone will not legitimate itself; cosmopolitanism is too weak a foundation on which to stand; the identity standard is emotive and arbitrary. We need to recover respect for global governance as a practice which makes it possible for human beings collectively to create the conditions for their safety, dignity, and flourishing.

Notes

1. Text of the official joint statement can be found through the online site of the *Hindu* at http://www.hindu.com/thehindu/nic/indousjoint.htm (accessed January 21, 2009).
2. I am grateful to Nick Onuf for this point.

12
Rules, Norms, Revisions?

Nicholas Rengger

Fritz Kratochwil's work stands as an eloquent rebuke to the narrowness, present mindedness and aridity that characterizes much modern scholarship, in International Relations (IR) as elsewhere in the human sciences. Richly interdisciplinary, drawing on political and social theory, history, law and philosophy as well as political science and IR, it gives those of us energetic enough to keep up with him, a *tour d'horizon* of many of the most important and salient aspects of the international condition and many possible trajectories for further exploration. And, in itself, it gives us a powerful and insightful vision of that condition and how we should understand it.

This view is usually characterized as "constructivist" in the contemporary *bricolage* that is international theory but my own view is that this term conceals far more than it illuminates and so I shall not use it here. Rather, I want to focus on what for me has always been one of the most interesting aspects of Kratochwil's *oeuvre*, to wit the way he reinterprets the tradition of philosophical jurisprudence that marked the classic writers "on the law of, and among, nations that runs from Grotius to Vattel and Triepel," as he puts it in *Rules, Norms, and Decisions* (1989a: 5). "By reviving a more philosophically oriented discussion which attempts to assess the role of norms in decision making" Kratochwil tells us, "we . . . gain a better picture of why actors in the international arena as we as in the domestic arena *have resort to norms*" (1989a: 5, his emphasis).

The clarification of, and implications of, this reality has been one of the central threads knitting together Kratochwil's work over several decades now and it has, as I say, been enormously fruitful. It has also, however, been controversial, to say the least. The controversy arises in part because of the ambitious character of the argument. For some it is, indeed, too ambitious. The *American Journal of International Law's* reviewer (David Bederman, then "of the District of Columbia Bar" and now a law professor at Emory University) noted, rather huffily, of *Rules, Norms, and Decisions*: "This is a book about international relations, sociology, logic, jurisprudence, rhetoric, game theory, language, politics and, oh yes, international law. Professor Kratochwil's effort defies easy characterization. It is also impervious to critical treatment, at least by this writer" (Bederman 1990). For others, however, the ambition is amply justified. *The American Political Science Review's* reviewer commented that "a short review cannot do justice to this literate and well written work" and added that "[the book] is an important contribution to the debate about rules and norms, their role in social action and their connection to law" (Brundage 1990: 1450).

It goes without saying that, if only for the once, I am on the side of *The American Political Science Review*. Indeed I would go further and suggest that—perhaps alongside Terry Nardin's *Law, Morality, and the Relations of States* (1983)—Kratochwil's book, and indeed his work more generally, is the most philosophically sophisticated account of norms and law that one can find in contemporary international relations theory and indeed beyond.[1] But there are also aspects of it that seem to me to be problematic and so I want, in this chapter, to probe some of the claims that issue from Kratochwil's major book, especially the claim that in central respects at least, the international legal order *is constitutive of* international relations; that, as Kratochwil puts it toward the end of *Rules, Norms, and Decisions*, "the international legal order exists simply by virtue of its role in defining the game of international relations" (1989a: 251).

I will thus start with a brief exposition of Kratochwil's main arguments in *Rules, Norms, and Decisions* and the links to his subsequent work before moving on to raise some concerns about aspects of that argument. These concerns address, first, the way in which Kratochwil understands and develops ideas relevant to moral rules and norms, and second, the way in which he understands and develops ideas relevant to legal rules and norms. I argue that, concerning both moral and legal rules and norms, Kratochwil's work breaks important ground in addressing concepts of legitimacy but should be pushed further in its conceptualization and inclusion of authority. In particular we might center on the twin questions of the *legitimacy* of laws and the *authority* they might be said to have; the first, as we shall see, is a matter of validity, the second a matter of justification.

The argument

The argument of *Rules, Norms and Decisions* is a complex one and it draws on a wide range of sources. Wittgenstein, Austin, Searle, Habermas, speech act theory and communicative rationality, alongside the philosophers of jurisprudence cited above—to say nothing of Hobbes, Hume, Durkheim and Freud—are all cited and discussed and fused into a construction (no pun intended) that is, nonetheless, very much Kratochwil's own.

The argument makes three initial assumptions. First, it is useful to start studying norms from a baseline that is an abstract initial situation defined essentially in public choice terms. Second, human action in general is rule governed, which means that "human action . . . becomes understandable against the background of norms embodied in conventions and rules which give meaning to an action." Third, "since rules and norms influence choices through the reasoning process, the processes of deliberation and interpretation deserve further attention" (1989a: 11). The first part of the book then develops these assumptions through an analysis—largely derived from speech act theory—of the prescriptive status of rules, an understanding of modes of reasoning—so called third party reasoning—and an analysis of rights essentially as claim rights (and though Hohfeld is recognizable, he is not, in fact, recognized).

The second half of the book then elaborates these discussions and concentrates on the way in which they might be deployed in the analysis of domestic and especially international law. As I pointed out above, it is this which is really the centerpiece of Kratochwil's argument. The earlier material is largely necessary to get us to be able to develop the "philosophical jurisprudence" that he is seeking to revive—though it is never less than interesting. In the process, he is able with tremendous clarity to show up the falsity of a simply materialist realism, of reductive attempt to conflate (or confuse) international law and policy (and/or politics) and of a simplistic (and "pure") black letter law or most conventional forms of legal positivism.

At the end of the book Kratochwil offers a powerful reflection on where he thinks his argument has led and what, therefore, are the next steps on the road. He is rightly critical of the tendency of much IR theory to equate the exception (which is the European states system) with the general rule and of the simplistic readings of "anarchy" that were so prevalent at the time. He maps out with vigor the trajectory that has largely concerned him ever since, concerned with the many varieties of praxis in the international context, ontologically, culturally, and institutionally.

So we have a profoundly important, and extremely powerful, rewriting of some of the central aspects of IR theory—and many other things as well, along the way—which has been and will remain rightly influential. But nothing is perfect, of course, and I want to meditate in the rest of this chapter on some of the areas where Kratochwil's arguments might be problematic and might need some revision.

Rules and moral rules[2]

I want to start by offering one observation that depends on one particular treatment of the idea of rules in contemporary (Anglophone) philosophy, on which Kratochwill avowedly draws, to wit Wittgenstein's. As is well known, his approach arises from his central idea that language is the medium through which we express understanding of the world, that "he speaking of language is part of an activity or a form of life" (Wittgenstein 1958: para. 23), a view that survived the transition from the *Tractatus* to the *Philosophical Investigations*, though its context and how Wittgenstein understood it changed profoundly in the process. In the latter work, famously, Wittgenstein refers to these forms of life as "language games" and they are endlessly multiple in human life. But there are at least two ways to interpret the notion of a game here. On one account, a game is simply a system of logically related symbols—a language having no social meaning on its own. On the second, however, a game has a logic (a language of utterance) to be sure, but it is not a game unless or until people play it. In both cases rules tell us how to "play the game," but in the first case they govern the game and any change of them alters the game (think of William Webb Ellis picking up the ball and running with it, thereby creating another game—rugby—not merely "changing the rules") while in the second case rules simply guide play.

One very well-known attempt to use this Wittgensteinian insight for the study of politics and society is Peter Winch's *The Idea of a Social Science* (1990). For Winch all meaningful behavior—therefore all specifically human behavior—is rule governed in a distinctively Wittgensteinian way. Winch's main target in his book is positivistic accounts of social science that seek to explain social phenomena in terms of "causes" where "meaning"—and thus rules—are largely unimportant. But he is also concerned to rebut the view he attributes to Michael Oakeshott (1990) that there can be meaningful forms of human behavior that reflect habit and custom but *do not* necessarily involve rules.

In this respect Kratochwil's argument parallels Winch's. He, like Winch, wants to assert that all meaningful (i.e. nonmechanical) human activity is rule governed. But there are, I think, some questions that might be raised here. In particular one might question whether it is possible to shrink all human moral action to rule-governed action. Traditional debates about moral rules, in Anglophone circles at least, have tended to revolve around debates between consequentialists and deontologists—with sometimes a few virtue ethicists thrown in for good measure. Part of this has its roots in the historically ambivalent attitude of the analytical tradition to the idea of moral (as opposed to general) rules. Wittgenstein was notoriously suspicious about the existence of moral "rules"—a suspicion that led directly to his celebrated dispute with Popper in the Cambridge Moral sciences club (Edmonds and Eidinow 2002) and which has borne considerable fruit in the work of his former student Stephen Toulmin (1950, 1992, 2001; Jonsen and Toulmin 1988).

Wittgenstein's objection to the idea of a *moral* rule was based on his objection to the more fundamental claim that the sphere of morality could be reduced to rule following, like all other aspects of human existence. Wittgenstein understood human life as deeply conventional—and thus rule governed—and so at this level one might be surprised that he did not think this of morality. However, to Wittgenstein morality is not constituted by rules as such at all. Rather they were either commands (in which case one followed them as such) or they were not obligatory at all and one could safely ignore them. In his excellent account of Wittgenstein's life, Ray Monk (1990) points out that Wittgenstein believed very strongly that there are morally obligatory responsibilities one undertook as a result of certain claims about oneself, but these could not be described as "rules." For Wittgenstein, moral understanding is conventional (that is nonnatural) but *not* rule governed—it is in this respect that the closing pages of the *Tractatus* marks a view from which Wittgenstein was never to deviate. Perhaps this is most clearly put in Proposition 6.421 which famously states "it is clear that ethics cannot be put into words; ethics is transcendental (ethics and aesthetics are one and the same)" (Wittgenstein 1921: 71). Similar remarks pepper the collection of occasional remarks Winch himself edited (Wittgenstein 1980) and even the *Investigations*.

Toulmin's variation on this theme mixes in some Aristotle with the Wittgenstein but the result is not dissimilar. For Toulmin, morally meaningful behavior can demonstrate a rule-like pattern—at least in certain contexts—but generally speaking we should develop an account of moral reasoning which is explicitly not rule governed but rather habitual; the kind of thing a certain sort of person would do in a certain sort of context *habitually* (because habituated to such behavior) rather than acting as the result of the application of a moral rule. Toulmin has nicely illustrated his argument with what he calls "the drowning baby" example. We should imagine a woman pushing a pram along a promenade whereupon the pram accidentally falls into the sea, threatening to drown the baby. A man dives is and then saves the child, at some risk to himself. Toulmin argues the appropriate answer to the question "why did you do that?" is simply a description of the event—the baby was drowning—not the invocation of a moral criterion for action.

The point here is not to suggest Wittgenstein was wholly correct is supposing this, only to suggest that the notion that all meaningful human action is rule following is not held even by one of the principal sources on which Kratochwil draws. And if one turns to Oakeshott—and especially to the first of the essays to which he gives the title "The Tower of Babel" (reprinted in 1991: 465–87)—one finds, I think an extremely subtle elucidation of the claim that moral behavior is, in general, of *two* sorts, only one which is rule governed—that which Oakeshott calls a form of the moral life "governed by the reflective application of a moral criterion" (1991: 472) and which appears in two common varieties: the self-conscious pursuit of moral ideals and the reflective observance of moral rules. Oakeshott contrasts such a form of the moral life with one which he thinks is shaped by a habit of affection and conduct. His point is that the moral life as we know it is a combination of both these but in its proper form should be seen as one where the former is recessive and the latter dominant, which he thinks is precisely the opposite of our own contemporary situation.

How might this be relevant in our current context? Simply because it suggests, if we are prepared to follow Oakeshott at least this far, that by starting with an framework where the choices are laid out in terms of the assumptions of public choice—as Kratochwil does at the opening of *Rules, Norms and Decisions*—we are *already assuming* that at least one form of the reflective application of a moral criterion is the only way to make sense of moral rules, and perhaps indeed of all rules. If this is not the case with forms of the moral life, it might not also be the case with other aspects of human life (art, for example). And if this is true, what becomes of Kratochwil's secondary assumption—to wit, that all forms of meaningful human action are rule governed? Is there, in other words, a place in Kratochwil's world for meaningful but not rule governed (in the relevant sense at least) behavior?

Rules and law

A second area where we might ask some awkward questions is in the area of law itself. The idea of a game also plays a central role in some of the leading accounts of legal rules that are expressly cited by Kratochwil. H. L. A. Hart is well known for the idea that law is a self-contained system of rules similar to that of a game such as chess, cricket or golf. This system contains two distinct types of rules (Hart 1961). The first type, which Hart calls primary rules, directly shape or govern behavior; the second type, secondary rules, are rules for the adjudication, change or recognition of the primary rules. So, the criminal law would be an instance of primary rules, constitutional laws an example of secondary rules. Hart's point here, among others, is that legal rules are *not* moral rules because their authority derives not from their content but from their source, which is, as Nicola Lacey puts it, "a distinctively institutionalised system of social recognition" (2004: 229). Hence, driving on the left is a valid rule in the UK, not because there is any intrinsic worth in driving on the left, but because there is an agreed set of criteria for recognition. In the same way, Hart argues, the legal prohibition on murder is not the same as, and derives its authority from a different source than, the moral injunction against unjustified killing.

As a number of Hart's critics both at the time of the publication of *The Concept of Law* and subsequently—Hans Kelsen, Lon Fuller and Ronald Dworkin, for example—have all pointed out, this notion of law seems to leave some very important questions unanswered.[3] Hart's system leaves the *justification* of any given set of legal rules—as opposed to their *validity*—very much up in the air. This was essentially the point of conflict between Hart and Fuller. The legal rules of Nazi Germany were, unquestionably, an example of a system where both primary and secondary rules worked. The Nuremberg laws, for example, were primary rules, the *Fuhrerprinzip*, a secondary one. Is this all there is to say on the matter? Is there no way we can say that some rules are "better" or "worse" than others?

The tradition of natural law (to which Fuller appealed in disagreeing with Hart) has always emphasized that for a system of legal rules to be properly valid, it needed to be (at least) not contrary to Natural Law: in other words, validity depended upon proper justification. But the content of this claim is highly contestable. Even Hart accepted what he famously termed a "minimal content" of natural law (roughly principles of formal justice, treating like cases alike and so on) but most natural law theorists would go much further (see, e.g. Finnis 1980). Then again, on Hart's view, legal rules are generally speaking "value free" and free standing. Dworkin has built a whole rival jurisprudence around the idea of the political role of judges and judgments, while Kelsen, though agreeing with Hart about the separation of law and morals, insists that the validity of legal rules depends upon constant reference to rules higher up in the system. This view ends up giving primacy to international law over domestic law and is a view not completely dissimilar to where Kratochwil ends up—though Kratochwil is no legal positivist.

In terms of international law, there is a very different claim which is increasingly influential. If one largely accepts the arguments of Marti Koskiniemmi (2002), then international law is itself a *political* project and one little more than a century old. Rather than standing outside politics—or framing politics in the sense Kratochwil suggests, international law—it is centrally political. Thus the "legal rules" generated by international lawyers are designed within a particular political context (in recent times mainly liberal) and designed with that context in mind. One should not be surprised, therefore, if the notions of rules in this project clash with other such notions derived from other kinds of projects.

It seems to me that the fundamental issue that is at stake in all of these cases is the relationship between the legitimacy of laws and the authority they might be said to have—or to put it in different terms, between their validity and their justification. Legitimacy is a very slippery concept if one takes its commonsense meaning, namely, that it simply denotes acceptance by those who are impacted by the institution or rule. Indeed, if legitimacy depends on just what individual perceivers believe it to be, there is no real metric by which to measure it, and it would appear to be an inherently contestable concept. It answers none of the more pressing concerns that swirl around international affairs: legitimate according to which criteria? in whose eyes? in which domains? and established how and by whom? What are the legitimate means of ensuring compliance with rules in whichever context, and how can the legitimacy of those means be established? Most importantly for consideration in an anarchic international system, do powerful actors ultimately define legitimacy in their own interests? What is the relationship (mutual and conflicting) between legitimacy and efficacy?

Thomas Franck has argued that international law is better understood as a system of rules rather than as law proper, rules that depend for their function on legitimacy. Franck makes not just a descriptive point about legal rules having legitimacy but an explanatory one about why states follow international law: "they believe the [international legal] rule and its institutional penumbra to have a high degree of legitimacy" (Franck 1990: 25). Franck argues that legitimacy does not derive from the substantive content of the rules but from certain elements of how rules are made. He narrows those elements down to four essential ones: determinacy, symbolic validation, coherence and adherence. When rules are clear, grounded in accepted patterns, coherent and adhered to, they have the sort of legitimacy that makes them workable.

Others, however, have argued that legitimacy cannot just rely on the procedural dimensions of rules. Rather there must be a substantive content to rules at the global level. Allen Buchanan has recently proposed a moral theory of international law that rests on the connection between justice and legitimacy. For Buchanan (2004), international law does not derive its legitimacy from consent but from the way in which those rules are just, which he extrapolates as adherence to human rights norms.

The concept of legitimacy, then, can arise either from the substantive content of rules or from the process that rules create for adjudicating claims among members of a community. The international legal system, as reflected in Frank's account, rests largely on legitimacy being a product of process, while recent interest in ethics at the global level, as demonstrated by Buchanan's account, reveals a focus on substantive criteria as providing legitimacy. Clarifying which assumption about legitimacy is operative in various appeals to rules is thus an essential component of how rules and law are conceptualized.

Buchanan's account also seeks to develop the relationship between legitimacy and authority. Authority must include legitimacy, but it also includes the further stipulation that those under a certain political system are *obliged* to obey its provisions. In other words, authority *combines* legitimacy with a further, nonjustificatory criterion. For this reason, Buchanan (2004: 237) argues that international law must be legitimate but it need not be authoritative, for he argues that in democracy obedience does not derive from a mystical relationship between the person and the state but from the rational justification that all those in the community understand and accept.

The question for Kratochwil is whether taking either of these tacks would do what Kratochwil claims, in *Rules, Norms, and Decisions*, international law does, which is *constitute* the game of international relations. And here it might be helpful to look briefly at the thought of Kratochwil's fellow constructivist pioneer, Nicholas Onuf. He shares a good deal with Kratochwil, although there are also instructive differences. Onuf's theoretical account of international relations, as is well known, argues that "our world and we continually remake each other" (2008: 466). We do that through the mediating properties of rules, which we should understand in terms of speech acts. It is in this sense that international relations (and IR) are constituted, as both Kratochwil and Onuf suggest, through the utterances people make about them. But surely the question, for both Kratochwil and for Onuf, is whether—as Buchanan suggests—one needs to have substantive criteria in order to ground legitimacy claims, or whether one can do it simply through "process." At times Onuf seems to suggest the former—as, for example, when he identifies himself as a "late modern" who believes in "the Enlightenment project" but also believes that it must be remade from the ground up (Onuf 2008: 298)—but Kratochwil seems less certain about this. But this question in itself simply raises a second—and perhaps ontologically prior—one: Is Buchanan (and thence Kratochwil and Onuf) consistent in resisting a stronger notion of authority, one that can not only validate but justify? One of the central questions, it seems to me, for thinkers in international (and indeed general) legal and political theory must surely be the relationship between authority understood as a systemic practice within rules and laws—how Kratochwil, Onuf and many others tend to treat it—and the wider authority claims that might be made (this law may be valid but it also immoral; does it, then, have obligatory force?). It is perhaps here, more than anywhere else in his work, that it would be interesting to see Kratochwil expand his analysis.

Conclusion

None of the above should be read as taking anything away from Kratochwil's achievement, not only in *Rules, Norms, and Decisions* but in his work more generally. Rather, I am hoping to push him to develop still further the fascinating and hugely fruitful account of the interrelations between law and politics in the international domain that has been central to his work throughout. My hunch is that the dominant trends in the contemporary philosophy of international law—law as policy (e.g. Higgins), law as procedure (e.g. Franck) and law as substantive moral category (e.g. Teson and Buchanan)—and all the most influential treatments of law in the literature of political science and IR—for example, the legalization literature Keohane has pioneered, Slaughter's neo-utilitarian functionalism and the increasingly "solidarist" readings of the "new" English school (e.g. Hurrell)—all lead away form the richness and depth that Kratochwil has been giving us. My chosen suggestion as a way to blunt that trajectory is that he needs to revise the account offered in *Rules, Norms, and Decisions* to take into account both meaningful action that is not rule governed and an understanding of law as requiring both validity and justification. So, Fritz, over to you.

Notes

I am grateful to Nick Onuf, Cecilia Lynch, Rod Hall and Oli Kessler for the invitation to participate in this project, to all of the other participants for their comments and, most of all, to Fritz Kratochwil for many years of animated and spirited disagreement (even the occasional agreement) and for an example of serious intellectual commitment—and serious *joie de vivre*—it would be hard to better.

1. I can think of no work in contemporary philosophy or in law that matches it in reach or range. The only contemporary legal thinkers who might be candidates, in my view, would be Marti Koskenniemi ([1989] 2005) and Philip Allott (1992), but each adopts a very different attitude to theory, and to law.
2. Aspects of the following argument were first developed in a joint paper with my colleagues Tony Lang and William Walker (Lang et al. 2006). However, I have developed my parts of that essay for this occasion in ways that I do not suppose my colleagues would either approve of or agree with and so I absolve them of any blame for the use to which I have put our collaboration in what follows.
3. See Fuller (1969) and Dworkin (1977). Kelsen did not, to my knowledge, comment in print about Hart's views, but debated with him on a visit to Berkeley in 1961 and criticized his theory as not taking seriously enough the idea that a norm can only be based on another norm (i.e. there must be a *grundnorm*). See the account of the Hart–Kelsen exchange in Lacey (2004: 249–53). Hart (1963) did comment on the exchange.

Part III

Building on Kratochwil: Persuasion, Order and Change

13
Norms, Persuasion and the New German Idealism in IR

Jens Steffek

> Earthly minds, like mud-walls, resist the strongest batteries: and though, perhaps, sometimes the force of a clear argument may make some impression, yet they nevertheless stand firm, keep out the enemy truth, that would captivate, or disturb them. . . . ["W]hat suits our wishes is forwardly believed", is, I suppose, what every one hath more than once experimented: and though men cannot always openly gain-say, or resist the force of manifest probabilities, that make against them; yet yield they not to the argument.
>
> John Locke, *Essay Concerning Human Understanding*, IV, xx, §12

With the constructivist turn in International Relations (IR) theory the study of social norms and norm-guided behavior has finally secured the prominent place on the research agenda that it deserves. It is beyond doubt that Fritz Kratochwil's extensive work on the nature and function of norms in politics and society has contributed enormously to this development. What makes reading Kratochwil exciting for the expert and sometimes frustrating for the novice seems to be his enormous versatility. He is one of the few authors who would not hesitate to adopt a Hobbesian perspective on social norms at one moment and a Freudian one in the next instance (Kratochwil 1989a: 113–28). Kratochwil works like a lighting technician in a theater who, by mastering all sorts of spotlights and color schemes, can change our perception of what we see on stage. And unlike many of the other lighting technicians in IR theory he never has stopped and put on one single spotlight, claiming that he has found the best illumination. What matters to Kratochwil in his study of social norms, it appears to me, is not the development of a concise, let alone parsimonious, theory. Rather, he strives to give a complete, and by necessity multifaceted, account of this very complex phenomenon.

Given the plurality of perspectives that he is willing and able to adopt, Kratochwil's reflections on norms are not an easy tool in the hands of the empirically minded researcher. In his work we find many reasons to be convinced that norms matter in international politics but little indication as to how exactly we should study them. Kratochwil's reflections on norms are an inspiration for empirical research, rather than a manual, as Antje Wiener points out in her chapter. Moreover, his multiperspective approach to social norms sits uncomfortably with the *praxis* of most scholars in IR, who engage in exercises of competitive theory-testing that put a premium on mutually exclusive explanations and fictions of monocausality (Kratochwil 2000a: 62–3; see also Kessler in this volume). It is therefore not surprising to see that other constructivist approaches have been more readily deployed than Kratochwil's in this respect.

Some constructivists in IR have adopted a Habermasian perspective that centers on processes of persuasion and communicative action as mechanisms of political change. As I argue below, this somewhat unexpected turn took place because Habermasian theorizing offers a radical alternative to the long-dominant rationalist approach in IR. In particular Habermas's bifurcation of the social world into distinct realms of strategic and communicative action makes his theorizing an attractive starting point for a challenge to rationalist theorizing in IR.

In this chapter I take issue with the tendency among some constructivists in IR to idealize processes of political change in Habermasian terms. My aim is not to refute Habermasian ideas as such, or to suggest we ban them from the agenda of IR. What I consider to be problematic and in need of rethinking is one specific adaptation of Habermasian thought in IR that envisages international norm change through deliberation and persuasion in international negotiation. More specifically, in this chapter I will discuss three unwarranted idealizations inherent in this line of Habermasian IR thinking. First is the assumption that there are fundamentally different modes of social interaction and that actors can switch from one to the other. Second is the idea that social norms spread through processes of persuasion. Third is the assumption that an act of agreement pertains to both the course of action and the motivating reasons for it. The two elements are logically connected by postulating that actors who share a normative belief will *therefore* take the same course of action.

These three idealizations all have roots in Habermasian social and political theory but were specifically adapted for use in IR. As instances of what I should like to call (with proverbial Teutonic irony) a "new German idealism," they might inflate our expectations of what norm-guided behavior in IR should look like. Frustrated that we do not find such behavior where we would expect to, we might dismiss the relevance of norms and communication in IR prematurely, or disregard aspects of norm-guided behavior that clearly do not fall into the category of "communicative action." Kratochwil's thinking on social norms is a good antidote to such unwarranted idealizations, as will become clear below.

How Habermas came to IR

As a resourceful social theorist, Jürgen Habermas has often taken sides in political debates on European integration and the consequences of globalization, but he is certainly not a typical IR scholar (Habermas 2007: 406–9). A disciplinary effort was required to bring his theorizing into IR. There was an early critical theory connection and a critique of realism in IR which I will not elaborate further here (but see Diez and Steans 2005). I will focus instead on the positivist rather than critical application of Habermasian thinking that entered IR by way of what was, in the beginning, a German debate (Humrich 2006). In the early 1990s several German IR constructivists sought to develop a theoretical alternative to rational choice as a theory of social action (the first was Müller 1994). They found inspiration in Habermas's seminal "Theory of Communicative Action," concentrating on one core aspect of it: the distinction between different modes of social action (1981, I: 273–337). Their ideas sparked the so-called ZIB-debate,[1] which kept German IR theory busy throughout the 1990s. The ramifications are still felt (Hanrieder 2008). The distinction between communicative and strategic action not only inspired debates at the theoretical and meta-theoretical level but was also applied to mainstream constructivist empirical research.

What I call mainstream constructivism is characterized by the assumptions that social norms motivate actors to choose courses of action and thus have causal effects that can be scientifically proven; and norm-based explanations can beat their rationalist rivals in exercises of competitive theory-testing (Checkel 1998: 342).[2] In recent years the center of debate between constructivists and rationalists "has moved to the challenge of explaining why some norms matter sometimes in some places and not others" (Price 2008: 193). Inherent in this conceptualization is, of course, the default assumption of traditional IR that there are many political situations in which norms do not matter—an assumption that more radical constructivists, including Kratochwil, would reject. Yet it paved the way for introducing Habermasian social theory to mainstream IR.

For mainstream constructivists, the central hypothesis is that communicative action or "arguing"[3] will result in persuasion, thereby making social norms effective and inducing political change (Deitelhoff 2009: 53).

> Arguing is also relevant for problem solving in the sense of seeking an optimal solution for a commonly perceived problem and for agreeing on a common normative framework. Seeking a reasoned consensus helps actors to overcome many collective action problems."
>
> (Risse 2000: 2)

In short, arguing thus conceived is a radical theoretical alternative to the rationalist search for a compromise negotiated between opposing interests. Since this alternative depends on the Habermasian bifurcation of the social world, it explains why Habermasian social theory is so attractive in a debate that pits rationalist explanations based on actors' self-interest against constructivist accounts that highlight the role of social norms.

In the following sections I will discuss the three problematic Habermasian idealizations deployed in recent research in IR. To repeat: "communicative action" is a distinct mode of social action; persuasion is a mechanism of norm diffusion; agreement to act jointly is "completely theorized" with respect to the joint action it produces. I do not claim that all of the authors I cite employ these three idealizations simultaneously or that these idealizations are exclusively made by Habermasians. They may also be found in the work of constructivists who do not explicitly link them to Habermas's writings.

Modes of social action

As explained above, the major point of reference for the reception of Habermas in constructivist IR was his monumental two-volume *Theory of Communicative Action* (1981). In the first volume of this study, Habermas develops the dichotomy of strategic versus communicative action. Strategic action is directed toward the attainment of goals by individuals through rational, instrumental calculation. Communicative action, in contrast, is a type of social behavior in which individuals coordinate their plans of action by means of rational communication. "The practice of reaching understanding differs from that of bargaining with respect to its intended aim: the desired agreement is understood in one case as consensus, in the other as a negotiated agreement or contract" (Habermas 1996a: 140). Unlike strategists, communicatively acting persons are oriented toward a reasoned consensus, not mere compromise, and they put their own beliefs and proposals for action to the test.

Habermas insists that this is not just an analytical distinction but a typology of actors' orientations that can be found in the real world, thus establishing a division of social behavior into realms of strategic and communicative action (Dorschel 1990). On closer inspection, this bifurcation is created in two different ways. The first way is to ground the distinction in the intentions of individuals. Actors are either oriented toward persuasion or toward reaching a bargained settlement. As Habermas explains: "I indeed assume that the actors can know in every phase of an interaction, even if only vaguely and intuitively, whether they are adopting a strategic and objectivating or a consensus-oriented attitude towards other participants" (Habermas 1984b: 544, my translation).

The second way to bifurcate strategic and communicative action is to ground it in the pragmatics of language use. Habermas posits that consensus-oriented communication can work only if actors reach an understanding on three "validity claims" underpinning a proposition: that what is being said is true, in the sense of being factually correct; that it is normatively right; and that the speakers mean what they say (truthfulness). How does strategic action relate to this? In an essay from 1976, Habermas conceptualizes strategic action as a derivative of communicative action (Habermas 1984a: 354). The key difference between the two is that in strategic action one validity claim is suspended: the claim to truthfulness. This illuminates well how some forms of rhetoric and deceit can function. An audience is manipulated by a speaker who pretends to be acting communicatively, in the sense of trying to persuade and being herself open to persuasion, but in reality is not.

In his later work, however, Habermas radicalizes his speech act theory and argues that in strategic action the three validity claims are suspended altogether (1984b: 544). This radicalization created some confusion because it makes it difficult to see how the strategic use of language can function in practice. This point needs some elaboration. In Habermas's theory of communicative action there is a somewhat obscure overlap between understanding the meaning of a speech act (*Verstehen*) and assent to what the speaker says (*Einverständnis*). The problem arises because Habermas equates the understanding of a proposition with the acceptance of the three validity claims of truth, rightness and truthfulness. If the addressee of a proposition responds with "yes," she supposedly agrees to the three validity claims. If she answers "no," she will be expected to challenge at least one of the validity claims made by the speaker. She may argue that the statement is factually wrong, that it is morally unacceptable, or that the speaker is not honest.

As an account of language use, this is quite enlightening. The problem is that Habermas connects it to a theory of social action and reserves the understanding of speech acts, as empirically evidenced by assent to a proposition, to the mode of communicative action. This leads to the conundrum of strategic communication because strategic social action seems to logically presuppose that actors understand their verbal messages correctly (Alexander 1988: 98). A threat, for instance, can only have the desired effect if the addressee understands it. What is more, the speaker obviously makes two validity claims while making a threat: first that her threat is true in the sense of being factually realizable—she has the means to carry out the threatened action—and, second, that she is truthful, in the sense that she is really committed to carrying out the threat and not just bluffing. In this example, only one validity claim, the moral rightness of the proposal, can be suspended.

Yet we need not even pick such an extreme example of forced assent. Even the normal practice of bargaining is full of references to social norms, which are only intelligible if we assume that actors can successfully discuss validity claims although they know that they are in a strategic situation. Jon Elster, for one, has highlighted this assumption in the case of collective wage bargaining:

> Norms of equality, equity and fair division shape the outcome of bargaining generally and of collective wage bargaining in particular. Sometimes appeal to a norm of distribution facilitates agreement, both in labour-capital bargaining and in labour-labour bargaining. Norms of fairness can force agreement on the division of earnings between shareholders and workers. . . . But norms can also be an obstacle to agreement. In the presence of competing norms that favour different groups, the self-righteousness conferred by belief in a norm can lead to a bargaining impasse.
>
> (Elster 1989: 215)

In this example, we cannot assume that successful bargainers really agree on a common conception of fairness and then decide what to do on that basis. Moral norms in this context function as focal points that render some possible solutions more salient than others (Kratochwil 1989a: 35). It is hard to account for such anchoring effects within the framework of Habermasian communicative action because actors are strategically oriented and they consciously refer to social norms that favor their interest. Nevertheless it might be difficult for the opponent to deny the validity of a focal point that enjoys a considerable pedigree. How can this be explained? Are actors "switching" here between the modes of communicative and strategic action? Habermas seems to think that frequent switching of a mode of "action orientation" is taking place in bargaining situations (Habermas 2007: 416–17).

Whether this assumption is warranted is an empirical question. It is important to note, however, that if we admit that strategically minded actors can communicate successfully, the distinction of two modes of social action collapses into a question of intentions (which Davis, Lynch and Bukovansky all discuss in this volume). As intentions are extremely difficult to monitor and empirically elusive, the bifurcation of social action that made Habermasian theory a good candidate for being adapted to the constructivist mainstream in IR reaches a dead end (Ulbert and Risse 2005; Müller and Deitelhoff 2005). As one of the proponents of argument as an alternative to strategic action acknowledged in recent years, Kratochwil's approach may be more useful than a Habermasian one because it allows for strategic communication to be governed by social norms (Müller 2004: 396). Kratochwil in fact does not associate certain types of language use to specific intentions of actors. This is particularly visible in his historically informed treatment of rhetoric, revealing that the perceived connection between rhetoric and strategic manipulation is a recent one (1989a: 40–3).

Persuasion

A second idealization usually complements the assumption that communicative action is a way in which norms and ideas are influential in international politics: persuasion. In constructivist IR theory, persuasion is conceptualized as a mechanism of change in actors' behavior (Johnston, 2001; for a critique, see Krebs and Jackson 2007). Persuasion implies that actors adopt new normative beliefs or change their perception of the situation when they are exposed to arguments made by others. This assumption is made by Habermasians such as Payne (2001) and Deitelhoff (2009) but also by other constructivists (Checkel 2001). The specific relevance of persuasion for constructivist IR is that it provides an explanation for the diffusion of norms (Risse 1999; Klotz 2002). In empirical research, however, it is notoriously hard to prove that persuasion has taken place (Krebs and Jackson 2007: 40). What we can observe is that participants adopt claims or normative arguments that they have been exposed to before. We might also observe that they simultaneously change their negotiation position. Yet it is hard to show that they really believe in the arguments they adopt and that changes in factual or normative beliefs actually cause changes in their negotiation position. As Payne reminds us, "apparent state acceptance of normative standards may reflect coercion or some other mechanism, rather than persuasion, at work" (2001: 39–40). In fact, an observed correlation of attempts at persuasion and changes in actors' behavior is not sufficient to prove the existence of a causal relationship between the two (Yee 1996: 72).

Since we cannot monitor the brains of negotiators to see if persuasion really takes place, we are left with second-best solutions, such as assessing the consistency of actors' utterances across several forums. This inability to pinpoint processes of persuasion first hand has left some constructivists with the rather desperate conclusion that

> our findings suggest that authentic persuasion did take place, and we assume that actors changed their orientation during the process of argumentation. At this stage, we are unable to methodologically and empirically prove this assumption: it is a theoretical paradise that is empirically lost!
>
> (Deitelhoff and Müller 2005: 177)

The difficulty in directly observing persuasion while it is happening surely is a serious methodological problem. It is especially serious in any context that obliges mainstream constructivists to show precisely when and how norms do the trick. However, my concern here is not only with how we might show that arguments matter. It is rather about how we think that arguments matter. In this respect, the major problem with the Habermasian approach to international communication seems to be that it puts great emphasis on a quite demanding causal mechanism: the change of beliefs. The idea that actors change their beliefs is particularly difficult to reconcile with international legal practice. In this context actors cannot be supposed to be open to persuasion or willing to put their own convictions to the test; they have no choice but to be strategically minded. Kratochwil's remarks on the functioning of practical and legal discourse are again illuminating here. The main purpose of persuasion in practical reasoning is not to make someone accept the validity of a norm but to agree that the norm is applicable in the specific circumstances of a case (1989a: 37–8). Persuasion may indeed take place quite often in international politics but not necessarily in the sense of norm diffusion or change of normative beliefs.

Consensus

The third idealization underpinning Habermasian thinking in IR is that consensual agreement to engage in argument anticipates a consensus on the outcome of the argument. In this mode of communication, participants coordinate their plans of action by means of "reasoned consensus" (Risse 2000: 7). The assumption is that persons who can agree on the reasons for action would also agree on what to do in practice. Otherwise arguing would be ineffectual as a way of resolving collective action problems. Therefore, in communicative action a problem of the practice-type (doing x or y?) is resolved by deliberating on the reasons for adopting options x or y. Such agreements, in which actors agree both on a proposal of the practice-type and on a logical connection with more abstract reasons (norms, values, principles) for adopting it may be called "completely theorized" (Sunstein 1995; Steffek 2005). The connection with Habermasian "communicative action" becomes clear when we confront it with bargaining. In a bargaining situation, agreements do not need to be completely theorized, and it is extremely unlikely that they are in practice. Bargaining actors only need to agree that a proposed solution of the practical type is sufficiently in line with their respective preferences to warrant strategic interaction. There is no need to harmonize these preferences or motivations.

The idea of completely theorized agreements is, quite like "communicative action" and "persuasion as belief change," a tremendous idealization. It assumes that political actors will be able to simultaneously agree on what to do and on why to do it. Empirically, however, this does not seem to be very likely, even under favorable circumstances. As a law scholar, Sunstein himself found that groups of judges acting together do not normally agree on a joint decision and simultaneously on the reasons for this decision. The possibility in some legal systems that a member of a judicial bench may give a separate yet "concurring opinion" testifies to the empirical importance of this situation.

Why do "concurring opinions" occur? Although individual judges may have some "preference" for a certain verdict, their deliberation does not resemble a real bargaining situation in which opponents with incompatible preferences (e.g. employers and trade unions) seek a practical settlement. The reason can instead be found in the narrow limits of rational inference. I am not alluding to different individual "rationalities" (ways of rational inference) or the plurality of possibly applicable norms and principles. The limits are imposed by the "horizontal" structure of practical reasoning that does not allow for a straightforward subsumption of concrete situations ("cases") under an abstract norm or law.

As Kratochwil reminds us, reasoning by precedent and analogy is an extremely important mechanism in both jurisprudence and diplomacy (1989a: 223–7). For instance, what international rules we think should govern outer space depends a good deal on what we think outer space is like (Peterson 1997). One might reply that this is a question of factual information to be resolved by way of arguing. But there is more to it than a question of factual proof that can be answered by reference to data or evidence. Data might help us determine characteristics of outer space such as density and temperature, but it is unlikely to help us determine if it is like Antarctica or the High Seas—a relevant question from a legal point of view. Our propensity to accept something as a good or convincing analogy will depend to a great extent upon our familiarity with certain social contexts, traditions and experiences (Chapman 1998). Kratochwil therefore concludes: "In particular, one has to inquire into the ways in which traditions, historical experiences, past cases, practices, ideologies, etc., provide support for 'reasons' that become socially dominant" (1989a: 33).

Conclusion

In this brief chapter I have used Kratochwil's broad approach to the study of norms in international relations to highlight some limitations of the new German idealism that is currently in vogue in constructivist IR. I have argued that much of the recent constructivist literature inspired by Habermasian thought is based on a set of idealized assumptions, in particular the triad of communicative action, persuasion and reasoned consensus. These idealizations were fostered and necessitated by the mainstreaming of constructivist IR, which created a demand for radical theoretical alternatives to rational choice and for well-specified empirical mechanisms. The need to bring convincing empirical evidence in theory-testing has posed great difficulties for constructivists and often been resolved in practice by saying that rationalist accounts remain deficient if not complemented by constructivist elements.

The move in mainstream constructivism to Habermasian social theory in order to complement or improve rational choice theory has some troublesome side effects. My concern is that an idealized conception of how norms work may narrow our view of what might be relevant phenomena for IR. In particular, it may lead us to understate, or even disregard, the extent to which norms stabilize existing international order and practices of exploitation, discrimination and inequality; the fact that the meaning of norms is contested and heavily dependent on context; that there are almost always strategic elements in the appeal to norms by social actors (see Larson's chapter in this volume); that the spread of, and adherence to, norms can function in ways other than persuasion; and that in practical matters a type of horizontal reasoning is very important that concentrates on analogies, comparisons and precedent rather than logical inference. The conclusion is not that IR scholars should forget Habermas. There are extremely interesting applications of Habermasian thought in IR that come without positivist strings attached, for instance on the shape and effects of an emergent global public sphere (Dryzek 2006; Mitzen 2005). For the study of international negotiation, diplomatic reasoning and the role of law in international relations, Kratochwil's broad approach to social norms should be our starting point.

Notes

1. The acronym ZIB stands for *Zeitschrift für internationale Beziehungen*, which is considered to be the flagship journal of German IR.
2. Constructivist research is not only about social norms and other types of prescriptions, but the mainstream empirical work places a heavy emphasis on them.
3. The use of the term "arguing" to denote the opposite of "bargaining" can be traced back to Jon Elster (1986) but was linked with Habermasian communicative action (Risse 2000).

14
Normative Baggage in International Encounters: Contestation all the Way

Antje Wiener

Introduction

In situations of crisis in world politics decisions have to be made on short notice. Usually, the process of decision making will involve heads of state or government, bringing together individuals who arrive from far afield and who are expected to act with reference to international law. Such international encounters bear a paradox, however. While it could be argued that the legitimacy of a decision increases with the diversity in a group's national makeup, empirical research cautions against assumptions about a causal link between diversity and legitimacy. If group diversity worsens the chances of acceptable compromise in international encounters, conflict may follow. This chapter seeks to shed light on this paradox by asking anew Kratochwil's erstwhile question, "how do norms work?" (Kratochwil 1984b). As legal scholars have pointed out, the implementation of the law requires social (read: shared) recognition that allows for an understanding of how to interpret legal texts within a particular social environment. That is, a norm X counts as Y in a specific context C only (Searle 2005: 10; see also Walker 2008). In the absence of social recognition the mere reference to legal texts leaves quite a margin for interpretation (Snyder 1990; Curtin 1999; Finnemore and Toope 2001).

This margin for diversity is likely to generate contestation in the best case and conflict in the worst-case scenario. The latter is most likely in situations of crisis, when decisions need to be taken fast. That is, there is neither time for engaging in the time-consuming processes of deliberation (Müller 2004), nor the possibility of drawing on the shared experience that is required to generate social recognition. Or so theories of social learning would tell us (Johnston 2001; Checkel 2001). If we follow Searle's dictum (2005: 12) about the constitutive role of language for all social institutions, it is the shortage of the time needed to find language that is acceptable to all parties which creates a problem in international encounters. To be sure, Habermasian scholars in International Relations (IR) have demonstrated that contestation and deliberation can lead to persuasion (Müller 2004; Risse 2000; also see Steffek's contribution to this volume), in turn leading to compromise and thus enhancing legitimacy (Tully 2002; Forst 2007; Brunnée and Toope 2009). However, contestation will be conducive to enhanced legitimacy only under certain conditions such as social interaction in a shared context over a prolonged period of time. In the worst-case scenario contestation in international relations potentially lays the ground for conflict, especially considering the multiplier function of encounters between higher-level civil servants and politicians.

When conceptualizing indicators for conflict in international relations it is therefore important to factor in the potential impact of diversity. To better understand the impact of diversity, I propose we consider international relations as the relations between actors of different national backgrounds. I empirically assess these international relations based on approaches that allow for the empirical appreciation of practice (Adler 2005; Pouliot 2008; Friedrichs and Kratochwil 2009e). These approaches focus on "background knowledge" (Adler 2005: 21) or individually held "normative baggage" to emphasize the implications of crossing sociocultural boundaries when acting internationally (Wiener 2008: Chapter 4). The underlying assumption is that in the absence of social recognition, where nothing seems intuitively appropriate (March and Olson 1989), individuals will turn to their individually held normative baggage for reference. In light of increasing international encounters and the strong likelihood of more rather than less diversity in the world, a better assessment of normative baggage is therefore crucial for understanding of normative conflict. It follows that instead of more or better law—or legal processes, for that matter—the legitimacy of international law may actually depend on sorting out the normative baggage brought to bear in international encounters.

Current contestations include diverging interpretations of international law in specific cases and subsequent practical decision making, diverging assessments of the utility of international organizations such as the United Nations and their law-making activities and diverging interpretations of norms in everyday processes of policymaking where international encounters take place. The issue at hand then is whether twenty-first century scholars in IR can reasonably and justifiably work with the assumption that the law is the law is the law. Consequently the question underlying today's debate about the future role of international law is whether what is accepted as formally valid is likely to be viewed as legitimate by all members of international society (also see Chris Brown's contribution to this volume). With the "meaning" of international law at stake (Walker 2008), the research question of which norms are powerful (Risse et al. 1999) stands to be replaced by the question of how do norms matter (Kratochwil 2000a) and whether they are perceived as legitimate by all those affected (Tully 2002; Brunnée and Toope 2010).

In a global context where fundamental norms such as human rights, democracy and the rule of law have become a rhetorical staple yet are often reduced to mere discursive reference points that have lost any particular meaning (Tamanha 2004), practice becomes all important (Kratochwil 2007). More specifically, I argue that to grapple with the challenge to the legitimacy of international law, it is important to engage in empirical research on the way meaning-in-use is enacted. This brings us back to Kratochwil's query about the way norms work. While IR has generated an impressive literature on how norms influence state behavior, this relatively narrow focus on norms research still leaves quite some margin for generating an answer to Kratochwil's erstwhile question. In teasing out the interactive perspective on norms in some more detail, this chapter advances an empirical contribution to that answer. To that end it applies the pluralist law-in-context approach as well as the critical constructivist approach supported by much of Kratochwil's work. As he has suggested, there is a certain attraction to the "normative pull of pluralism as a social ideal" (Kratochwil 2000a: 36). This pull, I would hold, is well placed within the framework of global constitutionalism as an academic construction and shared reference frame for debates on the future of international order (Walker 2008: 17; Weiler 1999; Tully et al. 2009).

This chapter elaborates on this argument with reference to Kratochwil's work on norms. It proceeds in three further sections. The first section reviews the discussion of norms in IR theory, focusing especially on the sequence of action and thus the theoretical contributions of those constructivists who refer to the logic of appropriateness and the logic of arguing. Drawing on these observations, the second section then turns to critically address the myopic handling of normativity in these contributions, a theme which will bring Kratochwil's call for a truly interdisciplinary normative IR theory back in. The last section takes up the call for empirical research to help evaluate theoretical claims and proposes to disaggregate norms research along the three dimensions of formal validity, social recognition and cultural validation.

Norms research in IR theory

Kratochwil's encompassing and substantive work on international relations has always engaged with both international political and legal theory. As he points out on the very first page of *Rules, Norms, and Decisions*,

> [t]o the extent that the focus is on interactions in the international arena, it is a book about international relations. To the extent that the investigation is interested in legal norms it is a book on *legal theory*. Insofar as issues of interpretation, precedent, and sources of law will be discussed, it is in a way a treatise on *jurisprudence*. To the extent that rules and norms are viewed as means to maintain *social order*, it is a book on social theory. Finally, to the extent that the analysis is occasioned by the re-reading of some of the classics of international law and political theory, it is—at least and without wanting to claim comprehensiveness or completeness—a study of *political thought*.
>
> (Kratochwil 1989a: 1, emphases added)

Notably, norms research in IR is found on one side of Kratochwil's theoretical coin. In the process the question of how do norms work has been rephrased in various ways. The soft positivist research design of modern constructivists focused on the research question of how norms impact on state behavior (Katzenstein 1996; Risse et al. 1999). The postpositivists, in turn, drew on the Wittgensteinian concept of mapping and rule making and were more interested in the research question of how rules emerge and, indeed, how to change and implement rules strategically (Fierke 1998). More recently, pluralists of varying provenance have begun to critically address the question of legality, legal obligation and the meaning of law (Brunnée and Toope 2009: Chapter 1; Walker 2008).

In principle, all approaches agree on the crucial aspect of interaction. Accordingly, they have engaged, albeit selectively, with the main points of the three constructivist pillars in IR (Kratochwil 1989a; Onuf 1989; Wendt 1987) while keeping positivist international relations theory at a distance. In practice, however, the concept of interaction has been explored with varying degrees of success, and, it has been noticed that the way interaction is conceived does not do justice to its full potential (Brunnée and Toope 2002; Herborth 2004; Klotz and Lynch 2007; Kessler in this volume). In fact, it could be argued that since Wendt's early proposal to de-ontologize the state based on Giddens' structuration theory (Wendt 1987) and Kratochwil and Ruggie's epistemological intervention on the constitutive impact of intersubjectivity in the international realm (Kratochwil and Ruggie 1986a), efforts to theorize interaction and apply the concept to the study of international relations confer on norms an ontological independence they do not possess as social constructions (Wiener 2004). In effect, norms were turned into something akin to a new billiard ball in IR theory. They were reduced to intervening variables rather than being acknowledged as part of the process.

The project of studying the impact of normative baggage seeks to reverse this process by peering into the ball, so to speak. Based on empirical research, it is possible to uncover the invisible properties which are constituted through the day-to-day process of enacting normative "structures of meaning-in-use" (Kratochwil 1989a: 18; Dworkin 1977: Chapter 2; Weldes and Saco 1996; Milliken 1999). Structures of meaning-in-use are defined as "intersubjective structures . . . that provide the categories through which we represent and understand the world" (Weldes 1998: 218). They therefore offer a reference frame for empirical studies that seek to reconstruct meaning which has been enacted at a particular point in time, and hence represent meaning that is actually in use. The practice of enacting that meaning and its impact on international encounters follow central constructivist assumptions about intersubjectivity (Kratochwil and Ruggie 1986a), relationality (Tilly 1975) and critical contestation (Tully 2002).

It follows that the importance of normative baggage is likely to grow with the decline of shared social references. Since it remains invisible to the agent who is carrying this baggage unless contested by others, it is likely to work as a spanner in the works in international encounters, especially in times of crisis. Normative baggage thus indicates the reference to the structural component of structures of meaning-in-use as well as the agentic component of individual enactment of this meaning. In the following, I am mainly concerned with advancing empirical research to address the apparent paradoxical development of increasingly contested fundamental norms and the growing need to legitimize actions within the international realm. In the absence of an all-encompassing transnationalization, international encounters are likely to generate more rather than less diversity.[1] To account for and work with this diversity, I identify interdisciplinary criteria that are understandable and acceptable within the three major involved strands of social science research on norms, that is, IR theory, international law and constitutionalism.

Bringing interaction back in

Various proposals have been made to bring interaction back in. With that project in view, since the early 1990s a number of research projects have taken the call to study interaction literally, as an invitation to study processes and practices rather than principles and rules in relations with norms. The resulting research has focused on processes of negotiation including strategies of bargaining and arguing which were studied with reference to communicative action theory, on the one hand, and on discursive practices of jurisgeneration, rule making and policy development, on the other. Both of these two perspectives have developed a highly sophisticated toolkit for studying the way norms work in international relations. The question this chapter raises is whether they have proceeded in too much isolation, given that they started out using constructivism as a meta-theory to enable better middle-range theorizing.

Reus-Smit's observation that the liberal dimension of international law has suffered a strange death puts a finger on what is, in my view, the deeper problem of mid-range theorizing that loses touch with the wider (theoretical) context (Reus-Smit 2001). The debate between Abbott et al.'s institutional approach to so-called legalization (2000) and Finnemore and Toope's call for studying law in context (2001) highlights the dilemma. What the former consider as legalization reflects, from the latter's point of view, a mere process of bureaucratic institutionalization. Where then does the 'legality' of a law-like institution begin (Brunnée and Toope 2010); how, if at all, can it be measured; and how does it matter? To assess the validity of each position, both approaches would need to be scrutinized with regard to their respective capability of assessing the relation between legality and legitimacy of the institutions (norms, principles, rules) in question.

In short, I believe that mid-range research on what might be called the logic of action has lost sight of key normative principles. For example, and explaining behavior with reference to the impact of norms, the logic of appropriateness replaced the explanatory power of the logic of consequence. Then, the logic of arguing was added on to the logic of appropriateness to explain the power to persuade others that ones own argument was more legitimate (Risse and Ulbert 2005; Müller and Deitelhoff 2005). Surely, these developments demonstrate how norms work in international relations. But, do they tell the whole story, for example, why norms don't work? While proceeding well beyond inter-state bargaining, Habermasian notions of deliberation in international negotiating settings leave some margin for improvement. Answering the question depends on how to incorporate interaction in a way that allows for empirical assessment. To that end, better empirical knowledge about the largely invisible impact of normative baggage is required. The following summarizes the key elements for such empirical work with a view to reversing the process of turning norms into a kind of thing they are not.

The de-ontologization of norms

At the core of the proposed approach is a typology of norms. The typology distinguishes fundamental norms, organizing principles and standardized procedures according to generalization and specificity. In addition I propose a disaggregation of norms according to three empirical dimensions of enacted meaning in use. These dimensions are formal validity (reference to officially documented texts), social recognition (enacting shared reference frames within a specific societal environment in which such texts are interpreted) and cultural validation (enacting individually held associative connotations). Cultural validation adds an individual perspective to the dimensions of formal validity and social recognition. With this conceptual innovation, it is now possible to empirically identify conditions under which conflict is more or less likely.

I argue that the dimension of cultural validation remains under-researched to this day despite Kratochwil's repeated calls for interactive approaches to norms. The conceptual innovation of cultural validation highlights the importance of context, thus picking up on research on contested norms which has evolved in IR theory and International Law, and which Kratochwil's work has done so much to inspire. By referring to this work, the concept of cultural validation highlights the way IR theory has deviated from Kratochwil's intentions and from the conceptual ground he explored in his complex work on rules, norms and decisions and later writings. And it argues that, if we see a paradoxical link between international encounters and increasing reference to as well as breaches of international law, then this is in part due to the pending full exploration of Kratochwil's argument.

Studies drawing on this typology have, for example, examined organizing principles such as accountability, the democratic audit, transparency and fundamental norms such as access to contestation, citizenship and representation in different policy sectors of nonstate governance. The degree of generality of norms is a measure of their moral and ethical scope. Fundamental norms include both core constitutional norms and basic procedural norms such as citizenship, human rights, the rule of law, democracy, as well as nonintervention, abstention from torture, and so forth. Organizing principles evolve through policy or political processes. They inform political procedures and guide policy practices and include such principles as legality, accountability, transparency, legitimacy and gender mainstreaming. Standardized procedures such as rules and provisions are the least likely to be contested on moral or ethical grounds as they entail prescriptions for action which are highly specific, such as instructions to assemble a "flat-pack piece of furniture" or electoral guidelines that call for qualified majority voting (Kratochwil 1989a).

Since "[n]o rules in international law are absolute," indeed, "[n]othing in this normative sphere is absolute" (Jackson 2003: 19), the expectation among international lawyers is that the substance of law depends on input through legal discourse, that is, deliberation, jurisprudence, learned opinion and other discursive interventions. The contested issue regarding the crucial input of discourse in international law lies in different legal traditions. These can generally be distinguished as a disposition among continental lawyers to interpret the letter of the law strictly, and a disposition among Anglo-American lawyers toward a generally flexible quality of international law understood as evolving through the process of jurisprudence (Scott 2003). Nonetheless it can be argued that while considering the input of discourse at different stages, lawyers would attribute a strong and constitutive role to discursive interventions in the process of international law. That emphasis on discourse as constitutive toward establishing substantive meaning of norms is not necessarily shared among political and social theorists who make conceptual distinctions between arguing, contestation, deliberation and discursive interventions. In IR theory the distinctive role of language as an intersubjective element in the process of the construction of norms was introduced by Kratochwil and Ruggie's paper (1986a) when they offered a constructivist, as opposed to a behavioral, approach to discourse—an approach foregoing needless conceptual distinctions even as it acknowledged the importance of politics, an approach abandoned as constructivism moved toward soft positivism.

The internationalization of political processes and policies indicates a change of the (quasi-)constitutional framework (formal validity), as well as the social environment (social recognition) in which politics takes place. In the absence of transnationalization, this process decouples legal validity and social recognition. That is, the social context of experience which provides the information required to generate shared recognition, on the one hand, and the context of norm interpretation, on the other, no longer overlap. Instead, individual actors take their normative baggage from their respective social environment to the political arena in which decision making takes place. While it is altogether likely that this arena also facilitates processes of social learning based on iterative interactions, this condition cannot be taken for granted in a globalized world of multiple and changing international organizational contexts in which international encounters take place. We therefore need to address empirically the spatial gap between formal validity (of norms) and social recognition. To address the consequences and discuss ways of remedying the spatial gap between formal validity and social recognition that is a common condition for international encounters, this section suggests that norms prompt individually held associative connotations. These interpretations offer an additional dimension that allows for empirical research to identify cultural validation based on everyday experience. The empirical focus is on the reconstruction of the way normative meaning-in-use is enacted individually.

The way norms work can be hypothesized according to two alternative views on the constitutive and regulative role of international law. The *community hypothesis* takes a utilitarian approach which has some appeal to liberal cosmopolitans. It expects compliance to increase with reference to a specific community, conceptualized either as treaty-based membership or as shared legal practices such as cross-referencing between constitutional courts (Slaughter 2003). The *diversity hypothesis* takes a pluralist perspective that considers social practices as constitutive for meaning. It holds that in the absence of all-encompassing transnationalization, international encounters have a selective rather than a harmonizing effect.

While the community hypothesis expects convergence with regard to the norms that matter, the diversity hypothesis expects conflict and contestation with regard to the meaning of norms. While both views would agree that the crucial aspect for the future role of international law as a shared reference for international encounters is to establish whether norms are accepted, they are likely to disagree on the question of whether norms matter because they are legal, or because they are perceived as legitimate, or both. In effect, the diversity hypothesis challenges the community hypothesis, pointing to its lack of context awareness. In this context, no one has argued more consistently than Kratochwil that the world is not better understood by ironing out the creases of complex social reality or by shying away from theoretical depth.

Conclusion

International encounters over fundamental norms are potentially conflictive since this situation involves bringing together a group of individuals who, by definition, do not share the same sociocultural memory. That is, contested meanings are expected when sociocultural boundaries are crossed. Cognitive neurological research has demonstrated that the description of shared events differs according to individual experience of the same event. In other words, what appears as a fact to one person is a questionable reversal of the facts to another (Roth 2002). Comparative research in the social sciences has demonstrated that individual experience is likely to generate diverse interpretations when studied with reference to the interpretation of fundamental norms in international relations such as human rights, democracy and the rule of law. This diversity emerges in particular when international interaction in negotiation or decision-making situations is moved out of domestic contexts and hence shared social recognition is undermined. This is particularly the case in situations where internationally composed committees are expected to make decisions on short notice. Here I have in mind crisis situations which require direct action according to international legal rules such as decisions with regard to terrorist threat, genocide or other crimes against humanity that require humanitarian intervention, or action with regard to Chapter VII of the UN Charter, that need to establish whether the condition of special threat requires immediate action. In such situations reference to international norms which are viewed as appropriate by members of the liberal international community may actually lead to quite substantial misunderstandings about the meaning of norms, souring relations among states in the process. This suggests that assumptions about the impact of shared social recognition remain to be further qualified with regard to contextual factors.

In the absence of time, resort to individual experience is conducive to a diversity of meaning, which forms the basis for conflict. If, to generate shared views, iterated interaction that involves the same individuals over an extended period of time (i.e. five or more years) is necessary, the input of processes of globalization or Europeanization does not necessarily generate harmonization in the short or medium term. If this were the case, the problem of conflicting interpretation of norms and hence contested legitimacy of international law would become increasingly obsolete over time. However, this is not likely according to recent research in the social sciences and legal studies (Wiener 2008; De Burca 2008). Against liberal expectations, even elites like the social group regularly engaging in international encounters do not develop shared interpretations of norms. This highlights the time-space relation of the constitution of international order (Walker 2008).

How do norms work?

As a critical appraisal, this chapter sought to highlight the advantages of Kratochwil's encompassing interdisciplinary and normative approach to norms, but it also raised questions about the empirical relevance of this work. While noting the increasing interdisciplinary engagement of political scientists and lawyers with regard to the input of norms, the point here was not only to straddle the boundaries between law and politics but to propose a terminology that makes interdisciplinary empirical research more accessible to both sides of the disciplinary boundary. This approach does not claim to do full justice to the width and depth of Kratochwil's work. It does, however, seek to advance interdisciplinary discussion that allows for more than a magpie foray into neighboring disciplines. Kratochwil's erstwhile question, "how do norms work?" has continued to influence his work and to inspire the work of others over the years. It is as topical as it could ever be. In light of a wealth of mid-range theorizing on norms which has dominated the constructivist research program in the 1990s, Kratochwil's emphasis on the way norms work remains a topical research program for the twenty-first century.

To conclude, this chapter argued that international interaction does not overcome diversity spontaneously but requires iterated interaction. This raises the normative problem of access to participation in international encounters. After all, transnational arenas that are constituted through iterated international interaction and which do create commonality remain exclusive. That is, they are accessible only to a limited group of participants who happen to be involved in specific contexts such as the working environments of some international institutions. For the most part, international interaction produces diversity by putting transnational arenas on a par with the already existing domestic arenas in which patterns of social recognition remain relatively stable. Diversity therefore needs to be considered as a condition for international relations and hence constitutive for international order.

Notes

This chapter had been first presented at FritzFest, Columbia University, February 14, 2009. I would like to thank all participants and especially Nick Onuf for very helpful comments; the responsibility for this version is mine.

1. This hypothesis was developed in Wiener 2008; see Chapters 8 and 9 for details.

15 Rules and Norms in a Post-Western World

Chris Brown

Introduction

Friedrich Kratochwil began to write about the normative foundations of international order at a time when a liberal world order was a stipulated ideal. The question of order was then typically framed in the context of international organization and understood in liberal institutionalist terms, but his concern then was with "the management of power" (1978: 1), a concern he shared with realists rather more than with liberal institutionalists. This chapter picks up the issue of the management of power, and aims to examine the normative foundations for the world order that will emerge over the coming decades, and to do so in a way that honors Fritz's enduring belief that normative projects are always politically motivated and political developments always normatively inflected, and which equally honors his engagement with "power politics" in the broadest sense of the term. Before proceeding to this task the underlying empirical assumptions upon which these speculations are based need to be made clear. There are two such assumptions; they can be stated briefly and are given here with only a very sketchy defense.

First, following the argument of William Wohlforth and Stephen Brooks, it is assumed that American military primacy will remain a feature of the architecture of twenty-first century international relations for the foreseeable future, that is, at least until mid-century (Wohlforth 1999; Brooks and Wohlforth, 2008). Primacy appears to be an objective to which the US political establishment is committed, and American military expenditures on hardware and R & D are such as to more or less guarantee the achievement of this objective, pace Chinese and Russian attempts to upgrade their forces. Severe economic hardship will affect all parties concerned, and, in any event, as Wohlforth and Brooks and Zbigniew Brzezinski argue, rivalries among the potential challengers to US power will be as salient a feature of the future world order as their putative opposition to the US (Brzezinski, 2004). The existence of nuclear weapons and minimum deterrence force-postures muddies the picture somewhat, which is why the US pursues anti-proliferation policies and may soon commit to the virtual elimination of nuclear weapons, but does not fundamentally change the fact that the US has force-projection capacities that no other state can match. In short, and contrary to the argument of structural realists such as John Mearsheimer or Kenneth Waltz, there will be no reemergence of traditional balance-of-power politics, because military power has always been central to such a balance (Mearsheimer, 1990; Waltz, 1993).

However, second, beyond the realm of military force it is assumed that something that does look a little more like a traditional balance of power will indeed emerge. China and India may not be able to challenge the US in military terms, but their current levels of economic growth and increasing technological sophistication—the former more apparent in China, the latter in India—mean that they will increasingly exert influence in other aspects of international relations, and these other aspects are, of course, of great, and perhaps increasing, significance. The November 2008 meeting of the G20 in New York to discuss the global economic crisis illustrates the point—clearly the voices of the emerging economies were heard there in a way they had never been heard before—and it is driven home by the role of China (and India) at the Copenhagen Summit on Climate Change in December 2009, which was decisive in the (rather unsatisfactory) end result of that conference. The other two BRIC countries—Brazil and Russia—have fewer guarantees of an influential future, but will still look to exert their influence in world politics when they can, as, of course, will the major West European powers and Japan.

The question that will be discussed here can now be formulated a little more precisely; what kind of normative foundations will exist if the emerging architecture of world politics is going to be characterized by the dispersal of real power among a number of actors, some of whom will be non-Western and some of whom will be authoritarian (Gat, 2007; Gat et al., 2009)? To anticipate the argument, the realist claim that this is, effectively, a nonquestion since norms of international conduct are of little significance and the characteristic patterns of world politics are not culture-specific will be examined; next, the constructivist rebuttal of this position which, especially in the version espoused by Friedrich Kratochwil, stresses the constitutive role of norms, and the importance of a deeper understanding of the political, legal and social context which underpin such norms will be set out; and then, at somewhat greater length, it will be asked whether Kratochwil's successful demolition of the realist position is, in fact, culture specific. To put the matter more succinctly, even if structural realism's account of the past and present international order is flawed, is it possible that this theory, or something similar, is actually the best guide we have for understanding how international politics will unfold in the twenty-first century? Ultimately the argument will be that it is not, but the issue is less clear-cut than might be expected.

The anarchy problematic

For structural realists—perhaps for any realist—the question posed here is of little interest, for two reasons. First, all anarchical systems are subject to the same imperatives. It matters not whether the great powers are Britain, France and Germany or the US, China and India; what matters is that they conduct their relations with one another under conditions of anarchy. To quote someone who was not a structural realist, indeed perhaps was not a realist at all, or at least only occasionally, "international politics is the realm of recurrence and repetition" with the same patterns reappearing in different eras (Wight, 1966: 26). And, second, in any event norms count for very little in international relations. States do what they must, and normative statements are best seen as rhetorical flourishes, not actual constraints on actions and certainly should not be taken seriously by analysts. China and India might, or might not, employ different rhetorics from each other and from the Western powers, but this matters very little, and certainly cannot be taken to indicate that the behavior of these states will be in any meaningful way different from that of their European predecessors as great powers.

The writer who most successfully brings together both of these arguments is Stephen Krasner (1995, 1999, 2001). In his *Sovereignty: Organized Hypocrisy* he begins by challenging the conventional notion that the nature of the European political order changed in a fundamental way during the course of the "long" sixteenth century; instead he argues that medieval rulers behaved in much the same way as the dynasts of the so-called Westphalia System. In both cases rulers confronted by the imperatives created by a desire to survive and prosper in a self-help system are obliged to behave similarly in response to similar structural pressures—although, possibly, medieval rulers had fewer resources at their disposal than their dynastic counterparts. In essence, states attempt to perform the same functions, even if they do so with different capabilities; this is true of any nonhierarchical system and medieval Europe was such a system.

Krasner appreciates, of course, that in the medieval era people thought differently about politics than they did in early modern times, and that whereas early modern rulers asserted their sovereignty, medieval rulers generally acknowledged that they existed within a chain of obligations that precluded such an assertion—European Christendom was an hierarchy in the sense that Empire and Papacy claimed superiority over other secular rulers, and those rulers rarely directly challenged this claim, at least not until the late fifteenth, early sixteenth centuries. But from Krasner's point of view, this matters little; following James March and Johann Olsen, he distinguishes between the "logic of expected consequences" and the "logic of appropriateness"—there are things we do in response to ends-means calculations, and there are things we do because we feel we ought to do them—and argues that in self-help systems, logics of consequence always trump logics of appropriateness (March and Olsen, 1989). Thus in the Westphalia System the norm of nonintervention is frequently invoked, but even more frequently violated—this, and other "[Principles] have been enduring yet violated"; hence this is a system of "organized hypocrisy" (Krasner, 1999: 90).

It should now be clear why, from a realist perspective, the question posed in this chapter is actually not worth posing, let alone trying to answer. The real international politics of our new century will be the same as those of the last and of every other era where there is no hierarchical, functionally differentiated system of "global" government—the rhetoric employed by the players may be different, but the game is the same.

The constructivist response

The realist argument set out above has never gone unchallenged. In fact, many writers who would generally be considered realist have allowed for a much more important role for norms than Krasner would suggest, and present a more historically nuanced account of the emergence of the current international order than a simple (and essentially unexplained) shift from hierarchy to anarchy at some unspecified time in the past. Hans J. Morgenthau certainly presents such a nuanced account, and in his discussion of morality and international relations is happy to use the term "international society" to convey the idea that this has not been simply the realm of power envisaged by Krasner—indeed, Morgenthau used the term international society freely before the work of "English School" figures such as Wight and Bull with which it is usually associated (Morgenthau, 1948; Bull, 1977; Wight, 1978). But the most sustained and elaborate critique of structural realism has been launched by constructivist writers. They have effectively critiqued the idea that states can be treated simply as placeholders within a structure—identities and values matter; as J. G. Ruggie argues, it mattered that the USA and not the USSR was the dominant power immediately after the World War II (Ruggie, 1998). Identities and interests cannot simply be seen as exogenously determined, nor can norms be dismissed simply as establishing standards of appropriate behavior that can be ignored at will. Norms may shape conduct by making certain kinds of action possible, and others inconceivable.

The constructivist theorist who offers the most ambitious and the most convincing account of this position, by way of an assault on the position Krasner exemplifies, is Kratochwil (1989a, 1993a, 1995a). Kratochwil demonstrates that Krasner fails to acknowledge the Wittgensteinian distinction between "regulative" and "constitutive" rules; those rules which actually constitute international society—such as the norm of nonintervention—make certain kinds of action possible and other kinds conceptually impossible, and this is not a matter that can be verified by empirical observation, nor is it a question of the relative importance of appropriateness as opposed to consequences, but rather a consequence of the logic of the practice in question. Krasner's response, that "[the] international system . . . does not have constitutive rules if such rules are conceived of as making some kinds of action possible, and precluding others" confirms that he misses the point that the international system could not be a system in any meaningful sense without the existence of constitutive rules (Krasner, 1999: 229).

Kratochwil wins this argument, but in "Sovereignty as 'Dominium'" (1995a) he also presents an argument confronting Krasner's elision of the differences between medieval and "Westphalian" rulers, and this argument, while apparently convincing, does raise some rather disturbing issues for the question which dominates the 1995 paper. Kratochwil traces the reemergence of Roman notions of property that accompanied the recovery of the Roman republican legacy during the Renaissance. Medieval notions of property always involved obligations to those above and below one—thus in the classic "feudal" system (never to be found in life in pure form), the local fief-holder would have obligations to those who worked his land and to his superior, the latter in turn would have obligations to the king, the king to the emperor, and the emperor to God. What one could and could not do with one's "property" was limited according to these obligations. The Roman notion of real property [*dominium*] was very different; the Roman property-owner could do more-or-less anything he (always a he in Rome) wished with it, so long as he did not infringe the rights of other property-holders to do whatever they wished with their property. Once such ideas gained currency, princes and kings were able to use them to make claims about their realms which could not have been expressed during a time when the older meaning of property held sway. The detail of this argument may be open to question, but the general thrust is clear and difficult to dispute (Holland, 2010).

It was, literally, inconceivable that a medieval monarch could claim to be a sovereign in the way that, for example, Louis XIV could in the seventeenth century. The norm of nonintervention flows from this new claim that rulers are able to make—just as my neighbor may not interfere with the way I dispose of my property, unless I do so in ways in which her property is adversely affected, so one sovereign has no basis for intervening in the internal policies of another sovereign unless those policies constitute, in the language of the UN Charter, a threat to international peace and security. For a sovereign to claim otherwise is to undermine the basis of his or her own sovereignty. At some later date, different notions of property and sovereignty may obtain, as has happened and may now be happening again—but the key point is not just that the norms of the system constrain the way in which sovereigns (and everyone else) think about politics but that these norms have a very specific history. The Westphalian political order is a product of both European Christendom and Neo-Roman political thought—from the latter comes the notion of sovereignty, which dominates but coexists uneasily with the residual idea, inherited from the former, that Europe is "one great republic," to use a term employed by both Edward Gibbon and Edmund Burke. It is this very specific history that has shaped the system and not the operation of logics of intended consequences in a self-help system, as structural realists have argued.

Socializing the newcomers?

The problem is that while this is the history of the European states that created Westphalia, it is not the history of most of the rest of the world. Indeed, the Europeans did not play the Westphalian game themselves when they were away from home, as Edward Keene has demonstrated (Keene, 2002). Of course, now is not 1648, and after 1945, the Westphalian system became genuinely global, with, in principle, the same rules applied to all—nonintervention being applied to non-Western states and the "standards of civilization" coming home to Europe itself in the form of the international human rights regime—but this process has not been without its difficulties, and, arguably, has worked as well as it has because the most important states in the system still remained European, or had populations of predominantly European origin. Once this ceases to be the case, as it is assumed it soon will, how will the system fare? Will an international *society* continue to be possible? And does Kratochwil's formulation of regulative versus constitutive rules, and the differences between medieval and Westphalian rulers, resolve the problems encountered in conceptualizing this society and understanding its forms of order?

A positive answer to this question is provided by "pluralist" English School theorists. The pluralist argument, as expressed with great clarity by Terry Nardin and Robert Jackson, is that the normative foundations of international society form the basis of an ethics of coexistence that is of general applicability (Nardin, 1983; Jackson, 2000). Nardin draws a distinction between those practices which presume no common project beyond the desire to coexist under conditions of peace and justice, and are designed to promote the conditions under which such coexistence can occur, and those practices that are orientated toward common purposes that go beyond coexistence. The former—exemplified by the law of treaties, or the practice of diplomatic immunity—are a necessary condition for the existence of an international society and their validity cannot be denied by those states that wish to be members of such a society. The latter—exemplified by cooperative institutions such as the WTO or NATO—are, by their nature, voluntary add-ons; no state can be obliged to sign-up for such projects. Jackson presents the argument somewhat differently but to much the same effect.

Interestingly, both Nardin and Jackson—Nardin more explicitly than Jackson—draw on the work of Michael Oakeshott to make their case (Oakeshott, 1975, 1991). In *On Human Conduct,* Oakeshott sets out a distinction between "civic associations" and "enterprise associations," which Nardin rebrands for his purposes as "practical" and "purposive" associations (Oakeshott, 1975). Identifying this influence draws attention immediately to some potential problems. First of all, it has to be noted that Oakeshott's attempt to limit the realm of the political to the terms of association of citizens (*cives*) has been singularly unsuccessful in domestic politics; all modern states actually engage extensively in enterprises on behalf of their citizens, attempting to providing social security, minimum levels of health care, and to manage the economy, all activities that Oakeshott believed improperly extended the realm of the political. At the international level, although much less successfully, states have engaged in similar enterprises, and it is by no means clear that such activity can any longer be described as simply the product of voluntary cooperation—the costs of abstaining from, for example, the WTO are sufficiently high that few states wish to be excluded from membership. But, rather more importantly for the purposes of this chapter, it also should be noted that Oakeshott's work is very explicitly grounded in the history of the modern European state—the distinction between civic and enterprise associations is not to be seen as plucked from the air, but rather as something developed by a tradition of European thought exemplified by Machiavelli, Hobbes and Hegel, the great political philosophers of the modern era. The obvious question is whether this distinction can be made meaningful for those who are not the inheritors of the European tradition.

To put the matter differently, Nardin argues that any state which wants to be considered a state in good standing in international society must adhere to the norms of practical association—but supposing there are "states" that don't want to be considered as members of international society and would rather assert their identities in different terms? Why should such polities—not really the right term—feel obliged to accept the terms of practical association in the absence of some form of coercion, even if we assume that practical association is the best way of describing international society? The pluralist argument is that those "polities" that do not want to consider themselves members of a society of states will be unable to sustain this position. The original social formations upon which such polities are built may have held different views, seeing themselves as "the Middle Kingdom" for example, or not having any sense of themselves as a polity at all prior to their membership of the system (true of many states created by decolonization), but their very existence as part of a functioning international society bears witness to the fact that they have been corralled, one way or another, into this status. But do they understand the implications of this status in the way that the pluralists assume they will? Will Kratochwil's broad agreement with Nardin's notion of international society as a "practical association" turn out to be overtaken and superseded by this shift (for other treatments of this question, see also the contributions by Lynch and Wiener in this volume)?

Sovereignty as the key norm

It seems quite clear that some such process of socialization has taken place. For example, while it may indeed be the case that some Chinese leaders still think of themselves as ruling the Middle Kingdom, there is very little evidence that this is any more salient with respect to actual behavior than is, say the French notion of a *mission civilatrice,* British myths about the beneficial nature of the *Pax Britannica,* or America's vision of itself as a "city on a hill." These national stereotypes may have some limited impact on the perceptions of decision-makers, but the unwillingness of the rest of the world to buy into the benign pictures they paint limits their actual influence and usually prevents national leaders from taking their own claims to a special status too seriously. In similar vein, contemporary Iran is never likely to forget that it is an Islamic Republic and occasionally makes claims to the effect that this status means that it is not bound by rules designed for less sanctified regimes—but in practice things are rather different and, at least in essentials, Iran behaves like a sovereign state among other sovereign states. It is worth noting that at the very height of the Islamic Revolution in 1979/80, when one of the core practices of international society, diplomatic immunity, was violated by the occupation of the American Embassy, aka the "nest of spies," the Iranian government maintained the fiction that this occupation was being conducted by revolutionary students and not by the state. Similarly, although Libya abolished its overseas embassies, replacing them with People's Bureaus, when in 1984 the personnel of the London Bureau fired shots which killed a police officer who was monitoring a demonstration by Libyan dissidents, Colonel Gaddafi was quick to claim diplomatic immunity on their behalf. One could go back to the way in which the USSR's original revolutionary ambitions were tamed to make the same point.

However, it seems equally clear this process of socialization has involved the internalization of a particular conception of the norms of international society, and in particular, has focused on that version of the sovereignty norms which were established in the long sixteenth century, and restated and endorsed by the UN Charter of 1945. More recent attempts to redefine the nature of sovereignty, for example by understanding sovereignty as incorporating human rights, or by asserting a generalized "Responsibility to Protect" (R2P) populations from extreme human rights abuse which lies in the first instance with sovereigns themselves, but then by default with the international community, have little resonance. To illustrate the point here, it is striking that when the notion of "Asian Values" was briefly popular in the early 1990s, the most vocal advocates of the view that there was a distinctive Asian take on human rights were Mahathir Mohamed and Lee Kuan Yew, leaders of Malaysia and Singapore respectively, and that neither the Indian nor the Chinese governments took more than a desultory interest in the movement (Bell, 2000). Whereas the leaders of Malaysia and Singapore were acknowledging the legitimacy of the contemporary international human rights regime, while attempting to shape it in ways that served their own interests (and possibly responded to their views of their populations), the two Asian giants simply took the high (or perhaps low) road by claiming that their domestic political and social arrangements were protected by their sovereignty and the "domestic jurisdiction" clause of the UN Charter, Article 2(7)—although, admittedly, in a half-hearted way China did also throw some Confucian arguments into the pot (Bell, 2008). In the case of China this stance is unsurprising since clearly many Chinese practices actually do violate contemporary human rights norms, but the Indian position is in some ways more interesting because the Indian constitution embraces international human rights standards and is generally respected by the Indian political class. Indeed, as Amartya Sen has argued, there is a long and influential tradition of Indian rationalism and respect for the individual which means that the idea of human rights is in no sense an alien importation (Sen, 2005, 2009). Still, when it comes to foreign policy, the Indian political class is deeply committed to a very strong, unrestricted notion of sovereignty and it is striking that in spite of its own, generally quite positive, record in the area of human rights, India has opposed every attempt to generate support for international humanitarian interventions to deal with large-scale human rights abuses, always on the grounds that they would violate the sovereignty of the state intervened against.

It is, of course, not remotely surprising that China and India should take this position. Both societies have suffered humiliation at the hands of Western powers over the last few centuries. The idea that these same powers should now announce their own moral superiority and consider themselves justified in criticizing the internal politics of their former victims is understandably hard to take—but the position taken by these states is not simply to be understood as a reaction to imperialism. If that were to be the case, one might have expected that as the colonial era recedes into the past, attitudes would gradually change and older resentments fade. In fact, this does not seem to be the trajectory that we have witnessed over the last half century. It seems to be the case that the secularist Western doctrines of Marxism (in China) and democratic socialism (in India) are actually less salient to those societies now than they were 50 years ago, and both are developing their own political forms with fewer references to the political movements that brought them into existence—but they remain committed to sovereignty as an ideal and as a practical goal of policy. To put the matter rather differently, some Western norms have stuck and indeed become reinforced, but they are the norms which cluster around the early, undoubtedly Western, notion of state sovereignty, and not the revisions to that notion that have accrued over time. The emerging powers have accepted the institutions of sovereignty and the nation-state but without taking on board the wider context within which these institutions developed in Europe; it was to that context that Martin Wight referred when he described the small but important difference between the morality of the jungle and the "traditions of Europe" (Wight 1978: 293).

Sovereignty and realism

Does the apparently firm commitment to an uncompromising notion of sovereignty on the part of the emerging great powers suggest that the structural realists are indeed the best guides to the new architecture of twenty-first century international politics? Perhaps not, since sovereignty still has to be seen as a constitutive norm of the system, contra Krasner—but the notion that a somewhat rigid notion of sovereignty is effectively the *only* normative principle of the system certainly has realist roots of a kind. But this is a position which has more in common with that of the blood-and-iron realists of the nineteenth century than with either the "righteous realists" or even the structural realists of the twentieth (Rosenthal, 1991). Thus while the latter could at least comprehend, and indeed in some cases actually support, the notion that sovereignty brings with it responsibilities for the condition of one's own people, for the former such ideas are meaningless, and institutional developments such as that of the international human rights regime a pointless irrelevance.

If this conception of international politics comes to dominate, a grim picture of the future emerges, but there are some reasons to be a little more positive. The underlying faith that history is on their side, that has characterized the thinking of advocates of global civil society and an ever more extensive human rights regime, may be misplaced, but the interdependencies that certainly characterize contemporary world politics cannot be disregarded. As suggested above, the emerging Great Powers will wish to preserve their sovereignty and will resist any attempt to redefine what that means in nontraditional terms, but the advantages of being part of an interdependent world economy are considerable, and unlikely to be risked unless core interests are at stake. Whereas in the past it was common for rising powers to feel that they had to define their new status by challenging existing power holders, building empires and "co-prosperity spheres" and the like, nowadays, pace John Mearsheimer, this is no longer necessary, and indeed may be even more counterproductive than previously. Thus former Russian president, current Prime Minister Putin's overt use of the energy card to buttress his position at home by making nationalist gestures abroad is actually (and quite predictably) causing Europeans to think of ways of reducing their dependence on Russian oil and gas. As numerous writers remarked at the time of the conjuncture of the conflict in Georgia with the Beijing Olympics in 2008, China is looking forward to exercising influence by going with the grain of the new century, while Russia seems unable to break contact with its imperial past. No prizes for guessing which strategy is actually more likely to bring dividends in the medium to long run.

To put these points in the context of IR theory, what may be happening is the return of something a lot like the models of complex interdependence that were popular in the 1970s, but which were swept aside by the triumph of neo-utilitarian theory in the 1980s (Keohane and Nye 1978). Multiple channels of access, the absence of a hierarchy of issues, generally low salience of military force, the importance of agenda setting and so on—these look like very promising topics, finding a middle way between the overoptimism of globalization theorists and the pessimism account of a contest between unitary rational egoists offered by modern realists. Perhaps, as G. John Ikenberry has argued, liberal internationalism is sufficiently resilient to cope with the shifts in relative power that are taking place, and a posthegemonic "Liberalism Internationalism 3.0" may emerge (Ikenberry 2009), but if so it is likely to be on the basis of economic interdependence and not any wider commitment to liberal values.

In short, this is still a system that relies heavily, almost exclusively, on material interests to tone down conflict and promote cooperation. The normative foundations of this regime look very thin; the absence of a common past and a common political vocabulary of the sort identified by Kratochwil make these foundations look even thinner than those required by the pluralism of Nardin or Jackson. The key question is whether the interdependencies that hold things together will continue to do so if things go seriously wrong with the world economy—the world is currently and painfully climbing out of recession, but if, as is possible, the situation worsens again, we may find an answer to this question. It is possible that the major economic powers, including China and India, will be able to deliver a collective response to the crisis, but if interdependencies shrivel and weaken, then, in the absence of a firmer normative basis for cooperative behavior, it is difficult to see what, if anything, will stand in the way of a return to the worst aspects of the politics of the old order.

Note

I am grateful to members of the International Relations Theory Workshop at LSE, to the participants in "Fritzfest," held in NYC February 2009, and to the editors of this collection for comments on earlier versions of this chapter. The usual disclaimers apply.

16

Understanding Change in International Politics, Again and Again and Again

Rey Koslowski

Introduction

In "Understanding Change in International Politics: The Soviet Empire's Demise and the International System" (Koslowski and Kratochwil 1994a), Friedrich Kratochwil and I argued that fundamental changes of the international system occur when actors through their practices change the rules and norms constitutive of international interaction and that the actions of the Soviet Union and the US in the ending of the Cold War represented such a fundamental transformation of the international system. We argued that any given international system does not exist because of immutable structures but rather the very structures are dependent for their reproduction on the practices of the actors.[1] Fundamental change of the international system occurs when actors, through their practices, change the rules and norms constitutive of international interaction. As we noted, leading international relations scholars had dismissed the significance of the end of the Cold War for international relations theory as a "single data point." Are there now perhaps more data points in political practice that have transformed the international system? Or does the end of the Cold War remain an outstanding anomaly?

Two obvious candidates for transformative "data points" are the "economic globalization" that became so prominent in the 1990s and the September 11, 2001 attacks of al-Qaeda on the US. As Kratochwil noted, "[w]hile only yesterday globalization was celebrated in public discourse as the virtually universal 'explanation' for a variety of phenomena, the terrorist attacks have placed security concerns on the front burner, and fears of a potential clash of civilizations seem to have displaced notions that globalization, working inexorably behind our backs, is fundamentally transforming our world" (Kratochwil 2002b: 25). Kratochwil further argued that globalization cannot be conceived of as an "actor" or "cause" of particular phenomena but rather several connected processes. Kratochwil acknowledged the centrality of new information technologies to these interconnected processes. "In the globalization discourse we come to terms with the implications of the *communications revolution* and probably also with that aspect that made the increasing speed and volume of transactions possible, *digitalization"* (Kratochwil 2002b: 28). With respect to the September 11 attacks, Kratochwil argued that the attacks had a deeper significance beyond shifting attention away from the global economy to security matters in that this terrorism "challenged the most basic assumptions underlying social life" and represented an existential threat to the institutional framework of the modern state and the system of states—that "Hobbesian project of modernity" (Kratochwil 2003c: 57).

Given that the information revolution has been a fundamental, if not the preeminent, feature of the interrelated processes that have come to be known as globalization, that new information technologies have increasingly been used by states and nonstate actors to pursue their interests and objectives on the international stage, and that many historians and international relations scholars have argued that technological innovations such as gunpowder and nuclear fission transformed the conduct of international politics in the past, I will also pay particular attention to the influence of recent technological innovations on changes in the practice of international politics as well as the ways technologies may shape international political practices in the future. Perhaps most noteworthy in this regard is nanotechnology—the study, design, creation, synthesis, manipulation and application of functional materials, devices and systems through control of matter at the scale of one billionth of a meter. Some analysts view nanotechnology as having great potential to transform production and economic development (see, e.g. Zakaria 2008), while others also consider the potential for nanotechnology to give rise to new more powerful weapons or even cause mass destruction by accident (Drexler 1986: Chapter 11).

Has there been anything that has happened in the past two decades that even comes close to the collapse of the Soviet Union in terms of changing the practices of international politics? In the pages that follow, I address this question by examining the social construction of technology and its role in international change. I then consider several developments, such as the information revolution and economic globalization and the "revolution in military affairs" associated with it; the September 11, 2001 attacks and the "war on terror"; and potential changes spurred by nanotechnology and the specter of "knowledge-enabled mass destruction" (KMD). I conclude with an evaluation of whether (and if so, how) the changes they represent approach the transformative nature of the end of the Cold War as well as consider some decisions to be made in the practice of world politics in the fast-approaching future.

Technology and change

As Kratochwil and I argued at the time (1994), international relations theories have largely been oriented toward stasis and only a handful of scholars explicitly focused their attention on change. It could also be argued that understandings of technology as a factor of change have often been subsumed into discussions of material factors and shifting military capabilities. That is, new technologies, particularly those applied to military objectives (e.g. gunpowder, nuclear fission) are considered material factors that can be considered "causes" for transformative changes. Therefore, analysis of technology and change has tended to fall on the "material side" of an ideational-material dichotomy that has developed in defining constructivism in relation to other theoretical approaches in international relations: constructivist scholarship has focused on ideas, speech acts and identity, in contrast to realism, which focuses on the distribution of capabilities and "hard power," or in contrast to liberal theorists who focus on material factors that shape world politics (e.g. Deudney 2007). The delineation of constructivism in terms of this ideational/material dichotomy (see e.g. Finnemore and Sikkink 2001) has been strongly criticized within constructivist ranks (see Klotz and Lynch 2007) and many chapters in this volume (including Chapters 1, 5, 6 and 13) take issue with such dichotomous thinking as well. To the extent that the ideational-material dichotomy relegates technology to the material, it is wrongheaded because technology is socially constructed, even if it is constructed within a set of physical constraints. Moreover, those physical constraints within which any given technology may be socially constructed are not necessarily fixed and may themselves change over time. Technologies, especially new information technologies, are just as "ideational" as they are "material."

With origins in the Greek *technē* (art, skill) and *logia* (saying), technology is commonly defined as "the practical application of knowledge especially in a particular area" (Merriam-Webster Dictionary). Although certain practical applications of knowledge may produce material things of great international consequence (cannon, nuclear weapons, etc.), the material things in and of themselves are not "technologies." Technologies only come into being through the human act of applying the knowledge in a particular way. For example, the wheel became a crucial transportation technology across Eurasia by 2000 BC but the wheel was only applied to children's toys in pre-Columbian civilizations in the Americas.

Many information technologies, like the Internet, are practical applications of knowledge that are not very "material" at all. The Internet is a "network of networks" that exists on computers connected by copper telephone lines, glass fiber-optic cables as well as electromagnetic transmissions and, therefore, in one sense, has a certain physicality. In technical terms, however, the Internet is not the computers and the wires but rather the Transmission Control Protocol/Internet Protocol (TCP/IP) suite of programs, which enables the operation of packet switching and movement of data from one computer host to another. These programs are series of symbols (0s and 1s) that may exist on a variety of physical media, such as cardboard punch cards, magnetic tape, CD-ROMs or computer hard drives—much as words exist on these same kinds of physical media.

The practical application of knowledge is a human act resulting from a human decision that may be motivated by a wide variety of social, religious and ideological reasons, the desire for amusement, or even a simple mistake. Many technologies, including military technologies, are "social constructions." The Internet's origins as a network that was funded by the US military in order to ensure command and control over nuclear weapons in the event of a Soviet first strike demonstrates the political dimensions of the practical application of knowledge (Herrera 2003). As this example vividly illustrates, however, it is a mistake to think that the development of any particular technology will automatically have a positive or negative effect on state capabilities and sovereignty. Human decisions to apply knowledge pragmatically (often in ways different than had been originally intended) may shape political practices that, in turn, shape the development of new technologies, that may themselves have completely unanticipated consequences.

The information revolution

Revolutionary changes in information technology, particularly the development of the Internet, propelled the economic globalization that undermined the ability of nation-states to influence macroeconomic trends with traditional monetary and fiscal policy instruments

(Kobrin 1997; Friedman 1999, 2005). At the same time, transnational corporations, international nongovernmental organizations (INGOs) and subnational governments have harnessed the same information technologies to pursue their interests on a global level and make their presence felt in forums of high politics, which had previously been the exclusive reserve of states and have, thereby, challenged state sovereignty (see e.g. Mathews 1997; Kobrin 1998; Deibert 2000).

During the 1990s, an increasing number of IR scholars like James Rosenau argued that the information revolution and globalization were transforming the international system (Rosenau 1995; Rosenau and Singh 2002). In sharp contrast, Kenneth Waltz reiterated arguments that globalization was not new, that international trade was not as extensive as in past eras and that globalization was geographically limited to the transatlantic area and Japan, and then proceeded to minimize the consequences of global economics on politics and the state (Waltz 1999). Kratochwil rejected Waltz's position that globalization was nothing new and therefore of little consequence. Kratochwil also took issue with the implications of Rosenau's argument that globalization was transformative when policymaker proponents of liberalization argued that globalization constrained action and choice to the extent that "[w]e either had to adjust or perish" (Kratochwil 2002b: 30–1). Kratochwil goes on to reflect on the argument made by Susan Strange in which the "units" (states) and their arrangement "is replaced by several interacting structures (security, production, credit, and knowledge) in order to capture the dynamics of change"(Kratochwil 2002b: 32–3) but pulls back from endorsing this argument by echoing one of Waltz's arguments and noting that while the market might be "global" for OECD states, it is not for other regions, most pointedly, sub-Saharan Africa. Kratochwil supports this argument by referring to the limited reach of the communications revolution and the fact that in the mid-1990s all of sub-Saharan Africa had as many telephone numbers as Manhattan. Much has changed since Kratochwil published in 2002 and he might reconsider his position. The "global digital divide" between those who have telephone and Internet access and those who do not has been closing at an accelerating rate largely due to declining transcontinental and transoceanic transmission costs resulting from the overbuilding of fiber optic cable capacity, spreading wireless Internet connectivity (including entire cities) and the rapid expansion of mobile telephone networks in developing countries that "leapfrog" expensive infrastructure investments in fixed copper wire landline telephone systems. Out of the world's population of 6.7 billion people, an estimated 1.6 billion use the Internet and 4 billion have mobile phones (2008 figures in CIA 2010).

The increasing use of information technologies in warfare has led to a so-called revolution in military affairs. Satellite surveillance combined with video and data from a wide variety of sensors render "information dominance" over theaters of operation and enable "smart" ordnance to inflict highly accurate strikes. Increasingly powerful and inexpensive microprocessors have also enabled rapid development of robotics used to neutralize roadside improvised explosive devices (IEDs) from a safe distance, run reconnaissance missions in difficult urban environments as well find and kill high-value targets in Pakistan with unmanned aerial vehicles (UAVs) that are remotely piloted from Nevada (Singer 2009).

At the same time, increasingly technologically sophisticated businesses, militaries and governments have also become increasingly dependent on these technologies. "The rapidly increasing interconnection of our information infrastructures and the growing reliance on them to 'steer' other infrastructures, ranging from energy flows to financial data and water supplies, also exponentially increase the vulnerability of our information-based societies" (Fuchs and Kratochwil 2002a: 230). Such vulnerabilities of critical information technology infrastructure upon which economies and militaries increasingly depend have enabled networked computers to become both weapon and target in the rapidly proliferating battlespaces of cyber-warfare and cyber-terrorism.

While it is clear that the information revolution has transformed the global economy and is rapidly changing many practices of warfare, to what extent, if any, have these economic and military changes as well as changes in political practice altered some (or all) of the constitutive norms and conventions of the international system? To begin with, the changes in domestic politics in Eastern Europe that ended the Cold War took place in the context of the information revolution; specifically the 1980s spread of the personal computer that decentralized computing around the world (Friedman 2005). The decentralization of computing, the digitization of information and its transmission via fax and then the Internet enabled those who opposed communist regimes to communicate and organize more effectively (Castells 1999). As communist regimes found it more difficult to stop radio and television beamed from the West, what little legitimacy they may have enjoyed was undermined, thereby facilitating the development of opposition movements and the "demonstration effect" that precipitated the rapid spread of democratization across Eastern Europe (Huntington 1993: 101–2).

With accelerating growth and the global spread of Internet hosts, as well as the launch of the World Wide Web in 1992 and the Mosiac graphical web browser in 1993, political movements increasingly used the Internet where it became available (Norris 2001). Blocking political communication via the Internet increasingly became a preoccupation of authoritarian regimes (Kalathil and Boas 2003), and political speech and practice increasingly moved from the streets to cyberspace. Moreover, the combination of texting on mobile phones, social networking sites (e.g. Facebook, Myspace, Twitter) and new media tools (YouTube) have proved effective in political organizing in the streets, as aptly demonstrated by Iranians who protested the outcome of the 2009 re-election of President Mahmoud Ahmadinejad. While totalitarian and authoritarian regimes were once able to erase such events from history books and consign protesters to oblivion, cell phone photos and video posted to the Internet enable the 1.6 billion people in the world with Internet access to see them the next day. If changing domestic political practices (e.g. practices that undermine totalitarianism and authoritarianism or lead to differing outcomes within a democracy) alter states' international practices that, in turn, lead to a new set of international conventions and norms, then one can say that changes in domestic politics enabled by new information technologies have had international systemic effects.

Ronald Deibert (1997) has demonstrated how information and communications environments enable some political practices to thrive and become institutionalized while others atrophy. The shift from writing on parchment to printing created an information and communications environment (e.g. printed laws, state records, maps, contracts and newspapers) that was conducive to the rise of a world order based on a system of nation-states. Similarly, the current information revolution is producing a shift to a hypermedia environment, epitomized by the Internet, which is more conducive to a world order of nonterritorial institutions and overlapping authorities akin to the neo-medievalism described by Hedley Bull (1977). To the extent that the information revolution has enabled the increasing volume of transnational and NGO activities, the "outsourcing" of states' functions to firms and NGOs and the production of "private authority" that transcends the territorial boundaries of states and becomes part and parcel of global governance (Hall and Biersteker 2002), the changing information and communication environment is shaping world orders as tremendous quantitative changes in transnational political practices yield qualitative changes in the way international politics are practiced.

The September 11, 2001 attacks and the "War on Terror"

In the immediate aftermath of the September 11, 2001 al-Qaeda attacks on the US, it was commonly said that "this changes everything" and "the world will never be the same." Compared with other conflicts around the world, the loss of life and property were not that large, definitely not enough to change the international distribution of capabilities. Nevertheless the attacks did prompt a major change in the international behavior of states. The attacks were even more significant in that they illuminated the latent reality of the technological empowerment of nonstate actors, thereby transforming policymakers' and citizens' understanding of the world.

While the distribution of capabilities among states clearly did not change just before the September 11 attacks, US foreign policy as well as international politics surrounding US actions clearly changed direction in the aftermath of the attacks. Initially, the Bush Administration's foreign policy largely focused on rebuilding military readiness depleted by Clinton-era humanitarian interventions, developing national missile defense, countering a rising China and dealing with a weak and incoherent Russia (Rice 2000). But then the US responded to the September 11 attacks with a "war on terror" directed first at Taliban-ruled Afghanistan and then Saddam Hussein's Iraq. The US took action in Iraq despite the fact that it was not in the US "national interest," as argued by international relations scholars, with prominent realists like Kenneth Waltz, John Mearsheimer and Stephen Walt among them (New York Times advertisement, 2002). Although foreign policy actions of the US may have had repercussions across the world, it is less clear whether these actions toward two relatively small powers have fundamentally changed the relations between the major actors within the international system.

In contrast to the actions taken by the US, the September 11 attacks themselves were perhaps much more revealing of systemic changes that were already well underway. While those who drew attention to the transformative factors of globalization pointed to the increasing role of NGOs such as Greenpeace and Amnesty International (Mathews 1997), the International Campaign to Ban Landmines (Deibert 2000), the networks of humanitarian actors (Lynch in this volume), and the campaign against a Multilateral Agreement on Investment (MAI-not) (Kobrin 1998), the September 11, 2001 attacks by al-Qaeda illuminated the "dark side" of globalization, highlighting a new challenge to the system of states. Just as environmental and human rights NGOs harnessed the Internet to organize locally and globally, al-Qaeda used the same technologies to organize its operations and function internationally like any other NGO. Moreover, the Hart-Rudman Commission warned in February 2001 that "[t]he combination of unconventional weapons proliferation with the persistence of international terrorism will end the relative invulnerability of the US homeland to catastrophic attack" (Hart-Rudman Commission 2001), but it was the September 11 attacks that brought home the fact that states could lose their monopoly control over certain mass casualty weapons technologies, and certain NGOs (including al-Qaeda) that do not follow the norms and conventions of states could acquire and use weapons of mass destruction (WMD).

As Kratochwil (2003c) pointed out, the September 11 attacks, in a sense, represent an existential challenge to the Hobbesian state and the state system largely because the phenomenon of international terrorism undermines the most quintessential institution of the international system—war. According to Hedley Bull (1977: 178),

> [w]ar is organized violence carried on by political units against each other. Violence is not war unless it is carried out in the name of a political unit; what distinguishes killing in war from murder is its vicarious and official character, the symbolic responsibility of the unit whose agent the killer is. Equally, violence carried out in the name of a political unit is not war unless it is directed against another political unit.

The September 11 attacks were not war because they had a "private character" directed not only at civilians of the enemy state but indiscriminately at "other groups and nations" as well (Kratochwil 2003c: 62). This form of international terrorism overturns the traditional Clausewitzian understanding of war as politics by other means by pursuing unlimited goals beyond that of a political settlement that can be achieved by traditional warfare. Moreover, "through the use of limited means, virtually unlimited goals are pursued and without compromise" (Kratochwil 2003c: 64).

Similarly, the violence inflicted on al-Qaeda by the US military is not war because al-Qaeda is not "another political unit." Although the Bush Administration's declaration of war on terrorism has been criticized as the nonsensical idea of waging war on a tactic (e.g. Gompert and Gordon 2008: 6), it can also be understood as a desperate act of redefining a phenomenon that defied international norms and conventions so as to better cope with it politically.

The problem posed by international terrorism goes beyond its private character to the weapons technologies and destructive capabilities that could potentially be wielded by these nonstate actors. That is, the institutions of nuclear deterrence that produced the "long peace" between the Soviet Union and the US and could, according to the logic of deterrence, stop India and Pakistan, or any other nuclear armed states for that matter, from going to war do not apply to suicidal terrorists armed with WMD. A nuclear attack by suicidal terrorists, like al-Qaeda, cannot be deterred because the terrorists that have conducted the attack, by definition, do not care about their own survival and there is no territory, no state apparatus, no population center to threaten with assured destruction of a second strike (Allison 2004). The September 11 attacks themselves did not change the international system in the way that the collapse of the Soviet Union did. However, the prospects of a nonstate actor wielding a WMD undermines the very institutions of the state and the state system, as the September 11 attacks so clearly demonstrated.

Nanotechnology and KMD

International relations scholars may rarely, if ever, see the term "nanotechnology" in IR journals and book series; however, nanotechnology may have the greatest potential to disrupt present expectations for scenarios of the future unfolding of world politics. To the extent that technology is socially constructed within certain physical constraints and information technology environments shape political practice, nanotechnology may expand the physical bounds of information technology and thereby enable political practices within and between states as well as nonstate actors that, in turn, may have major international consequences. Nanotechnology may influence developments in a wide variety of areas ranging from cheaper energy and economic growth to new arms races and the empowerment of malevolent nonstate actors, which in turn will impinge on the relations between states.

Nanotechnology was initially conceived by Richard Feynman who envisioned "infinitesimal machines" that could build complex products like miniature computers with wires "10 or 100 atoms in diameter" (Feynman 1959). As the term "nanotechnology" was increasingly applied more broadly beginning in the 1990s to describe the development of materials and devices at the size of 100 nanometers or smaller, the original conceptualization of nanotechnology has come to be referred to as "molecular nanotechnology" or "molecular manufacturing." The distinction is that the "ordinary" nanotechnology that exists today is about making nanoscale materials and products, whereas the original concept is about making nanoscale productive systems.

Feynman's original idea was further articulated by Eric Drexler in the first book on the subject, *Engines of Creation: The Coming Era of Nanotechnology* (1986). Drexler considered the operation of proteins as machines that manipulate matter at the molecular level and then, through an analogy of artificial proteins, he envisioned engineering and mass manufacturing that would move and manipulate one atom, one molecule at a time by what he calls "universal assemblers."

> [These] enzyme-like second-generation machines will be able to use as "tools" almost any of the reactive molecules used by chemists—but they will wield them with the precision of programmed machines. They will be able to bond atoms together in virtually any stable pattern, adding a few at a time to the surface of a workpiece until a complex structure is complete. Because assemblers will let us place atoms in almost any reasonable arrangement, they will let us build almost anything that the laws of nature allow to exist. In particular, they will let us build almost anything we can design—including more assemblers. The consequences of this will be profound, because our crude tools have let us explore only a small part of the range of possibilities that natural law permits. Assemblers will open a world of new technologies.
>
> (Drexler 1986: Chapter 1)

Molecular manufacturing envisions using molecule-sized assemblers to build more assemblers that, through parallel processes, fabricate the materials that are subsequently assembled into finished products. As envisioned by Feynman and Drexler, molecular manufacturing largely remains more of a vision than a reality.

In contrast, presently existing "ordinary" nanotechnology builds nanoscale components or materials into larger scale products through conventional manufacturing processes. Ordinary nanotechnology has produced nanoscale materials that are currently used in hundreds of commercial products, ranging from microprocessors, photovoltaic cells and engine oil to antibacterial food containers, baby pacifiers, sunscreen, golf clubs and hearing aids (PEN 2009). Ordinary nanotechnology may produce significant political consequences in the near future through increasing computer power, reducing the costs of solar and other renewable energy sources that would reduce dependence on fossil fuels from conflict-prone regions like the Middle East, or through precipitating international disputes over global environmental regulation of nanoscale particles and materials similar to disputes over high-atmosphere ozone, acid rain, genetically modified foods, greenhouse gases, etc.

To a certain extent, ordinary nanotechnology is already changing the physical constraints within which other technologies are socially constructed. For example, the advance of many information technologies is constrained by the bounds of hardware development. Information technologies have developed rapidly over the past decades due to the fact that over the past 50 years the number of transistors on a microcircuit double approximately every 18 to 24 months (Moore's Law). It was anticipated that the physical constraints of conventional semi-conductor manufacturing (etching transistors on silicon), would make Moore's Law obsolete by increasing the number of years necessary for doubling the number of transistors on a microchip. However, all microprocessor manufacturers have incorporated nanoscale features into their chips thereby maintaining Moore's Law into the present (Economist 2005). Moreover, IBM researchers have used nanotechnology to create vacuums a few nanometers wide that keep the billions of tiny copper wires in a chip from touching one another, instead of putting down a layer of insulating material and trying to align it effectively at the nanoscale (Fitzgerald 2008). By enabling more transistors to be squeezed onto silicon wafers, such new applications of nanotechnology will help extend Moore's Law further into the future.

The increasing computing power made possible by ordinary nanotechnology alone will sharpen the resolution of satellite imagery, increase the effective sensitivity of sensors, better guide ordnance to targets, make robots smarter as well as enable the development of ever more ingenious social networking and political organizing applications on mobile devices. The current horizon for the expansion of computing imposed by the physical constraints of conventional microelectronic technologies yields a corresponding set of constraints on the surveillance, sensing, robotics and social networking technologies that utilize the computing power of microprocessors. By breaking those physical constraints of microelectronics, ordinary nanotechnology is expanding the scope for the social construction, development and expansion of all these (and other) technologies based on computing. The continued expansion and development of new information technologies enabled by ordinary nanotechnology's extension of Moore's Law may have future political consequences rivaling, if not exceeding, those resulting from the Internet.

It is the original concept of nanotechnology as molecular manufacturing, however, that has the greatest potential for stretching physical constraints on the social construction of technologies and on international systems transformation. A crucial feature of molecular manufacturing is that assemblers "will let us build almost anything we can design—including more assemblers." Replicating assemblers that multiply exponentially would be sufficient to convert simple raw materials into finished products similar to products that we are familiar with now. For example, molecular manufacturing contained in a desktop-sized device might produce a laptop computer with a billion Central Processing Units (CPUs)—as depicted in a short animated video, "Productive Nanosystems: From Molecules to Superproducts" (available at http://www.foresight.org/nano/general.html).

The potential of impact of molecular manufacturing on information technology development would be exponentially greater than any previous advance in computing power. This is because molecular manufacturing would not only enable the etching of nanoscale circuitry on silicon it would also enable mass manufacturing of microprocessors by arranging all the atoms of the microprocessors themselves. Currently a desktop or laptop computer might have a single microprocessor CPU or two or four processing units on one chip operating in a parallel configuration to increase processing speed and performance. By building microprocessors one atom, one molecule at a time, molecular manufacturing enables the production of microprocessors that would be infinitesimal in size. Such microprocessors could become components of computing systems that use billions of such microprocessors in parallel processing—all in a package the size of today's laptops. Should molecular nanotechnology become a reality, the physical constraints on Moore's Law that ordinary nanotechnology had pushed to new limits would, likewise, be overcome but to a tremendously greater degree of magnitude. Such exponentially increased computing power may mean new and unforeseen innovations by those researchers and firms in states with high technology industries. Or, it may mean that those tasks accomplished by the most advanced technologies of today will be accomplished much more cheaply in an ever greater number of the world's states by a greater percentage of the world's population, thereby having distributional effects across the international system.

The potential consequences of molecular manufacturing for international security may, however, be much more direct than the military uses of extremely powerful computers. Given that molecular manufacturing utilizes nanoscale universal assemblers that can build any number of objects, including themselves, assemblers can become self-replicating. "States could also use replicating assemblers to build arsenals of advanced weapons, swiftly, easily, and in vast quantity" (Drexler 1986: Chapter 4). It should come as no surprise that nanotechnology is among the new technologies receiving increasing funding for science and technology connected to military applications (Paarlberg 2004: 133, Carafano and Gudgel 2007: 3) and that analysts within the US officer corps think that the development of nanotechnology could trigger a new arms race (Vandermolen 2006: 100).

Drexler also identified a threat that nanotechnology could pose if replicating assemblers were to somehow be released into the environment and self-replicate uncontrollably. Replicating assemblers that were powered by sunlight could make almost anything (including themselves) out of common materials. Such replicating assemblers have the potential to push organisms out of the environmental niches in which they currently survive. As Drexler explains, "'[p]lants' with 'leaves' no more efficient than today's solar cells could out-compete real plants, crowding the biosphere with inedible foliage. Tough, omnivorous 'bacteria' could out-compete real bacteria: they could spread like blowing pollen, replicate swiftly, and reduce the biosphere to dust in a matter of days" (Drexler 1986: Chapter 11). This scenario, known as the "gray goo problem" means that if replicating assemblers were to be developed they would need to be very carefully controlled—that is, a lab accident could spell extinction.

The existential dangers of such a technology led computer scientist Bill Joy to consider a new class of WMDs based on genetics, nanotechnology and robotics (GNR) technologies that are so powerful, especially in potential combinations of even greater effect, that they enable what he termed KMD. "For the first time, these accidents and abuses are widely within the reach of individuals or small groups. They will not require large facilities or rare raw materials. Knowledge alone will enable the use of them" (Joy 2000). Joy argues that preempting the destructive potential of nanotechnology through relinquishment or arms control will be extremely challenging because nanotechnology is not easily differentiated into commercial and military purposes and since the key ingredient to weapons development is knowledge, verification of relinquishment "will have to occur in cyberspace as well as physical facilities." He concludes with an ethical injunction to scientists to reexamine "the open access to and unlimited development of knowledge . . . if it puts us all in danger of extinction."

The potential of knowledge-enabled mass destruction depends on the decisions to apply knowledge of genetics, nanoscale science and robotics to certain human endeavors. Scientists like Joy may individually decide to give up pursuing certain lines of scientific inquiry in order to reduce the risk of extinction and policymakers may collectively decide to limit the development of certain technologies for the same reason. Just as military applications of nanotechnology may precipitate arms races among states, nanotechnologies can be wielded by terrorists. Both of these possibilities have led to calls for international cooperation to regulate the development and control of nanotechnology (Vandermolen 2006).

Conclusion

"Understanding Change in International Politics: The Case of Rule-Governed Change," was first presented at the American Political Science Association Meeting in September 1990 and it took over three years of reviews, rebuttals and revisions before our paper appeared as an article in *International Organization* (Koslowski and Kratochwil 1994a). One of the most interesting criticisms we faced was the argument made at a 1991 conference that the end of the Cold War was a single "data point." We provided our counterargument in the article but given the passing of two decades since we initially wrote paper, it is worth placing the end of the Cold War in a broader comparative perspective. The end of the Cold War was unique in the sense that there has been nothing quite as palpable and obvious like the shift from a bipolar world to post-Cold War unipolarity (Wohlforth 1999) or multipolarity (Mearsheimer 2003: 380) or "uni-multipolarity" (Huntington 1999: 36) or "something else," whatever it might be. There has been no similar dramatic change in the international system like that occasioned by the end of the Cold War and resulting in an inability of analysts to satisfactorily describe the world in the established terminology of polarity and the balance of power. Nevertheless there have been other kinds of changes that are transformative in effect.

While the term "globalization" may be a convenient label for a collection of interrelated processes that upon inspection is very problematic (Kratochwil 2002b), these information technology-enabled processes have continued and deepened despite the shift toward security concerns after the attacks of September 11, 2001. The September 11 attacks come closest in terms of an event that could be considered as a similar historical turning point in the political practices of great powers that could be considered transformational. However, it was less the event itself, and the military responses to the event, and more the potential of terrorists acquiring WMD that have changed the way that policy-makers and citizens perceive the world, which is, in turn, changing the way that states relate to each other and with nonstate actors.

Implications of such terrorism for the Hobbesian project of the modern state that Kratochwil (2003b) highlighted are changing the way that we think of security and changing the way that policymakers attempt to provide it. Although there is no one event that one could point to as having changed the international system, technology-enabled globalization, technology-driven military transformation and technologically empowered nonstate actors have all contributed to the "something else" that the post-Cold War world has become.

Moreover, we can anticipate more, not less, in the way of change emanating from human technological ingenuity. In and of itself, nanotechnology has yet to have any major direct political consequences, domestically or internationally; however, applications of nanoscale science to certain manufacturing processes changes the material context for other technological developments, like the Internet, that have already very significant political consequences.

Onuf (1989) and Kratochwil (1989a) broke open the overly deterministic thinking in international relations inherent in structural theories of the time that were bent on proving continuity rather than being open to the possibility of change. Onuf and Kratochwil showed us that the world was of our making—though practices resulting from human decisions influenced by norms. In the coming years, however, decisions to be made by policymakers with respect to the development of nanotechnology may have tremendous consequences that have the potential to transform international systems in ways we may not yet be able to imagine. Whether nanoscale science is translated into practical applications of mass production and/or mass destruction will depend on political practices within, among and around states. The technologies that subsequently come into being will, in turn, help shape the world of our making, if not destroy it.

Notes

This chapter was written while I was a Fellow of the Transatlantic Academy in Washington, DC. I greatly appreciate the support of the academy. Many thanks to Friedrich Kratochwil and to an anonymous reviewer for the helpful comments and suggestions as well as to Nicholas Onuf for excellent editorial guidance and substantive suggestions.

1. See Chapter 6 for a discussion of the "practice turn" and Chapter 8 for a discussion of "rules in practice."

17

The "Inter" according to Fritz: Rethinking IR's Proverbial Toolbox

Mathias Albert and Yosef Lapid

Any attempt to make sense of Friedrich Kratochwil's evolving life-work will quickly lead to the conclusion that he is a prolific but hard-to-classify IR thinker. This conclusion is rendered inevitable by the sheer diversity and massive scope of his research interests and contributions and by his unique scholarly temperament and intellectual style.[1] For instance, to the extent that the International Relations (IR) discipline now boasts at least three vibrant intellectual communities—International Theory, International Political Theory and International Law (see Snidal and Wendt 2009)—Kratochwil clearly qualifies as one of a handful of IR scholars with significant contributions in all of them. Similarly, "Kratochwil stands out as one of the very few thinkers in IR whose work tries to understand the implications of thinking and making assumptions about ontology, social theory and science in tandem" (Guzzini, this volume). To further complicate matters, Kratochwil's work highlights the need to pay due respect to the irreducible complexities of social life without losing hope of making sense of the human condition and tries to unite history with theory without inflicting undue injustices on either. Add to this list Kratochwil's rejection of reified concepts and static maps, his reliance on nuanced conceptual tools for monitoring ever-changing spatial and temporal forms and his insistence on the responsibility of social theorists to constantly refine conceptual tools and cognitive maps in view of new experiences, and you get an initial understanding of why his work is always hard-to-classify and sometimes hard to digest.

In this chapter, we shall focus on some of Kratochwil's efforts to transform IR into a more reflexive discipline with a more nuanced understanding of the underlying temporal and spatial premises which inform its scholarly undertakings. We will do so by focusing on Kratochwil's sustained fascination with the "inter" in (Inter)national Relations and his explicit reference to this prefix in the titles of some of his recent work (see Kratochwil 2005a, 2007d). We will do so in three consecutive steps. First, we will address the "Why Inter?" question. Here we will argue that Kratochwil's rationale for singling out this prefix can be traced back to his conviction that rethinking and fine-tuning the "inter" can yield a richer understanding of "the political," "the disciplinary" and "the transformative" in the study and practice of international relations. Next, we will engage the "How?" question by addressing three sets (i.e. spatial, temporal and semantic) of fine-tuning operations entailed in Kratochwil's eclectic comments on the "inter." Finally, we will conclude with a brief evaluation of Kratochwil's "re-thinking the inter" project in the context of his larger contributions to IR theory as reflected in this volume.

Why "Inter?"

As one of the three terms—that is, the "inter", the "national" and the "relational"—used by the IR scholarly community to constitute and to demarcate a distinct subject matter for their investigation, the "inter" has shown remarkable resilience in face of massive empirical transformations and mounting normative challenges. After all these years—and despite endless discussions of globalization and transnationalism—the community of scholars who shares a declared interest in world politics and global affairs continues to understand itself predominantly as an "inter-type" discipline or subfield. As put by Ole Wæver, powerful challenges notwithstanding, "there will be a discipline called IR . . . and most likely a set of theories known as IR theories will go together with this field" (Wæver 2007: 294). In view of the above, it is somewhat surprising to note that by comparison with the other two terms, the "inter" has failed to attract significant scholarly attention in its own right. Whereas the "national" and the "relational" have been subjected to extensive scrutiny and rethinking, the "inter" was barely able to maintain its position as an (indispensable) descriptive prefix in the disciplinary self-designation of a perennially insecure scholarly field (see Lapid and Kratochwil 1996a; Jackson and Nexon 1999).

In this context, Kratochwil stands out as an IR scholar with a declared interest in "the different ways we conceive of the 'inter' in our discourses" (Kratochwil 2007d: 498). Noteworthy, in particular, is his insistence that this interest is not limited to the "inter-national" or any other (reified) "referent," for that matter (2007d: 498). It is the prefix itself (the inter), and not its typically invoked referent (the national), which now presumably requires serious conceptual, theoretical and meta-theoretical elucidation. If so, the question of "Why Inter?" clearly presents itself.

In this chapter we shall argue that Kratochwil's rationale for singling out this prefix can be traced back to his conviction that rethinking and fine-tuning the "inter" can yield a richer understanding of "the political," "the disciplinary" and "the transformative" (i.e. epochal change) in the study and practice of international relations. Although space constraints will allow only a skeletal reconstruction of this rationale, we find it persuasive and well worth pursuing.

In his work, Kratochwil detects a massive and still lingering confusion regarding the proper definition of the "political." This is problematic because, in Kratochwil's view, the "political" serves as a key criterion for establishing disciplinary relevance in International Relations. He insists, therefore, that "the discipline . . . must develop the skills appropriate for its object" (Kratochwil 2007f: 1). In fact, Kratochwil goes so far as saying that a better understanding of the "political" is a prerequisite for "generating a discipline that finally makes progress" (2007f: 1). However, and unlike some of his colleagues who are satisfied with pointing out the "essentially contested" nature of the "political" and end up endorsing a "broad" (but often circular or arbitrary) definition (Snidal and Wendt 2009: 8), Kratochwil highlights the need for serious semantic elucidation and conceptual innovation.

It is in this context that we can best understand Kratochwil's growing fascination with the "inter." His line of reasoning directs our attention to the ways in which different configurations of the "inter" may result in different types (i.e. "old" versus "new") of politics (Kratochwil 2007d: 496). In other words, a better understanding of the "inter" is a prerequisite for generating a better understanding of the "political" and a better understanding of the political is, in turn, a prerequisite for a better understanding of the "disciplinary" in the context of epochal change. In sum, Kratochwil's growing fascination with the "inter" is partially related to his hope to use this prefix as a springboard for conceptual elucidation and theoretical innovation involving core disciplinary matters such as the rethinking of the political.

Our comments in the previous paragraph have already hinted at some ways in which a more nuanced understanding of the "inter" may also facilitate a more productive engagement with the "disciplinary" (i.e. the problem of discipline) in International Relations. In what follows, we shall briefly shift our attention from the ontological to the epistemological relevance of the "inter" in Kratochwil's work. More specifically we will glance at the balance between disciplinarity and (inter)disciplinarity in his theoretical reflections. In a recently published book on "key IR thinkers," Robert Keohane and Friedrich Kratochwil are identified respectively as the principal "gate-keeper" and "gate-breaker" in present day IR theory (Griffiths et al. 2009: 126). The authors aptly clarify, however, that as a "gate-breaker" Kratochwil has been neither "deconstructive" (in a Nietzschean sense) nor "anti-disciplinary." Rather, his main ambition has been "to ensure that we maintain an open-ended dialogue about what constitutes social knowledge and what reproduces social life in international relations" (ibid.). Without further elaboration, we posit that Kratochwil's reflective and flexible understanding of the "inter" has also enhanced his ability to walk the fine line between "disciplinarity" and "inter-disciplinarity" in International Relations.[2]

Historicizing the inter: Rethinking temporal premises and assumptions

Together with other social sciences, the IR discipline has been undergoing a "historical turn" of sorts (McCourt 2007) in recent years. Although a process which rests on many shoulders, Kratochwil in this context certainly qualifies as one of the most persistent and vocal IR scholars advocating a "serious" engagement with the "historical." To be sure, for Kratochwil a serious engagement with history must go well beyond the distilling of putative "lessons" from the past or the "testing" of theories by presumably unadulterated "facts." History does happen in the past, but this fact alone does not necessarily render it a "fixed" or "secure" source of knowledge. To seriously engage with the historical, we must realize that historical facts are always constituted through memory and historical reflection. They are always remembered from a certain perspective as part of a "story."

In pursuing this line of reasoning, Kratochwil issues a frontal challenge to traditional definitions of history which see the connection between the past, present and future as "fixed" or "pre-given." To be sure, he is hardly alone in his advocacy for a radically new understanding of time and memory. As pointed out by Michalis Kontopodis in his editorial introduction to a recent issue of *Memory Studies*: "There is no past, no present, and no future as such; the relation between the past, the present and the future is always made from some point of view and must be expressed or enacted for the past, the present and future to emerge" (Kontopodis 2009: 6). Noteworthy in this context is the fact that such a reading of history leaves the door open for the insertion of the political into our understanding of temporality. As emphasized by Kratochwil, how something is memorized and recalled, that is, what story about transformations in international relations (and elsewhere) is told, is part and parcel of contemporary political understandings and projects (Kratochwil 2006b: 13). In his words, "in this reflection we establish our identities as agents and societies and understand ourselves the 'same' despite all the changes. In this sense, 'history' is the encounter with 'self' rather than simply a storehouse of data" (2006b: 15).[3]

The core question now becomes: Is it possible to harness Kratochwil's understanding of history and time to enrich and to fine-tune our understanding of the "inter"? Our answer is that we can, provided we take seriously his suggestions regarding history and temporality. The following three benefits, in particular, deserve our attention.

First, in as far as the constituent units of the "inter" are constituted through memory (and historical reflection), the historicity of collective actors becomes very important for a more nuanced, less reified and more open (basically processual) understanding of the "inter." In other words, the configuration of the "inter" depends on how the connection between past, present and future—which, to reiterate, is never "fixed" or "pre-given"—is enacted. It follows that Kratochwil has no use for a transhistorical "inter" fixed from the standpoint of the (Westphalian) present. Rather, his interest lies with an "inter" that "is shaping and shaped by the temporal and contingent more than by what is universal and trans-historically valid" (Kratochwil 2007d: 499).

Second, Kratochwil's reading of history and temporality also requires us to pay due attention to the key role played by political contestation in the production and reproduction of the "inter." It reminds us, for instance, that there are always multiple stories to be told about the past, the present and the future, thus calling attention to the fact that at any point in time the evolution of the "inter" may be shaped by plural, coexisting and/or contradictory temporalities. Qualitative transformations in the configuration of the "inter" are therefore always possible though never predestined.

Finally, Kratochwil's work reminds us that whereas the temporality of any one of the possible referents of the "inter" (i.e. the nation, the state, etc.) may indeed be deteriorating (Sassen 2000: 215), the temporality of the "inter" itself is for the time being quite robust. For the foreseeable future, we will be dwelling in "inter"-type configurations.

Locating the inter: Rethinking spatial premises and assumptions

It seems fair to say that while Kratochwil's contributions on "historicizing" the inter play on themes which only fairly recently have received a more widespread attention in the discipline (e.g. process philosophy, historical sociology of IR), his thoughts on the spatial and territorial configurations and premises of international relations in the mid-1980s were a core inspiration for a broad "spatial turn" in the discipline which has taken place over the last two decades. In contrast to his thoughts on historicizing the inter, which are spread over a large variety of texts, his thoughts on the territorial and spatial premises and assumptions informing the inter can be found in a condensed fashion in a seminal single-authored article published in 1986 which served as an inspiration to John Ruggie's article "Territoriality and Beyond" published seven years later (Ruggie 1993).

In his 1986 article, Kratochwil (1986b) proposes a boundary-focused type of spatial analysis for the study of international politics. International politics is understood to be space-based, involving spatially delineated "units" and the space "between" them (the "inter"). Unlike most IR scholars at the time, that is, before a "spatial turn" took place in the discipline, Kratochwil avoids the spatial assumptions famously characterized by Agnew (1994) as a "territorial trap" for our thoughts about what politics is about and where the political is located. Most importantly in this context, he alerts us to the fact that the spaces of international relations are not just "there" to be discovered. They are produced; they are constructed, lived and enacted; and they are *politically contested.*

Linking to a rich tradition in philosophy and social theory, Kratochwil shows that it is insufficient to treat space as "flat" and internally divided by simple territorial lines. Rather, space is dynamic, multidimensional and historically emergent. Like the concept of property—which is semantically and structurally linked to the concept of territorial sovereignty—space is never as solid and simple as it sometimes appears. Property and sovereignty are both claims whose extent is continually being tested and limited by competing counterclaims. As put by Kratochwil, "territoriality, like property, is not a simple concept, but comprises a variety of social arrangements that have to be examined in greater detail" (Kratochwil 1986b: 28).

Such a view forces to quite radically engage with the issues of a plurality of spaces which constitute the "inter," including but also going beyond the sovereign territorial state. For both Kratochwil (1986b) and Ruggie (1993), political spaces that stand in tension to the space of sovereign territoriality are important because they can provide a venue of exploration of contemporary international transformation. Those spaces are part of the process of "unbundling" territoriality. Long before much of the "globalist" hype of the 1990s, Kratwochil and Ruggie alert us to the fact that a far-reaching "de-territorialization" of social relations has never been at stake. Rather, shifting processes in the reconfiguration of territorial space provide an important key to understand far-reaching changes in the international system. While traditionally scholars understood the "inter" to mean relations between Westphalian states and grounded their analysis in an ontology of states as territorially based "power containers" and of the international system as a realm of "great power competition," in his 1986 article Kratochwil opens the way to a more nuanced picture of the "international" and its "units." In his words: "By focusing on the changing function of borders rather than on the configuration and number of actors . . . the present approach provides a richer and more detailed treatment of the historical material while preserving parsimony and explanatory power" (Kratochwil 1986b: 52).

In sum, Kratochwil's contributions to spatial analysis can be easily added to and combined with his temporal insights to energize and to facilitate a richer and more nuanced understanding of the "inter" in international relations. The spaces through which the "inter" is constituted and reproduced are not simply "out there." Rather, they are configured and reconfigured by the (re-)drawing of specific boundaries, which typically also play important roles in the construction of collective identities. In his 1986 article, Kratochwil takes boundaries and their dynamics as his point of departure and shows that human societies have made sense of political boundaries in different ways at different times. "On the most basic level," he remarks at another point, "the 'inter' marks the place where we as agents come into contact with each other and realize that the outcome of the encounter is dependent on whether we are able to orient our actions meaningfully towards each other" (2007d: 500). In thinking about the "inter," Kratochwil urges us to keep in mind that spatial and ascriptive distinctions are interdependent and define the changing nature of the political game. And because politics deals with the particular and the contingent, both "time" and "space" emerge as important dimensions of the "inter" in international relations.

Situating the inter: Rethinking global semantics

Binding together and going beyond efforts to "historicize" and "locate" the inter in a more fruitful way is Kratochwil's sensitivity to context and his diagnosis that there "seems to be a growing disparity between the practices which comprise international relations, and the conceptual apparatus with which we attempt to analyze these practices" (Kratochwil 2000d: 143). While this could be said to be a driving motive behind much of conceptual and theoretical innovation in any academic field, Kratochwil goes to some lengths in order to demonstrate that the disjuncture between practices and the conceptual apparatus employed toward their analysis is not a temporary shortcoming to be remedied and then left aside at some point. Rather, catching up with practices conceptually is a somehow never-ending task: the analyst constantly refines her or his conceptual apparatus only to find her/himself being surpassed by practices once again. However, the analyst in this sense is not a modern academic Sisyphus as the latter would imply that there is a final top to reach in the end. Yet, and this could be said to form a driving motive of Kratochwil's work, *practices never come to an end*. As they continue, so must efforts toward refining conceptual tools.

However, such efforts must not be limited to tracing conceptual problems back to a failure of correspondence with a presumably pre-existing world. Indeed, Kratochwil insists that concepts simply do not do their work by "reference" or by "mirroring." Rather, they are embedded in historically (and locally) variable semantic fields, leading to asynchronous and asymmetrical adjustments of their meanings. It is in this sense that Kratochwil attunes us to the necessity to understand the meaning of central concepts such as "politics" or "legitimacy" in their relevant "semantic fields" (Kratochwil 2006d). In other words, in engaging conceptual problems, Kratochwil urges us to turn our attention toward "the manner in which our political terms function within a larger semantic field, the links and connections they establish and [the] actual practices they thereby authorize, support or legitimize" (Kratochwil 2007d: 498).

It stands to reason that Kratochwil would approach the conceptual challenges associated with the "inter" in a similar manner. He would be less concerned with putative mirroring failures regarding the "real" referents of the "inter-" (national or other), and more concerned with configuring a fertile "semantic field" for the prefix itself. Concepts such as sovereignty, citizenship and legitimacy—which are in Kratochwil's view crucial to an understanding of the contemporary contours of politics—would surface as prime candidates in this context. However, in as far as these concepts form subsets of more general meaning clusters underlying the construction of *Identities*, *Borders*, and *Orders* (*IBO*) (see Albert et al. 2001), the IBO triad can arguably offer a particularly attractive semantic field for the "inter" in an era of epochal change. Such is the case because the IBO triad "identifies three key 'moments' central to the stabilization of any conceivable world" (Lapid 2001: 7).

It follows from these observations that the question of whether there actually "is" a fundamental change going on in the world for Kratochwil is nonsensical. Thus where others may bemoan diagnoses of constant change and novelty (see, e.g. Krasner 1994), for Kratochwil that is all there is. However, of course, change comes at various speeds and happens in complex semantic fields which underlie the formation of meaning. And this is exactly why Kratochwil will never come down to a referential "definition," or even only a temporary fixation, of the meaning of the "inter." Rather, the "inter" is constantly reworked and reconfigured in various semantic fields. And yet, as with renovating old houses, tracing its evolution is a rewarding yet never finished struggle.

Mission impossible? Friedrich Kratochwil and the IR project

The contours in which we situated Kratochwil's work in the preceding paragraphs should have made it clear that he does not sit easy within the majority of contemporary IR discourses: his work proceeds by permanently undermining the endeavors to arrive at stable definitions or understandings of the "inter" which underlie the entire academic project of a discipline of International Relations. Why he remains in the disciplinary orbit of such a discipline may thus come to be seen as rather surprising. And possibly it can only be explained by an ironic twist underlying his work which prevents him to throw out the "inter" altogether. He thus reminds us that the task is not (or at least not always has to be) a wholesale renovation of social theorizing, but that such renovations always need to be connected to the existing practices of (international) politics. However, Kratochwil also reminds us that the intellectual house of IR cannot successfully go ahead by just refurbishing single rooms here and there, but that sometimes it is necessary to tackle the cracks in the foundations. What makes him stand out is that despite a great number of colleagues who would not acknowledge that there is a problem with the foundations, Fritz Kratochwil does not simply move away to build a new house somewhere else, but attempts the almost impossible restoration of the old one on the existing site. Strangely enough, as in the movie with the same title, although such a mission may be next to "impossible," so far it has succeeded.

Notes

1. Elaborating on Isaiah Berlin, Ellias Khalil proposes a fox/hedgehog/owl typology of intellectual temperaments differentiated by the type of questions different scholars ask and by the way they treat the problem of time. Kratochwil does not easily fit into the fox or hedgehog categories. The owl category may be more suitable; see Khalil (1992).
2. In this context Kratochwil qualifies as a scholar who engages the problem of discipline in International Relations with a "flexible mindset." See Lapid (2002: 2–4).
3. Although referring to it only in passing, Kratochwil is very close to the Bielefeld School of historical semantics and *Begriffsgeschichte* around Reinhart Koselleck when he points out that an engagement with the historical and historical reflection makes us "aware of the 'dialectic of choice' in which from the present the past is recollected and joined with the future by means of a political 'project'" (Kratochwil 2006b: 8).

Friedrich Kratochwil's Published Work, 1971–2010

(1971) "Politik und Politische Wissenschaft," *Zeitschrift für Politik*, vol. 18: 113–23.

(1972a) "Strukturfunktionalismus und Methodologische Probleme der Politischen Entwicklungslehre," *Zeitschrift für Politik*, vol. 19: 32–48. Reprinted in Franz Nuscheler (ed.), *Politikwissenschaftliche Entwick-lungsländerforschung*, Wege der Forschung, vol. 379 (Darmstadt: Wissenschaftliche Buchgesellschaft, 1986), pp. 74–98.

(1972b) "Amerika, hast du es besser?" *Zeitschrift für Politik*, vol. 20: 73–81.

(1978) *International Order and Foreign Policy* (Boulder, CO: Westview Pres).

(1981a) *The Humean Conception of International Relations*, World Order Studies Program, Occasional Paper no. 9 (Center of International Studies, Princeton University).

(1981b) "Alternative Criteria for Evaluating Foreign Policy," *International Interaction*, vol. 8: 105–22.

(1982) "On the Notion of 'Interest' in International Relations," *International Organization*, vol. 36: 1–30.

(1983a) "Is International Law 'Proper Law?'" *Archiv für Rechts- und Sozialphilosophie*, vol. 69: 13–46.

(1983b) "Thrasymmachos Revisited: On the Relevance of Norms and the Study of Law for International Relations," *Journal of International Affairs*, vol. 36: 343–56. Reprinted as ch. 10 in Peter A. Toma and Robert Gorman (eds), *International Relations: Understanding Global Issues* (Pacific Grove, CA: Brooks-Cole Publishers, 1990). Reprinted as ch. 3 in Martti Koskenniemi (ed.), *International* (Aldershot: Dartmouth, 1992).

(1984a) "Errors Have Their Advantages," *International Organization*, vol. 38: 305–20.

(1984b) "The Force of Prescriptions," *International Organization*, vol. 38: 685–708.

(1985a) edited with Richard Falk and Saul H. Mendlovitz, *International Law: A Contemporary Perspective* (Boulder, CO: Westview Press).

(1985b) "The Role of Domestic Courts as Agencies of the International Legal Order," pp. 236–63, in Richard Falk, Friedrich Kratochwil and Saul H. Mendlovitz (eds), *International Law: A Contemporary Perspective* (Boulder, CO: Westview Press).

(1985c) "Of Law and Human Action: A Jurisprudential Plea for a World Order Perspective in International Legal Studies," pp. 639–50, in Richard Falk, Friedrich Kratochwil and Saul H. Mendlovitz (eds), *International Law: A Contemporary Perspective* (Boulder, CO: Westview Press).

(1985d) with Paul Rohrlich and Harpreet Mahajan, *Peace and Disputed Sovereignty, Reflections on Conflict over Territory* (Lanham, MD: University of Press of America, 1985).

(1985e) "Rethinking the Sources of International Law," *Columbia Journal of Transnational Law*, vol. 23: 705–12.

(1986a) with John Gerard Ruggie, "International Organization: A State of the Art or an Art of the State," *International Organization*, vol. 40: 753–76. Reprinted, pp. 17–27, in Paul Diehl (ed.), *The Politics of International Organizations: Patterns and Insights* (Chicago: Dorsey Press, 1989, pp. 17–27). Reprinted, pp. 290–306, in Oran R. Young (ed.), *The International Political Economy and International Institutions* (Cheltenham: Edward Elgar, 1996). Reprinted, pp. 341–65, in Lisa Martin and Beth Simmons (eds), *International Institutions* (Cambridge, MA: MIT Press, 2001). Reprinted, pp. 37–52, in Friedrich V. Kratochwil and Edward. D. Mansfield (eds), *International Organization and Global Governance* (New York: Pearson Longman, 2005).

(1986b) "Of Systems and Boundaries, Reflections on the Formation of the State System," *World Politics*, vol. 39: 27–52.

(1987a) "Norms and Values: Rethinking the Domestic Analogy," *Ethics and International Affairs*, vol. 1: 135–59.

(1987b) "Rules, Norms, Values and the Limits of 'Rationality'," *Archiv für Rechts- und Sozialphilosophie*, vol. 73: 301–29.

(1988a) "Diritto e principi di natura: Pufendorf e le leggi di natura come condizioni transcendentali di un discorso sulle dispute," *Teoria Politica*, vol. 4: 3–27.

(1988b) "Regimes, Interpretation and the 'Science' of Politics", *Millennium*, vol. 17: 263–84.

(1988c) "Protagorean Quest: Community, Justice, and the 'Oughts and Musts' of International Politics," *International Journal*, vol. 43: 205–40.

(1989a) *Rules, Norms and Decisions, On the Conditions of Practical and Legal Reasoning in International Relations and Domestic Affairs* (Cambridge: Cambridge University Press).

(1989b) "The Challenge of Security in a Changing World," *Journal of International Affairs*, vol. 43: 19–41.

(1992) "International Order and Individual Liberty," *Constitutional Political Economy*, vol. 3: 39–50.

(1993a) "The Embarrassment of Changes: Neo-Realism as the Science of *Realpolitik* without Politics," *Review of International Studies*, vol. 19: 63–80.

(1993b) "Norms vs. Numbers, Multilateralism and the Rationalist and Reflexivist Approaches to Institution— A Unilateral Plea for Communicative Rationality," pp. 443–74, in John Gerard Ruggie (ed.), *Multilateralism Matters: Theory and Praxis of an International Form* (New York: Columbia University Press).

(1993c) edited with Edward D. Mansfield, *International Organization: A Reader* (New York: HarperCollins).

(1993d) "Constitutional Thought vs. Value-based Thought in World Order Studies," ch. 11, in Richard A. Falk, Robert C. Johansen and Samuel S. Kim (eds), *The Constitutional Foundations of World Peace* (Albany: State University of New York Press).

(1993e) with Rodney Bruce Hall, "Medieval Tales: Neorealist "Science" and the Abuse of History," *International Organization*, vol. 47: 479–92.

(1993f) "Contract and Regimes: Do Issue Specificity and Variations of Formality Matter?" pp. 73–93, in Volker Rittberger (ed.), *Regime Theory and International Relations* (Oxford: Clarendon Press).

(1994a) with Rey Koslowski, "Understanding Change in International Politics: The Soviet Empire's Demise and the International System," *International Organization*, vol. 48: 215–48.

(1994b) "The Limits of Contract," *European Journal of International Law*, vol. 5: 465–91. Reprinted, pp. 24–53, in Cecelia Lynch and Michael Loriaux (eds),

Law and Moral Action in World Politics (Minneapolis: University of Minnesota Press, 2000).

(1994c) "Citizenship: On the Border of Order?" *Alternatives*, vol. 19: 485–506. Reprinted, pp. 181–97, in Yosef Lapid and Friedrich Kratochwil (eds), *The Return of Culture and Identity in IR Theory* (Boulder, CO: Lynne Rienner).

(1994d) "Changing Relations between State, Market, and Society, and the Problem of Knowledge," *Pacific Focus*, vol. 9: 43–60.

(1995a) "Sovereignty as 'Dominium': Is there a Right of Humanitarian Intervention?" pp. 21–42, in Gene M. Lyons and Michael Mastanduno (eds), *Beyond Westphalia? National Sovereignty and International Intervention* (Baltimore: Johns Hopkins University Press).

(1995b) "Was wissen wir über den Wandel der Beziehungen zwischen Staat, Markt und Gesellschaft?" *Welttrends*, no. 7: 114–32.

(1995c) "Why Sisyphus Is Happy: Reflections on the 'Third Debate' and on Theorizing as a Vocation," *The Sejong Review* vol. 3: 3–36.

(1996a) edited with Yosef Lapid, *The Return of Culture and Identity in IR Theory* (Boulder, CO: Lynne Rienner).

(1996b) "Revisiting the 'National': Toward an Identity Agenda in Neorealism?" pp. 105–28, in Yosef Lapid and Friedrich Kratochwil (eds), *The Return of Culture and Identity in IR Theory* (Boulder, CO: Lynne Rienner).

(1996c) "Is the Ship of Culture at Sea or Returning?" pp. 201–22, in Yosef Lapid and Friedrich Kratochwil (eds), *The Return of Culture and Identity in IR Theory* (Boulder, CO: Lynne Rienner).

(1997a) "Globalization and the Disappearance of 'Publics'," ch. 4, in Jin–Young Chung (ed.), *Global Governance: The Role of International Institutions in A Changing World* (Seoul: Sejong Institute).

(1997b) "Awakening or Somnambulation," *Millennium*, vol. 26: 1–6.

(1998a) "Politics, Norms, and Peaceful Change: Two Moves to Institutions," *Review of International Studies*, vol. 24: 193–218. Reprinted, pp. 193–218, in Tim Dunne, Michael Cox and Ken Booth (eds), *The Eighty Years' Crisis* (Cambridge: Cambridge University Press). Reprinted, pp. 106–119, in Friedrich Kratochwil and Edward D. Mansfield (eds), *International Organization and Global Governance* (New York: Pearson, Longman, 2005).

(1998b) "Vergeßt Kant! Reflexionen zur Debatte über Ethik und Internationale Politik," pp. 96–149, in Christine Chwaszcza and Wolfgang Kersting (eds), *Politische Philosophie der Internationalen Beziehungen*. (Frankfurt am Main: Suhrkamp).

(1999) "Acción y Conocimiento Histórico: La Construcción de Teorías de las Relaciones Internácionales," *Foro Internacional*, vol. 39: 588–610.

(2000a) "How Do Norms Matter?" pp. 35–68, in Michael Byers (ed.), *The Role of Law in International Politics* (Oxford: Oxford University Press).

(2000b) "Theory and Political Practice: Reflections on Theory-Building in International Relations," pp. 50–64, in Paul Wapner and Lester Edwin J. Ruiz (eds), *Principled World Politics: The Challenge of Normative International Relations* (Lanham, MD: Rowman and Littlefield).

(2000c) "Constructing a New Orthodoxy? Wendt's 'Social Theory of International Politics' and the Constructivist Challenge," *Millennium*, vol. 29: 73–101.

(2000d) "The Politics of Place and Origin: An Inquiry into the Changing Boundaries of Representation, Citizenship, and Legitimacy," pp. 185–211, in Beverly Neufeld and Michi Ebata (eds), *Confronting the Political in International Relations* (London: Macmillan). Reprinted in *International Relations of the Asia-Pacific*, vol. 1, 2001: 143–65.

(2001a) "Constructivism as an Approach to Interdisciplinary Study," pp. 13–35, in Karin M. Fierke and Knud Erik Jørgensen (eds), *Constructing International Relations: The Next Generation* (Armonk, NY: M.E. Sharpe).

(2001b) "International Law as an Approach to International Ethics: A Plea for a Jurisprudential Diagnostics," pp. 14–41, in by Jean-Marc Coicaud and Daniel Warner (eds), *Ethics and International Affairs* (Tokyo: United Nations University Press).

(2001c) with Mathias Albert, "Conclusion," pp. 275–91, in Mathias Albert, David Jacobson and Yosef Lapid (eds), *Identities, Borders, Orders: Rethinking International Relations Theory* (Minneapolis: University of Minnesota Press).

(2001d) with T. Hopf and R. N. Lebow, "Reflexivity: Method and Evidence," pp. 12884–8, in *International Encyclopedia of the Social & Behavioral Sciences* (Oxford: Elsevier Science).

(2002a) edited with Doris Fuchs, *Transformative Change and Global Order* (Muenster: LT-Verlag; New Brunswick, NJ: Transaction Books).

(2002b) "Globalization: What It Is and What It Is Not: Some Critical Reflections on the Discursive Formations Dealing with Transformative Change," pp. 25–44, in Doris A. Fuchs and Friedrich Kratochwil (eds), *Transformative Change and Global Order* (Muenster: LIT Verlag; New Brunswick, NJ: Transaction Books).

(2002c) "Souveränität und Moderne. Eine begriffliche Analyse des semantischen Feldes," pp. 29–51, in Markus Jachtenfuchs and Michèle Knodt (eds), *Regieren in internationalen Institutionen* (Opladen: Leske + Budrich).

(2003a) *Reflections on Theory and Practice*, European University Institute Working Paper, SPS No.2003/16.

(2003b) "11. September: Das Ende des Hobbesischen Projekts?" pp. 109–25, in Ellen Bos and Antje Helmerich (eds), *Neue Bedrohung Terrorismus. Der 11. September 2001 und die* (Muenster: LIT Verlag).

(2003c) "Moles, Martyrs and Sleepers: The End of the Hobbesian Project?" *Ethnologia Europaea*, vol. 33: 57–68. Reprinted, pp. 57–68, in Regina Bendix and John Bendix (eds), *Sleepers, Moles, and Martyrs: Secret Identifications, Societal Integration, and The Differing Meanings Of Freedom* (Copenhagen: Museum Tusculum Press, 2004).

(2003d) "The Monologue of 'Science'," *International Studies Review*, vol. 5: 123–53.

(2003e) "The 'Legalization' of World Politics?" *Leiden Journal of International Law*, vol. 16: 878–84.

(2005a) "Religion and (Inter-)National Politics: On the Heuristics of Identities, Structures, and Agents," *Alternatives*, vol. 30: 113–40.

(2005b) edited with Edward D. Mansfield, *International Organization and Global Governance: A Reader* (New York: Pearson Longman). Chinese translation (Pearson, Asia and Peking University Press, 2007).

(2006a) "Constructing a New Orthodoxy," pp. 21–47, in Stefano Guzzini and Anna Leander (eds), *Constructivism and International Relations* (London: Routledge).

(2006b) "History, Action and Identity: Revisiting the 'Second' Great Debate and Assessing its Importance for Social Theory," *European Journal of International Relations*, vol. 12: 5–29.

(2006c) "Global Governance and the Emergence of a 'World Society'," ch. 14, in Nathalie Karagiannis and Peter Wagner (eds), *Varieties of World Making: Beyond Globalization* (Liverpool: Liverpool University Press).

(2006d) "On Legitimacy," *International Relations*, vol. 20: 302–8.

(2006e) "The Genealogy of Multilateralism: Reflections on an Organizational Form and its Crisis," ch. 8, in Edward Newman, Ramesh Chandra Thakur and John Tirman (eds), *Multilateralism Under Challenge? Power, International Order and Structural Change* (Tokyo: United Nations University Press).

(2007a) "Of False Promises and Safe Bets: A Plea for a Pragmatic Perspective in Theory Building (The Tartu Lecture)," *Journal of International Relations and Development*, vol. 10: 1–15.

(2007b) "Of Communities, Gangs, Historicity, and the Problem of Santa Claus: Replies to My Critics," *Journal of International Relations and Development*, vol. 10: 57–78.

(2007c) "Looking Back from Somewhere: Reflections on What Remains 'Critical' in Critical Theory," *Review of International Studies*, vol. 33, Supp. 1: 25–45. Reprinted, pp. 25–45, in Nicholas Rengger and Ben Thirkell-White (eds), *Critical International Relations Theory after 25 Years* (Cambridge: Cambridge University Press).

(2007d) "Rethinking the 'Inter' in International Politics," *Millennium*, vol. 35: 495–511.

(2007e) "Evidence, Inference, and Truth as Problems of Theory-Building in the Social Sciences," pp. 25–41, in Richard Ned Lebow and Mark Irving Lichbach (eds), *Theory and Evidence in Comparative Politics and International Relations* (New York: Palgrave Macmillan).

(2008a) "Sociological Approaches to International Relations," pp. 444–61, in Christian Reus-Smit and Duncan Snidal (eds), *The Oxford Handbook of International Relations* (Oxford: Oxford University Press).

(2008b) "Constructivism: What It Is (Not) and How It Matters," pp. 88–99, in Donatella della Porta and Michael Keating (eds), *Approaches and Methodologies in the Social Sciences: A Pluralist Perspective* (Cambridge: Cambridge University Press).

(2008c) with Mariano Barbato, *Habermas's Notion of a Post-Secular Society: A Perspective from International Relations*, European University Institute Working Papers, MWP 2008/25.

(2008d) "Ten Points to Ponder About Pragmatism: Some Critical Reflections on Knowledge-Generation in the Social Sciences," pp. 11–25, in Harry Bauer and Elisabetta Brighi (eds), *Pragmatism and International Relations* (London: Routledge).

(2009a) "Legal Theory and International Law," pp. 55–67, in David Armstrong (ed.), *Routledge Handbook of International Law* (London: Routledge).

(2009b) "Has the Rule of Law Become a Rule of Lawyers? An Inquiry into the Uses and Abuses of an Ancient *Topos* in Contemporary Debates," pp. 171–96, in Gianluigi Palombella and Neil Walker (eds), *Relocating the Rule of Law* (Oxford: Hart Publishing).

(2009c) with Mariano Barbato "Towards a Post-Secular Political Order? *European Political Science Review*, vol. 1: 1–24.

(2009d) "How (Il)liberal is the Liberal Theory of Law? Some Critical Remarks on Slaughter's Approach," *Comparative Sociology*, vol. 9: 120–45.

(2009e) with Jörg Friedrichs, "On Acting and Knowing: How Pragmatism Can Advance International Relations Research and Methodology," *International Organization*, vol. 63: 701–31.

(2010) with Oliver Kessler, "Between Explaining and Understanding: What is New in the New Systems Theory?" pp. 23–42, in Mathias Albert, Lars-Erik Cederman and Alexander Wendt (eds), *New Systems Theories of World Politics* (New York: Palgrave Macmillan).

Book reviews, conference papers, consultancy reports and occasional pieces not included.

References

For all references to Kratochwil's publications, including co-authored pieces, see Friedrich Kratochwil's Published Work, 1971–2009

Abbott, A. (1995) "Things of Boundaries," *Social Research*, vol. 62: 857–82.

Abbott, K. W., R. O. Keohane, A. Moravcsik, A.-M. Slaughter, and D. Snidal (2000) "The Concept of Legalization," *International Organization*, vol. 54: 401–45.

Abrahamsen, R. and M. C. Williams (2008) "Selling Security: Assessing the Impact of Military Privatization," *Review of International Political Economy*, vol. 15: 131–46.

Adler, E. (1992) "The Emergence of Cooperation: National Epistemic Communities and the International Evolution of the Idea of Nuclear Arms Control," *International Organization*, vol. 46: 101–45.

Adler, E. (2005) *Communitarian International Relations: The Epistemic Foundations of International Relations* (London: Routledge).

Adler, E., and M. Barnett (1998) "Security Communities in Theoretical Perspectives," pp. 3–28, in E. Adler (ed.) *Security Communities* (Cambridge: Cambridge University Press).

Adler, E., and P. M. Haas (1992) "Conclusion: Epistemic Communities, World Order and the Creation of a Reflective Research Program," *International Organization*, vol. 46: 367–90.

Agnew, J. (1994) "The Territorial Trap: The Geographical Assumptions of International Relations Theory," *Review of International Political Economy*, vol. 1: 53–80.

Albert, M., D. Jacobson, and Y. Lapid (2001) *Identities, Borders, Orders: Rethinking International Relations Theory* (Minneapolis: University of Minnesota Press).

Alexander, J. (1988) "Habermas' neue kritische Theorie: Anspruch und Probleme," pp. 73–109, in A. Honneth and H. Joas (eds), *Kommunikatives Handeln, Beiträge zu Jürgen Habermas' Theorie des kommunikativen Handelns* (Frankfurt am Main: Suhrkamp).

Allison, G. (2004) *Nuclear Terrorism: The Ultimate Preventable Catastrophe* (New York: New York Times Books).

Allott, P. (1992) *Eunomia: New Order for a New World* (Oxford: Oxford University Press).

Aristotle (1908) *Nichomachean Ethics*, trans. W. D. Ross (Oxford: Clarendon Press).

Aristotle (1953) *The Ethics of Aristotle*, trans. J. A. K. Thomson (Middlesex: Penguin Books).

Aristotle (1984a) *The Complete Works of Aristotle: The Revised Oxford Translation*, ed. J. Barnes (Princeton: Princeton University Press).

Aristotle (1984b) "On the Soul," trans. J. A. Smith, pp. 641–92, in Aristotle (1984a).

Aristotle (1999) *Nicomachean Ethics*, 2nd edn trans. T. Irwin (Indianapolis, IN: Hackett).

Aristotle (2000) *Nicomachean Ethics*, trans. R. Crisp (Cambridge: Cambridge University Press).

Aron, R. (1962) *Paix et guerre entre les nations*, 8th edn (Paris: Calmann-Lévy).

Axelrod, R. (1984) *The Evolution of Cooperation* (New York: Basic Books).

Baldwin, D. A. (1971) "Money and Power," *Journal of Politics*, vol. 33: 578–614.

Baldwin, D. A. (1978) "Power and Social Exchange," *American Political Science Review*, vol. 72: 1229–42.

Baldwin, D. A. (1985) *Economic Statecraft* (Princeton: Princeton University Press).

Bauer, H., and E. Brighi, (eds) (2008) *Pragmatism in International Relations* (London: Routledge).

Bederman, D. (1990) "Review," *American Journal of International Law*, vol. 84: 775.

Behnke, A. (2001) "Grand Theory in the Age of Its Impossibility: Contemplations on Alexander Wendt," *Cooperation and Conflict*, vol. 36: 121–34.

Bell, D. A. (2000) *East Meets West: Human Rights and Democracy in East Asia* (Princeton, NJ: Princeton University Press).

Bell, D. A. (2008) *China's New Confucianism: Politics and Everyday Life in a Changing Society* (Princeton, NJ: Princeton University Press).

Bell, D. S. A. (2001) "International Relations: The Dawn of a Historiographical Turn?" *British Journal of Politics and International Relations*, vol. 3: 115–26.

Benhabib, S. (2007) "Twilight of Sovereignty or the Emergence of Cosmopolitan Norms? Rethinking Citizenship in Volatile Times," *Citizenship Studies*, vol. 11: 19–36.

Berger, J. (1982) "Die Versprachlichung des Sakralen und die Entsprachlichung der Ökonomie," *Zeitschrift für Soziologie*, vol. 11: 353–65.

Berger, P. L., and T. Luckmann (1966) *The Social Construction of Reality: A Treatise in the Sociology of Knowledge* (Garden City, NY: Doubleday).

Berkowitz, L. (1968) "Responsibility, Reciprocity, and Social Distance in Help Giving: An Experimental Investigation of English Social Class Differences," *Journal of Experimental Social Psychology*, vol. 4: 46–63.

Berkowitz, L., and P. Friedman (1967) "Some Social Class Differences in Helping Behavior," *Journal of Personality and Social Psychology*, vol. 5: 217–24.

Bernstein, R. J. (1983) *Beyond Objectivism and Relativism: Science, Hermeneutics and Praxis* (Philadelphia: University of Pennsylvania Press).

Bernstein, S., R. N. Lebow, J. G. Stein, and S. Weber, "Social Science as Case-Based Diagnostics," pp. 229–60 in R. N. Lebow and M. I. Lichbach (eds), *Theory and Evidence in Comparative Politics and International Relations* (New York: Palgrave Macmillan).

Bigo, D. (2002) "Security and Immigration: Toward a Critique of the Governmentality of Unease," *Alternatives*, vol. 27: 63–92.

Blau, P. M. (1964a) *Exchange and Power in Social Life* (New York: Wiley).

Blau, P. M. (1964b) "Justice in Social Exchange," *Sociological Inquiry*, vol. 34: 193–206.

Blau, P. M. (1968) "Interaction: Social Exchange," in D. L. Sills (ed.), *International Encyclopedia of the Social Sciences* (New York: Free Press).

Bleiker, R. (2001) "The Aesthetic Turn in International Political Theory," *Millennium: Journal of International Studies*, vol. 30: 509–33.

Bloch, M. (1990) *The Royal Touch* (New York: Dorset).
Bohr, N. (1984) "Über die Erkenntnisfragen der Quantenphysik," in K. Baumann and R. Sexl (eds), *Die Deutungen der Quantumtheorie* (Braunschweig: Vieweg).
Bourdieu, P. (1977) *Outline of a Theory of Practice*, trans. R. Nice (Cambridge: Cambridge University Press).
Bourdieu, P. (1984) *Distinction*, trans. R. Nice (Cambridge, MA: Harvard University Press).
Bourdieu, P. (1990) *The Logic of Practice*, trans. R. Nice (Stanford: Stanford University Press).
Bourdieu, P. (1991) "The Peculiar History of Scientific Reason," *Sociological Forum* 6: 3–26.
Brickman, P., L. J. Becker, and S. Castle (1979) "Making Trust Easier and Harder Through Two Forms of Sequential Interaction," *Journal of Personality and Social Psychology*, vol. 37: 515–21.
Brooks, S. G., and W. Wohlforth (2008) *World Out of Balance: International Relations and the Challenge of American Primacy* (Princeton: Princeton University Press).
Brown, C. (2000) "Cultural Diversity and International Political Theory: From the *Requirement* to 'Mutual Respect?'" *Review of International Studies*, vol. 26: 199–213.
Brundage, S. (1990) Review, *American Political Science Review*, vol. 90: 1450–1.
Brunnée, J., and S. J. Toope (2000) "International Law and Constructivism: Elements of an Interactional Theory of International Law," *Columbia Journal of Transnational Law*, vol. 39: 19–74.
Brunnée, J., and S. J. Toope (2002) "The Changing Nile Basin Regime: Does Law Matter?" *Harvard International Law Journal*, vol. 43: 105–59.
Brunnée, J., and S. J. Toope (2005) "Norms, Institutions and UN Reform: The Responsibility to Protect," *Journal of International Law & International Relations*, vol. 2: 121–37.
Brunnée, J., and S. J. Toope (2010) *Legitimacy and Legality in International Law: An Interactional Account* (Cambridge: Cambridge University Press).
Brzezinski, Z. (2004) *The Choice* (New York: Basic Books).
Buchanan, A. (2004) *Justice, Legitimacy, and Self-Determination: Moral Foundations for International Law* (Oxford: Oxford University Press).
Budz, M. (2009) "A Heterotopian Analysis of Maritime Refugee Incidents," *International Political Sociology*, vol. 3: 18–35.
Bueno de Mesquita, B. (1985) "Towards a Scientific Understanding of International Conflict: A Personal View," *International Studies Quarterly*, vol. 24: 121–36.
Bukovansky, M. (2007) "Liberal States, International Order, and Legitimacy: An Appeal for Persuasion over Prescription," *International Politics*, vol. 44: 175–93.
Bukovansky, M. (2010) "Institutionalized Hypocrisy and the Politics of Agricultural Trade," in R. Abdelal, M. Blyth, and C. Parsons (eds) *Constructing the International Economy* (Ithaca: Cornell University Press).
Bull, H. (1977) *The Anarchical Society: A Study of Order in World Politics* (New York: Columbia University Press).
Bull, H. (1980) "International Order and Foreign Policy: A Theoretical Sketch of Postwar International Politics by Frederick V. Kratochwil," *Third World Quarterly*, vol. 2: 134–7.

Burchell, G., C. Gordon, and P. Miller (eds) (1991) *The Foucault Effect: Studies in Governmentality* (Chicago: University of Chicago Press).

Burton, J. W. (1962) *Peace Theory: Preconditions of Disarmament* (New York: Knopf).

Byers, M. (2002) "The Shifting Foundations of International Law," *European Journal of International Law*, vol. 13: 21–41.

Byers, M. (ed.) (2000) *The Role of Law in International Politics: Essays in International Relations and International Law* (Oxford: Oxford University Press).

Calhoun, C. (2007) *Nations Matter: Citizenship, Solidarity, and the Cosmopolitan Dream* (London: Routledge).

Camus, A. (1942) *Le mythe de Sisyphe: Essai sur l'absurde* (Paris: Gallimard).

Carafano, J. J., and A. Gudgel (2007) "Nanotechnology and National Security: Small Changes, Big Impact," Heritage Foundation Backgrounder, no. 2071.

Carr, E. H. (1964) *The Twenty Years Crisis* (New York: Harper).

Cassin, B. (2004) "'Dynamis,' 'energeia' 'entelekheia' et la définition aristotélicienne du mouvement" in B. Cassin (ed.), *Vocabulaire européen des philosophies* (Paris: Seuil, Dictionnaires Robert).

Castells, M. (1999) *The Information Age: Economy, Society and Culture* (Oxford: Blackwell).

Central Intelligence Agency (2010) *The World Factbook*, at https://www.cia.gov/library/publications/the-world-factbook.

Certeau, M. de (1984) *The Practice of Everyday Life*, trans. S. Rendall (Berkeley and Los Angeles: University of California Press).

Chadwick-Jones, J. K. (1976) *Social Exchange Theory: Its Structure and Influence in Social Psychology* (London: Academic Press).

Chalmers, A. F. (1976) *What Is This Thing Called Science?* (Indianapolis, IN: Hackett).

Chapman, B. (1998) "More Easily Done Than Said: Rules, Reasons and Rational Social Choice," *Oxford Journal of Legal Studies*, vol. 18: 293–329.

Checkel, J. (2002) *Persuasion in International Institutions*, Working Paper 02/14 (Oslo: Arena).

Checkel, J. T. (1998) "The Constructivist Turn in International Relations Theory," *World Politics*, vol. 50: 324–48.

Checkel, J. T. (2001) "Why Comply? Social Learning and European Identity Change," *International Organization*, vol. 53: 553–88.

Claude, I. L., Jr. (1989) "The Balance of Power Revisited," *Review of International Studies*, vol. 15: 77–85.

Claude, I. L., Jr. (1962) *Power and International Relations* (New York: Random House).

Cohen, J. (2004) "Minimalism about Human Rights: The Most We Can Hope For?" *Journal of Political Philosophy*, vol. 12: 190–213.

Cohen, J. L. (2004) "Whose Sovereignty? Empire versus International Law," *Ethics and International Affairs*, vol. 18: 1–24.

Cohen, J. L. (2008) "A Gobal State of Emergency or the Further Constitutionalization of International Law: A Pluralist Approach," *Constellations*, vol. 15: 456–84.

Connor, W. R. (1984) *Thucydides* (Princeton: Princeton University Press).

Constantinou, C. M., O. P. Richmond, A. Watson (2008) *Cultures and Politics of Global Communication* (Cambridge: Cambridge University Press).

Cortell, A. P., and Davis J. W. (2000) "Understanding the Domestic Impact of International Norms: A Research Agenda," *International Studies Review*, vol. 2: 65–87.

Crawford, N. C. (2002) *Argument and Change in World Politics: Ethics, Decolonization, and Humanitarian Intervention* (Cambridge: Cambridge University Press).

Curtin, D. M. (1999) "'Civil Society' and the European Union: Opening Spaces for Deliberative Democracy?" pp. 185–280, in *Collected Courses of the Academy of European Law*, vol. 7, book 1 (Dordrecht: Kluwer).

Daston, L., and P. Gallison (2007) *Objectivity* (New York: Zone Books).

David, P. (2004) "Nature," in B. Cassin (ed.), *Vocabulaire Européen des Philosophies* (Paris: Seuil, Dictionnaires Robert).

Davis, J. W. (2005) *Terms of Inquiry: On the Theory and Practice of Political Science* (Baltimore: Johns Hopkins University Press).

De Burca, G. (2008) *Europe's Judicial Resolution and the UN Security Council*, Paper Series (New York: Fordham Law School).

Debrix, F. (1999) *Re-Envisioning Peacekeeping: The United States and the Mobilization of Ideology* (Minneapolis: University of Minnesota Press).

Deibert, R. J. (1997) *Parchment, Printing, and Hypermedia: Communication in World Order Transformation* (New York: Columbia University Press).

Deibert, R. J. (2000) "International Plug n' Play? Citizen Activism, the Internet, and Global Public Policy," *International Studies Perspectives*, vol. 1: 255–72.

Deitelhoff, N. (2006) *Überzeugung in der Politik. Gründzüge einer Diskurstheorie internationalen Regierens* (Frankfurt am Main: Suhrkamp).

Deitelhoff, N. (2009) "The Discursive Process of Legalization: Charting Islands of Persuasion in the ICC Case," *International Organization*, vol. 63: 33–65.

Descartes, R. (1996) *Discourse on Method*, in D. Weissman (ed.), *Discourse on Method and Meditations on First Philosophy* (New Haven: Yale University Press).

Deudney, D. H. (2007) *Bounding Power: Republican Security Theory from the Polis to the Global Village* (Princeton: Princeton University Press).

Deutsch, K. W. (1954) *Political Community at the International Level: Problems of Definition and Measurement* (Garden City, NY: Doubleday).

Deutsch, M. (1973) *The Resolution of Conflict: Constructive and Destructive Processes* (New Haven: Yale University Press).

DeWitt, B. S. (1970) "Quantum Mechanics and Reality," *Physics Today*, vol. 23: 30–5.

Diez, T., and J. Steans (2005) "A Useful Dialogue? Habermas and International Relations," *Review of International Studies*, vol. 31: 127–40.

Dilthey, W. (2002) *The Formation of the Historical World in Human Sciences*, Selected Works, vol. 3, ed. R. A. Makkreel and F. Rodi (Princeton: Princeton University Press).

Dorschel, A. (1990) 'Handlungstypen und Kriterien', *Zeitschrift für philosophische Forschung*, vol. 44: 220–52.

Drexler, K. E. (1986) *Engines of Creation: The Coming Era of Nanotechnology* (New York: Anchor Books), at: http://e-drexler.com/d/06/00/EOC/EOC_Table_of_Contents.html.

Dryzek, J. S. (2006) *Deliberative Global Politics* (Cambridge: Polity Press).

Durkheim, E. (1982 [1895]) *The Rules of Sociological Method* (New York: Free Press).

Dworkin, R. (1986) *Law's Empire* (London: Fontana Press).

Dworkin, R. M. (1977) *Taking Rights Seriously* (Cambridge, MA: Harvard University Press).

Easton, D. (1953) *The Political System: An Inquiry into the State of Political Science* (Chicago: University of Chicago Press).

Easton, D. (1971) *The Political System: An Inquiry on the State of Political Science*, 2nd edn (New York: Knopf).

The Economist (2005) "A Survey of Nanotechnology: Apply Here," vol. 374, issue 8407: 5.

Edelman, M. (1988) *Constructing the Political Spectacle* (Chicago: University of Chicago Press).

Edelman, M. (1995) *From Art to Politics* (Chicago: University of Chicago Press).

Elster, J. (1986) "The Market and the Forum," pp. 103–32, in Elster and A. Hylland (eds), *Foundations of Social Choice Theory* (Cambridge: Cambridge University Press).

Elster, J. (1989) *The Cement of Society* (Cambridge: Cambridge University Press).

Etzioni, A. (1967) "The Kennedy Experiment," *Western Political Quarterly*, vol. 20: 361–80.

Ferguson, Y. H., and R. W. Mansbach (1988) *The Elusive Quest: Theory and International Politics* (Columbia: University of South Carolina Press).

Feynman, R. (1959) "There's Plenty of Room at the Bottom," Meeting of the American Physical Society, California Institute of Technology, December 29, 1959, at http://www.its.caltech.edu/~feynman.

Fierke, K. M. (1998) *Changing Games, Changing Strategies: Critical Investigations in Security* (Manchester: Manchester University Press).

Finnemore, M., and K. Sikkink (2001) "Taking Stock: The Constructivist Research Program in International Relations and Comparative Politics," *Annual Review of Political Science*, vol. 4: 391–416.

Finnemore, M., and S. J. Toope (2001) "Alternatives to 'Legalization': Richer Views of Law and Politics," *International Organization*, vol. 55: 743–58.

Finnis, J. (1980) *Natural Law and Natural Rights* (Oxford: Clarendon Press).

Fish, S. (1989) *Doing What Comes Naturally: Change, Rhetoric, and the Practice of Theory in Literary and Legal Studies* (Durham, NC: Duke University Press).

Fitzgerald, M. (2008) "Trying to Put New Zip into Moore's Law," *New York Times*, February 24, 2008.

Forst, R (2007) *Das Recht auf Rechtfertigung* (Frankfurt am Main: Suhrkamp).

Franck, T. (1990) *The Power of Legitimacy among Nations* (Oxford: Oxford University Press).

Frankel, S. H. (1977) *Money, Two Philosophies: The Conflict of Trust and Authority* (Oxford: Basil Blackwell).

Frei, C. (2001) *Hans J. Morgenthau: An Intellectual Biography* (Baton Rouge: Louisiana State University Press).

Friedman T. L. (1999) *The Lexus and the Olive Tree* (New York: HarperCollins).

Friedman T. L. (2005) *The World is Flat: A Brief History of the Twenty-First Century* (New York: Farrar Straus & Giroux).

Friedman, M. (1953) "The Methodology of Positive Economics," in Friedman, *Essays in Positive Economics* (Chicago: Chicago University Press).

Friedrichs, J. (2000) *Aufschlußreiche Rhetorik: Ein Versuch über die Redekultur und ihren Verfall bei Thukydides* (Würzburg, Ergon).

Fuller, L. (1969) *The Morality of Law* (New Haven: Yale University Press).

Gadamer, H.-G. (2004) *Truth and Method*, 2nd edn, trans. J. Weinsheimer and D. G. Marshall (New York: Continuum).

Gat, A. (2007) "The Return of Authoritarian Great Powers," *Foreign Affairs*, vol. 86, no. 4: 59–70.

Gat, A., D. Deudney, G. J. Ikenberry, and R. Inglehart (2009) "Which Way is History Marching? Debating the Authoritarian Revival," *Foreign Affairs*, vol. 88, no. 4: 150–9.

George, A. L. (ed.) (1983) *Managing US-Soviet Rivalry: Problems of Crisis Prevention* (Boulder, CO: Westview Press).

Gergen, K. J., P. Ellsworth, C. Maslach, and M. Seipel (1975) "Obligation, Donor Resources and Reactions to Aid in Three Cultures," *Journal of Personal and Social Psychology*, vol. 31: 390–400.

Giddens, A. (1982) "Labour and Interaction," pp. 149–61, in J. B. Thompson and D. Held (eds), *Habermas: Critical Debates* (London: Macmillan).

Gompert, D. C., and J. Gordon IV (2008) *War by Other Means: Building Complete and Balanced Capabilities for Counterinsurgency* (Santa Monica, CA: RAND).

Goodman, N., M. Douglas, and D. L. Hull (1992) *How Classification Works: Nelson Goodman among the Social Sciences* (Edinburgh: Edinburgh University Press).

Goranson, R. E., and L. Berkowitz (1966) "Reciprocity and Responsibility Reactions to Prior Help," *Journal of Personality and Social Psychology*, vol. 3: 227–32.

Gouldner, A. W. (1960) "The Norm of Reciprocity: A Preliminary Statement," *American Sociological Review*, vol. 24: 161–78.

Gramsci, A. (1971) *Selections from the Prison Notebooks*, ed. and trans. Q. Hoare and G. Nowell Smith (New York: International Publishers).

Greenberg, M. S. (1980) "A Theory of Indebtedness," pp. 3–26, in K. J. Gergen, M. S. Greenberg, and R. H. Willis (eds), *Social Exchange: Advances in Theory and Research* (New York: Plenum Press).

Greenberg. M. S., and S. P. Shapiro (1971) "Indebtedness: An Adverse Aspect of Asking for and Receiving Help," *Sociometry*, vol. 34: 290–301.

Greider, W. (1987) *Secrets of the Temple: How the Federal Reserve Runs the Country* (New York: Touchstone).

Griffiths, M., S. C. Roach, and M. S. Solomon (2009) *Fifty Key Thinkers in International Relations* (London: Routledge).

Guzzini, S. (1993) "Structural Power: The Limits of Neorealist Power Analysis," *International Organization*, vol. 47: 443–78.

Guzzini, S. (2000) "A Reconstruction of Constructivism in International Relations," *European Journal of International Relations*, vol. 6: 147–82.

Habermas, J. (1973) *Theory and Practice*, trans. J. Viertel (Boston: Beacon Press).

Habermas, J. (1981) *Theorie des kommunikativen Handelns*, 2 vols. (Frankfurt am Main: Suhrkamp).

Habermas, J. (1984a) "Was heißt Universalpragmatik?" pp. 353–440, in Habermas, *Vorstudien und Ergänzungen zur Theorie des kommunikativen Handelns* (Frankfurt am Main: Suhrkamp).

Habermas, J. (1984b) "Replik auf Einwände," pp. 475–570, in Habermas, *Vorstudien und Ergänzungen zur Theorie des kommunikativen Handelns* (Frankfurt am Main: Suhrkamp).

Habermas, J. (1988) "Entgegnung," pp. 327–405, in A. Honneth and H. Joas (eds), *Kommunikatives Handeln, Beiträge zu Jürgen Habermas' 'Theorie des kommunikativen Handelns'* (Frankfurt am Main: Suhrkamp).

Habermas, J. (1996) "Sprechakttheoretische Erläuterungen zur kommunikativen Rationalität," *Zeitschrift für philosophische Forschung*, vol. 50: 65–91.

Habermas, J. (2004) *Wahrheit und Rechtfertigung. Philosophische Aufsätze*, 2nd edn (Frankfurt am Main: Suhrkamp).

Habermas, J. (2007) "Kommunikative Rationalität und grenzüberschreitende Politik: eine Replik," pp. 406–59, in P. Niesen and B. Herborth (eds), *Anarchie der kommunikativen Freiheit* (Frankfurt am Main: Suhrkamp).

Hacking, I. (1999) *The Social Construction of What?* (Cambridge, MA: Harvard University Press).

Hall, R. B. (2008) *Central Banking as Global Governance: Constructing Financial Credibility* (Cambridge: Cambridge University Press).

Hall, R. B., and T. J. Biersteker (eds) (2002) *The Emergence of Private Authority in Global Governance* (Cambridge University Press).

Hanrieder, T. (2008) "Moralische Argumente in den Internationalen Beziehungen: Grenzen einer verständigungstheoretischen 'Erklärung' moralischer Debatten," *Zeitschrift für internationale Beziehungen*, vol. 15: 161–86.

Hardin, R. (2003) *Indeterminacy and Society* (Princeton: Princeton University Press).

Hart, H. L. A. (1961) *The Concept of Law* (Oxford: Clarendon Press).

Hart, H. L. A. (1963) "Kelsen Visited," UCLA Law Review, vol. 10: 709–28.

Hart-Rudman Commission (2001) *Road Map for National Security: Imperative for Change, The Phase III Report of the US Commission on National Security/21st Century*.

Heath, A. (1976) *Rational Choice and Social Exchange* (Cambridge: Cambridge University Press).

Heidegger, M. (1993) *Basic Writings*, ed. D. F. Krell (San Francisco: Harper).

Heppt, A. (2007) "The Promise of the Better Argument: On the Analysis of Argumentation in International Relations," unpublished manuscript, St. Gallen.

Herborth, B. (2004) "Die via media als konstitutionstheoretische Einbahnstraße: Zur Entwicklung des Akteur-Struktur-Problems bei Alexander Wendt," *Zeitschrift für Internationale Beziehungen*, vol. 11: 61–88.

Herrera, G. L. (2003) "Technology and International Systems," *Millennium: Journal of International Studies*, vol. 32: 559–93.

Herrnstein, R., and C. Murray (1994) *The Bell Curve* (New York: Free Press).

Hesse, M. (1978) "Theory and Value in the Social Sciences," pp. 1–16, in C. Hookway and P. Pettit, *Action and Interpretation* (Cambridge: Cambridge University Press).

Hobbes, T. (1968) *Leviathan*, ed. C. B. Macpherson (Baltimore: Penguin).

Hobbes, T. (1996) *Leviathan*, ed. R. Tuck (Cambridge: Cambridge University Press).

Hoffmann, J., and G. S. Rosenkrantz (1997) *Substance: Its Nature and Existence* (London: Routledge).

Holland, B. (2010) "Sovereignty as Dominium? Reconstructing the Constructivist Roman Law Thesis," *International Studies Quarterly*, vol. 54: 449–80.

Hollis, M., and S. Smith (1994) "Two Stories about Structure and Agency," *Review of International Studies*, vol. 20: 241–51.

Holsti, O. R. (1967) "Cognitive Dynamics and Images of the Enemy: Dulles and Russia," in D. J. Finlay, O. R. Holsti, and R. R. Fagen (eds), *Enemies in Politics* (Chicago: Rand McNally).

Hughes, E. J. (n.d.) Papers: Hughes Diary, Princeton University Library.
Huizinga, J. (1950) *Homo Ludens* (Boston: Beacon).
Hume, D. (2000 [1740]) *Treatise of Human Nature* (Oxford: Oxford University Press).
Humrich, C. (2006) "Germany," pp. 72–99, in K. E. Jørgensen and T. B. Knudsen (eds), *International Relations in Europe* (London: Routledge).
Huntington, S. P. (1993) *The Third Wave: Democratization in the Late Twentieth Century* (Norman: University of Oklahoma Press).
Huntington, S. P. (1999) "The Lonely Superpower," *Foreign Affairs*, vol. 78, no. 2: pp. 35–49.
Hurd, I. (2008) "Constructivism," pp. 298–316, in C. Reus-Smit and D. Snidal (eds), *The Oxford Handbook of International Relations* (Oxford: Oxford University Press).
Hurrell, A. (2002) "Norms and Ethics in International Relations," pp. 137–54, in W. Carlsnaes, T. Risse, and B. A. Simmons (eds), *Handbook of International Relations* (London: Sage).
Ikenberry, G. J. (2009) "Liberal Internationalism 3.0: America and the Dilemmas of Liberal World Order," *Perspectives on Politics*, vol. 7: 71–87.
Iklé, F. C., and N. Leites (1962) "Political Negotiation as a Process of Modifying Utilities," *Journal of Conflict Resolution*, vol. 6: 19–28.
Jackson, P. T., and D. H. Nexon (1999) "Relations before States: Substance, Process, and the Study of World Politics," *European Journal of International Relations*, vol. 5: 291–332.
Jackson, P. T., and R. R. Krebs (2003) "Twisting Tongues and Twisting Arms: The Power of Political Rhetoric," paper presented at the annual meeting of the American Political Science Association.
Jackson, R. (2000) *The Global Covenant* (Oxford: Oxford University Press).
Jervis, R. (1976) *Perception and Misperception in International Politics* (Princeton: Princeton University Press).
Jervis, R. (1978) "Cooperation under the Security Dilemma," *World Politics*, vol. 30: 167–214.
Jervis, R. (2010) "Identity and the Cold War," pp. 22–43, in M. P. Leffler and O. A. Westad (eds), *The Cambridge History of the Cold War*, vol. 2, *Crises and Détente* (Cambridge: Cambridge University Press).
Johnson, J. (1991) "Habermas on Strategic and Communicative Action," *Political Theory*, vol. 19: 181–201.
Johnston, A. I. (2001) "Treating International Institutions as Social Environments," *International Studies Quarterly*, vol. 45: 487–515.
Jolivet, R. (1929) *La notion de substance: Essai historique et critique sur le développement des doctrines d'Aristote à nos jours* (Paris: Gabriel Beauchesne).
Jonsen, A, R., and S Toulmin (1988) *The Abuse of Casuistry: A History of Moral Reasoning* (Berkeley and Los Angeles: University of California Press).
Joy, B. (2000) "Why the Future Doesn't Need Us," *Wired*, issue 8.04 (April, at http://www.wired.com/wired/archive/8.04/joy_pr.html).
Kalathil, S., and T. C. Boas (2003) *Open Networks, Closed Regimes* (Washington: Carnegie Endowment for International Peace).
Kaplan, M. A. (1966) "The New Great Debate: Traditionalism vs. Science in International Relations," *World Politics*, vol. 19: 1–20.
Katzenstein, P. J. (1996) *Cultural Norms and National Security: Police and Military in Post War Japan* (Ithaca: Cornell University Press).

Keene, E. (2002) *Beyond the Anarchical Society: Grotius, Colonialism and Order in World Politics* (Cambridge: Cambridge University Press).

Kelley. H. H., and J. W. Thibaut (1978) *Interpersonal Relations: A Theory of Interdependence* (New York: Wiley).

Keohane, R. O. (1986) "Reciprocity in International Relations," *International Organization*, vol. 40: 1–28.

Keohane, R. O., and J. S. Nye (1977) *Power and Interdependence* (Boston: Little Brown).

Kessler, O. (2007) "From Agents and Structures to Minds and Bodies," *Journal of International Relations and Development*, vol. 10: 243–71.

Khalil, E. (1992) "Fox, Hedgehog, and Owl: Three Temperaments of Economic Discourse," *Methodus*, vol. 4: 101–9.

King, G., R. O. Keohane, and S. Verba (1994) *Designing Social Inquiry: Scientific Inference in Qualitative Research* (Princeton: Princeton University Press).

Kissinger, H. A. (1957) *A World Restored: The Politics of Conservatism in a Revolutionary Era* (London: Gollancz).

Klotz, A. (1995) *Norms in International Relations: The Struggle against Apartheid* (Ithaca: Cornell University Press).

Klotz, A. (2002) "Transnational Activism and Global Transformations: The Anti-Apartheid and Abolitionist Experiences," *European Journal of International Relations*, vol. 8: 49–76.

Klotz, A., and C. Lynch (2006) "Translating Terminologies," *International Studies Review*, vol. 8: 356–62.

Klotz, A., and C. Lynch (2007) *Strategies for Research in Constructivist International Relations* (Armonk, NY: M. E. Sharpe).

Kobrin, S. J. (1997) "The Architecture of Globalization: State Sovereignty in a Networked Global Economy," in J. H. Dunning (ed.), *Governments, Globalization and International Business* (Oxford: Oxford University Press).

Kobrin, S. J. (1998) "The MAI and the Clash of Globalizations," *Foreign Policy*, no. 112: 97–109.

Komorita, S. S. (1973) "Concession-Making and Conflict Resolution," *Journal of Conflict Resolution*, vol. 17: 745–62.

Kontopodis, M. (2009) "Editorial: Time, Matter, Multiplicity," *Memory Studies*, vol. 2: 5–10.

Koskenniemi, M. (2002) *The Gentle Civiliser of Nations: The Rise and Fall of International Law, 1870–1960* (Cambridge: Cambridge University Press).

Koskenniemi, M. (2006 [1989]) *From Apology to Utopia: The Structure of International Legal Argument* (Cambridge: Cambridge University Press).

Krasner, S. (1994) "International Political Economy: Abiding Discord," *Review of International Political Economy*, vol. 1: 13–19.

Krasner, S. (1995) "Sovereignty and Intervention," in G. M. Lyons and M. Mastanduno (eds), *Beyond Westphalia? State Sovereignty and International Intervention* (Baltimore: Johns Hopkins University Press).

Krasner, S. (1999) *Sovereignty: Organized Hypocrisy* (Princeton: Princeton University Press).

Krasner, S. (2001) "Rethinking the Sovereign State Model," *Review of International Studies*, vol. 27, 17–42.

Kratochwil (1971–2010) See "Friedrich Kratochwil's Published Work, 1971–2010," pp. 252–257, in this volume.

Kratochwil, F. (2007) "Leaving Sovereignty Behind? An Inquiry into the Politics of Post-Modernity," unpublished manuscript, European University Institute.

Kuhn, T. (1970a) *The Structure of Scientific Revolutions*, 2nd edn (Chicago: University of Chicago Press).

Kuhn, T. (1970b) "Reflections on my Critics," pp. 231–78, in I. Lakatos and A. Musgrave, (eds), *Criticism and the Growth of Knowledge* (Cambridge: Cambridge University Press).

Kydd, A. H. (2000) "Trust, Reassurance, and Cooperation," *International Organization*, vol. 54: 325–57.

Kydd, A. H. (2005) *Trust and Mistrust in International Relations* (Princeton: Princeton University Press)

Lacey, N. (2004) *A Life of H. L. A. Hart: The Nightmare and the Noble Dream* (Oxford: Oxford University Press).

Lakatos, I. (1970) "Falsification and the Methodology of Scientific Research Programmes," pp. 91–196, in I. Lakatos and A. Musgrave (eds), *Criticism and the Growth of Knowledge* (Cambridge: Cambridge University Press).

Lakoff, G. (1987) *Women, Fire, and Dangerous Things: What Categories Reveal about the Mind* (Chicago: University of Chicago Press).

Lakoff, G., and M. Johnson (1980) *Metaphors We Live By* (Chicago: University of Chicago Press).

Lang, Jr., A. F., N. Rengger, and W. Walker (2006) "The Role(s) of Rules: Some Conceptual Clarifications," *International Relations*, vol. 20: 274–94.

Lapid, Y. (2002) "Sculpting the Academic Identity: Disciplinary Reflections at the Dawn of a New Millennium," pp. 1–15, in D. Puchala (ed.), *Visions of International Relations: Assessing an Academic Field* (Columbia: University of South Carolina Press).

Lapid, Y. (2001) "Identities, Borders, Orders: Nudging International Relations Theory in a New Direction," pp. 1–20, in Albert et al. (eds) (2001).

Lasswell, H. D. (1936) *Politics: Who Gets What, When, How* (New York: McGraw-Hill).

Latour, B., and S. Woolgar (1986) *Laboratory Life: The Social Construction of Scientific Facts* (Princeton: Princeton University Press).

Laudan, L. (1986) *Science and Values* (Berkeley: University of California Press).

Laudan, L. (1996) *Beyond Positivism and Relativism* (Boulder, CO: Westview).

Leander, A. (2005) "The Power to Construct International Security: On the Significance of Private Military Companies," *Millennium Journal of International Studies*, vol. 33: 803–26.

Lebow, R. N. (2003) *The Tragic Vision of Politics: Ethics, Interests and Orders* (Cambridge: Cambridge University Press).

Lebow, R. N. (2007) "Science as an Ethical Practice," *Journal of International Relations and Development*, vol. 10: 16–24.

Levy Jr., M. J. (1969) "Does It Matter If He's Naked? Bawled the Child," in K. Knorr and J. N. Rosenau (eds), *Contending Approaches to International Politics* (Princeton: Princeton University Press).

Lieberman, B. (1964) "I-Trust: A Notion of Trust in Three-Person Games and International Affairs," *Journal of Conflict Resolution*, vol. 3: 271–80.

Luhmann, N. (1975) *Macht* (Stuttgart: Enke Verlag).

Luhmann, N. (1979) *Trust and Power: Two Works*, trans. H. Davis, J. Raffan, and K. Rooney (New York: Wiley).

Luhmann, N. (1990) *Die Wissenschaft der Gesellschaft* (Frankfurt am Main: Suhrkamp).
Luhmann, N. (1997) *Die Gesellschaft der Gesellschaft* (Frankfurt am Main: Suhrkamp).
Lynch, C. (1994) "Kant, the Republican Peace, and Moral Guidance in International Law," *Ethics & International Affairs*, vol. 8: 39–58.
Lynch, C. (1998) "Social Movements and the Problem of Globalization," *Alternatives*, vol. 23: 149–73.
Lynch, C. (1999) *Beyond Appeasement: Interpreting Interwar Peace Movements in World Politics* (Ithaca: Cornell University Press).
Lynch, C. (2000) "Acting on Belief: Christian Perspectives on Suffering and Violence," *Ethics & International Affairs*, vol. 14: 83–98.
Lynch, C. (2005) "The 'R' Word, Narrative, and Perestroika: A Critique of Language and Method," pp. 154–66, in K. R. Monroe (ed.), *Perestroika! The Raucous Rebellion in Political Science* (New Haven: Yale University Press).
Lynch, C. (2009) "Liberalism and the Contradictions of Global Civil Society," pp. 35–50, in A. Franceschet (ed.), *The Ethics of Global Governance* (Boulder, CO: Lynne Rienner).
Lynch, C. (2010) "Religion, Identity, and the War on Terror: Insights from Religious Humanitarianism," in P. James (ed.), *Religion, Identity, and Global Governance* (Toronto: University of Toronto Press).
Lyotard, J.-F. (1954) *La Phénoménologie* (Paris: Presses Universitaires de France).
MacIntyre, A. (1981) *After Virtue: A Study in Moral Theory*, 3rd edn (Notre Dame, IN: University of Notre Dame Press).
MacIntyre, A. (1990) *Three Rival Versions of Moral Enquiry: Encyclopaedia, Genealogy, and Tradition* (Notre Dame, IN: University of Notre Dame Press).
March, J. G., and J. P. Olsen (1989) *Rediscovering Institutions: The Organizational Basis of Politics* (New York: Free Press).
Marx, K. (1969a) "Thesen über Feuerbach," in K. Marx und F. Engels, *Werke*, Bd. 3 (Berlin: Dietz), pp. 5–7.
Marx, K. (1969b) "Theses on Feuerbach," in K. Marx and F. Engels, *Selected Works*, vol. 1 (Moscow: Progress Publishers), pp. 13–15.
Mathews, J. (1997) "Power Shift," *Foreign Affairs*, vol. 76, no. 1: 50–66.
Mauss, M. (1954) *The Gift*, trans. I. Cunnison (Glencoe, IL: Free Press).
Mazower, M. (2000) *Dark Continent: Europe's Twentieth Century* (New York: Vintage).
McClintock, C. D., and S. P. McNeill (1966a) "Reward and Score Feedback as Determinants of Cooperative Game Behavior," *Journal of Personality and Social Psychology*, vol. 4: 606–13.
McClintock, C. D., and S. P. McNeill (1966b) "Reward Level and Game Playing Behavior," *Journal of Conflict Resolution*, vol. 10: 98–102.
McCourt, D. (2007) "The Historical Turn in International Relations," Working Papers, SPS no. 2007/06 (Fiesole: European University Institute).
Mearsheimer, J. (1990) "Back to the Future: Instability in Europe after the Cold War," *International Security*, vol. 15: 5–56.
Mearsheimer, J. J. (2003) *The Tragedy of Great Power Politics* (New York: Norton).
Milliken, J. (1999) "The Study of Discourse in International Relations: A Critique of Research and Methods," *European Journal of International Relations*, vol. 5: 225–54.

Mitzen, J. (2005) "Reading Habermas in Anarchy: Multilateral Diplomacy and Global Public Spheres," *American Political Science Review*, vol. 99: 401–17.

Monk, R. (1990) *Ludwig Wittgenstein: The Duty of Genius* (London: Cape).

Monoson, S., and M. Loriaux (2006) "The Illusion of Power and the Disruption of Moral Norms: Thucydides' Critique of Periclean Policy," pp. 27–51, in B. Jahn (ed.), *Classical Theory in International Relations* (Cambridge: Cambridge University Press).

Morgenthau, H. J. (1933) *La notion du "politique" et la théorie des différends internationaux* (Paris: Sirey).

Morgenthau, H. J. (1935) "Théorie des sanctions internationales," *Revue de droit international et de législation comparée*, vol. 3–4: 474–503.

Morgenthau, H. J. (1948) *Politics among Nations: The Struggle for Power and Peace*, 1st edn (New York: Knopf).

Morgenthau, H. J. (1966a) *Politics among Nations: The Struggle for Power and Peace*, 3rd edn (New York: Knopf).

Morgenthau, H. J. (1966b) "The Purpose of Political Science," pp. 63–79, in J. C. Charlesworth (ed.), *A Design for Political Science: Scope, Objectives and Methods* (Philadelphia: American Academy of Political and Social Science).

Morris, S., and S. Rosen (1973) "Effects of Felt Adequacy and Opportunity to Reciprocate on Help Seeking," *Journal of Experimental Social Psychology*, vol. 9: 265–70.

Mosse, G. (1981) *The Crisis of German Ideology: Intellectual Origins of the Third Reich* (New York: H. Fertig).

Mosse, G. (ed.), (1966) *Nazi Culture: Intellectual, Cultural, and Social Life in the Third Reich* (London: W. H. Allen).

Müller, H. (1994) "Internationale Beziehungen als kommunikatives Handeln: Zur Kritik der utilitaristischen Handlungstheorie," *Zeitschrift für internationale Beziehungen*, vol. 1: 15–44.

Müller, H. (2004) "Arguing, Bargaining and All That: Communicative Action, Rationalist Theory and the Logic of Appropriateness in International Relations," *European Journal of International Relations*, vol. 10: 395–435.

Müller, H., and Deitelhoff, N. (2005) "Theoretical Paradise – Empirically Lost? Arguing with Habermas," *Review of International Studies*, vol. 31: 167–80.

Nardin, T. (1983) *Law, Morality, and the Relations of States* (Princeton: Princeton University Press).

Nemeth, C. (1970) "Bargaining and Reciprocity," *Psychological Bulletin*, vol. 74: 297–308.

Neumann, I. (2002) "Returning Practice to the Linguistic Turn: the Case of Diplomacy," *Millennium: Journal of International Studies*, vol. 31: 627–51.

New York Times (2002) "War with Iraq is Not in America's National Interest," advertisement on the op-ed page of the 26 September edition signed by 33 scholars.

Nexon, D. H. and I. B. Neumann (eds) (2006) *Harry Potter and International Relations* (Lanham, MD: Rowman and Littlefield).

Nietzsche, F. (1995) Vorlesungsaufzeichnungen, Abt. 2 Bd. 5, F. Bornmann and M. Carpitella (eds), in G. Colli and M. Montenari (eds), *Nietzsche Werke* (Berlin: Walter de Gruyter).

Nietzsche, F. (1997) *On the Genealogy of Morality*, trans. C. Diethe (Cambridge: Cambridge University Press).

Norris, P. (2001) *Digital Divide: Civic Engagement, Information Poverty, and the Internet Worldwide* (Cambridge University Press).
Oakeshott, M. (1975) *On Human Conduct* (Oxford: Clarendon Press).
Oakeshott, M. (1991) *Rationalism in Politics and Other Essays*, new edn (Indianapolis, IN: Liberty Press).
Onuf, N. (1989) *World of Our Making: Rules and Rule in Social Theory and International Relations* (Columbia: University of South Carolina Press).
Onuf, N. (1998a) "Constructivism: A User's Manual," pp. 58–78, in V. Kubálková, N. Onuf, and P. Kowert (eds), *International Relations in a Constructed World* (Armonk, NY: M. E. Sharpe).
Onuf, N. (1998b) *The Republican Legacy in International Thought* (Cambridge: Cambridge University Press).
Onuf, N. (2001) "Speaking of Policy," pp. 77–95, in V. Kubálková (ed.), *Foreign Policy in a Constructed World* (Armonk, NY: M. E. Sharpe, 2001).
Onuf, N. (2004) "Humanitarian Intervention: The Early Years," *Florida Journal of International Law*, vol. 16: 753–87.
Onuf, N. (2008) *International Legal Theory: Essays and Engagements, 1966–2006* (Abingdon: Routledge-Cavendish).
Onuf, N. (2009) "Structure, What Structure?" *International Relations*, vol. 23: 183–99.
Onuf, N., and P. Onuf (2006) *Nations, Markets and War: Modern History and the American Civil War* (Charlottesville: University of Virginia Press).
Oppenheim, F. E. (1981) *Political Concepts: A Reconstruction* (Oxford: Basil Blackwell).
Oye, K. A. (1985) *Cooperation under Anarchy* (Princeton: Princeton University Press).
Paarlberg, R. L. (2004) "Knowledge as Power: Science, Military Dominance, and US Security," *International Security*, vol. 29: 122–51.
Patomäki, H. (1996) "How to Tell Better Stories about World Politics," *European Journal of International Relations*, vol. 2: 105–33.
Patomäki, H., and C. Wight (2000) "After Postpositivism? The Promises of Critical Realism," *International Studies Quarterly*, vol. 44: 213–37.
Payne, R. A. (2001) "Persuasion, Frames and Norm Construction," *European Journal of International Relations*, vol. 7: 37–61.
Pearson, K. (1892) *The Grammar of Science* (London: Walter Scott).
PEN (2009) The Project on Emerging Nanotechnologies, "Consumer Products: An Inventory of Nanotechnology-Based Consumer Products Currently on the Market," http://www.nanotechproject.org/inventories/consumer.
Peterson, M. J. (1997) "The Use of Analogies in Developing Outer Space Law," *International Organization*, vol. 51: 245–74.
Pettit, P. (1997) *Republicanism: A Theory of Freedom and Government* (Oxford: Clarendon Press).
Polanyi, M. (1958) *Personal Knowledge: Towards a Post Critical Philosophy* (London: Routledge).
Popper, K. R. (1959) *The Logic of Scientific Discovery* (London: Hutchinson).
Popper, K. R. (1968) *The Logic of Scientific Discovery*, 3rd ed. (New York: Harper).
Popper, K. R. (1972) *Objective Knowledge: An Evolutionary Approach* (Oxford: Oxford University Press.
Potter, W. C. (2005) "India and the New Look of US Nonproliferation Policy," *Nonproliferation Review*, vol. 12: 343–54.

Pouliot, Vincent (2008), "The Logic of Practicality: A Theory of Practice of Security Communities," *International Organization*, vol. 62: 257–88.
Price, R., and Reus–Smit, C. (1998) "Dangerous Liaisons? Critical International Theory and Constructivism," *European Journal of International Relations*, vol. 4: 259–94.
Price, R. (2008) "Moral Limit and Possibility in World Politics," *International Organization*, vol. 62: 191–220.
Pruitt, D. G. (1968) "Reciprocity and Credit Building in a Laboratory Dyad," *Journal of Personality and Social Psychology*, vol. 8: 143–7.
Pruitt, D. G. (1981) *Negotiation Behavior* (New York: Academic Press).
Pufendorf, S. (2005 [1729]) *Of the Law of Nature and Nations: Eight Books*, 4th English edn, trans. B. Kennett, photo-reprint (Clark, NJ: The Lawbook Exchange).
Ragin, C. (2000) *Fuzzy Set Social Science* (Chicago: University of Chicago Press).
Rapoport, A. (1970) "Conflict Resolution in the Light of Game Theory and Beyond," pp. 1–42, in P. Swingle (ed.), *The Structure of Conflict* (New York: Academic Press).
Reiss, H. (ed.) (1991) *Kant: Political Writings*, 2nd edn, trans. H. B. Nisbet (Cambridge: Cambridge University Press).
Rescher, N. (1996) *Process Metaphysics: An Introduction to Process Philosophy* (Albany: State University of New York Press).
Reus-Smit, C. (1997) "The Constitutional Structure of International Society and the Nature of Fundamental Institutions," *International Organization*, vol. 51: 555–89.
Reus-Smit, C. (2001) "The Strange Death of Liberal International Theory," *European Journal of International Law*, vol. 12: 573–93.
Rice, C. (2000) "Promoting the National Interest," *Foreign Affairs*, vol. 79, no. 1: 45–62.
Riker, W. H. (1974) "The Nature of Trust," pp. 53–81, in J. T. Tedeschi (ed.), *Perspectives on Social Power* (Chicago: Aldine).
Risse, T. (1999) "International Norms and Domestic Change: Arguing and Communicative Behavior in the Human Rights Area," *Politics and Society*, vol. 27: 526–56.
Risse, T. (2000) "'Let's Argue': Communicative Action in World Politics," *International Organization*, vol. 54: 1–39.
Risse, T., and C. Ulbert (2005) "Deliberately Changing the Discourse: What Does Make Arguing Effective?" *Acta Politica*, vol. 40: 351–67.
Risse, T., S. C. Ropp, and K. Sikkink (eds) (1999) *The Power of Human Rights: International Norms and Domestic Change* (Cambridge: Cambridge University Press).
Rittberger, V., and P. Mayer (eds) (1993) *Regime Theory and International Relations* (Oxford: Clarendon Press).
Ritter, G. (1947) *Die Dämonie der Macht: Betrachtungen über Geschichte und Wesen des Machtproblems im Politischen Denken der Neuzeit* (Stuttgart: Hannsmann).
Rorty, R. (ed.) (1967) *The Linguistic Turn: Recent Essays in Philosophical Method* (Chicago: Chicago University Press).
Rose, N., P. O'Malley, and M. Valverde (2006) 'Governmentality', *Annual Review of Law and Social Science*, vol. 2: 83–104.

Rosenau, J. N. (1995) "Governance in the Twenty-First Century," *Global Governance*, vol. 1: 13–43.

Rosenau, J. N., and E.-O. Czempiel (eds) (1992) *Governance without Government: Order and Change in World Politics* (Cambridge: Cambridge University Press).

Rosenau, J. N., and J. P. Singh (eds) (2002) *Information Technologies and Global Politics: The Changing Scope of Power and Governance* (Albany, NY: SUNY Press).

Rosenfeld, M. (1994) "Modern Constitutionalism as Interplay between Identity and Diversity," pp. 3–38, in M. Rosenfeld (ed.), *Constitutionalism, Identity, Difference and Legitimacy: Theoretical Perspectives* (Durham, NC: Duke University Press).

Rosenthal, J. (1991) *Righteous Realists* (Baton Rouge: University of Louisiana Press).

Rouse, J. (1987) *Knowledge and Power: Toward a Political Philosophy of Science* (Ithaca: Cornell University Press).

Ruggie, J. G. (1993) "Territoriality and Beyond: Problematizing Modernity in International Relations," *International Organization*, vol. 47: 139–74.

Ruggie, J. G. (1998) *Constructing the World Polity* (London: Routledge).

Sartori, G. (1970) "Concept Misinformation in Comparative Politics," *American Political Science Review*, vol. 64: 1033–52.

Sassen, S. (2000) "Spatialities and Temporalities of the Global: Elements for a Theorization," *Public Culture*, vol. 12: 215–32.

Schatzki, T., K. K. Cetina, and E. Von Savigny (eds) (2001) *The Practice Turn in Ccontemporary Theory* (London: Routledge).

Schelling, T. C. (1960) *The Strategy of Conflict* (Cambridge, MA: Harvard University Press).

Schelling, T. C. (1968) "Game Theory and the Study of Ethical Systems," *Journal of Conflict Resolution*, vol. 12: 35–44.

Schimmelfennig, F. (2003) *The EU, NATO and the Integration of Europe: Rules and Rhetoric* (Cambridge: Cambridge University Press).

Schmitt, C. (1963) *Der Begriff des Politischen* (München: Duncker und Humblot).

Schmitt, C. (2005) *Political Theolog: Four Chapters on the Concept of Sovereignty*, trans. G. Schwab (Chicago: University of Chicago Press).

Schopler, J., and V. D. Thompson (1968) "Role of Attribution Processes in Mediating Amount of Reciprocity for a Favor," *Journal of Personality and Social Psychology*, vol. 2: 243–50.

Scott, S. V. (2005) "Identifying the Source and Nature of a State's Political Obligation towards International Law," *Journal of International Law and International Relations*, vol. 1: 49–60.

Searle, J. R. (2005) "What Is an Institution?" *Journal of Institutional Economics*, vol.1: 1–22.

Sen, A. (2005) *The Argumentative Indian* (London: Allen Lane).

Sen, A. (2009) *The Idea of Justice* (London: Allen Lane).

Sending, O. J., and I. B. Neumann (2006) "Governance to Governmentality: Analyzing NGOs, States, and Power," *International Studies Quarterly*, vol. 50: 651–72.

Shapiro, I. (2002) "Problems, Methods, and Theories in the Study of Politics, or What's Wrong with Political Science and What to Do about It," *Political Theory*, vol. 30: 596–619.

Shklar, J. N. (1984) *Ordinary Vices* (Cambridge, MA: Harvard University Press).

Shubik, M. (1970) "Game Theory, Behavior, and the Paradox of the Prisoner's Dilemma: Three Solutions," *Journal of Conflict Resolution*, vol. 4: 181–94.

Simons, H. W. (ed.) (1990) *The Rhetorical Turn: Invention and Persuasion in the Conduct of Inquiry* (Chicago: University of Chicago Press).

Sinclair, T. J. (2005) *The New Masters of Capital: American Bond Rating Agencies and the Politics of Creditworthiness* (Ithaca: Cornell University Press).

Singer, J. D. (1961) "The Level of Analysis Problem in International Relations," *World Politics*, vol. 14: 77–92.

Singer, J. D. (1969) "The Incompleat Theorist: Insight without Evidence," pp. 62–86, in K. Knorr and J. N. Rosenau (eds), *Contending Approaches to International Relations* (Princeton: Princeton University Press).

Singer, P. W. (2009) *Wired for War: The Robotics Revolution and Conflict in the 21st Century* (New York: Penguin).

Slaughter, A.-M. (2003) "A Global Community of Courts," *Harvard International Law Journal*, vol. 44: 191–219.

Slaughter, A.-M. (2005) "Security, Solidarity, and Sovereignty: The Grand Themes of UN Reform," *American Journal of International Law*, vol. 99: 619–31.

Slaughter, A.-M., and W. Burke-White (2002) "An International Constitutional Moment," *Harvard International Law Journal*, vol. 43: 1–21.

Slingerland, E. (2001) "Virtue Ethics, the *Analects*, and the Problem of Commensurability," *Journal of Religious Ethics*, vol. 29: 95–125.

Snidal, D. (1985) "Coordination versus Prisoner's Dilemma: Implications for International Cooperation and Regimes," *American Political Science Review*, vol. 79: 923–42.

Snidal, D., and A. Wendt (2009), "Why There is International Theory Now," *International Theory*, vol.1: 1–14.

Snyder, F. (1990) *New Directions in European Community Law* (London: Weidenfeld and Nicholson).

Snyder, J. L. (1984/1985) "Richness, Rigor, and Relevance in the Study of Soviet Foreign Policy," *International Security*, vol. 9: 89–108.

Stapp, H. P. (1972) "The Copenhagen Interpretation," *American Journal of Physics*, vol. 40: 1098–116.

Staub, E., and L. Sherk (1970) "Need Approval, Children's Sharing Behavior, and Reciprocity in Sharing," *Child Development*, vol. 41: 243–53.

Steele, B. J. (2008) *Ontological Security in International Relations: Self-Identity and the IR State* (Abingdon: Routledge).

Steffek, J. (2005) "Incomplete Agreements and the Limits of Persuasion in International Politics," *Journal of International Relations and Development*, vol. 8: 229–56.

Stein, A. A. (1983) "Coordination and Collaboration: Regimes in an Anarchic World," in S. D. Krasner (ed.), *International Regimes* (Ithaca: Cornell University Press).

Strassler, R, B. (ed.) (1998) The Landmark Thucydides, trans. R. Crawley (New York: Touchstone).

Struett, M. (2004) "The Meaning of the International Criminal Court," *Peace Review*, vol. 16: 317–21.

Sunstein, C. R. (1995) "Incompletely Theorized Agreements," *Harvard Law Review*, vol. 108: 1733–72.

Swinth, R. L. (1967) "The Establishment of the Trust Relationship," *Journal of Conflict Resolution*, vol. 11: 335–44.

Tamanha, B. Z. (2004) *On The Rule of Law: History, Politics, Theory* (Cambridge: Cambridge University Press).

Taylor, M. (1976) *Anarchy and Cooperation* (London: Wiley).

Tesser, R, R. Gatewood, and M. Driver (1968) "Some Determinants of Gratitude," *Journal of Personality and Social Psychology*, vol. 9: 233–6.

Thompson, J. (2008) *Rapporteur's Report of the Annual UNHCR Consultation with NGOs* (Geneva: International Council of Voluntary Agencies).

Thucydides (1996) *The Landmark Thucydides: A Comprehensive Guide to the Peloponnesian War*, ed. R. B. Strassler (New York: Free Press).

Tilly, C. (1975) *The Formation of National States in Western Europe* (Princeton: Princeton University Press).

Toope, S. J. (2000) "Emerging Patterns of Governance and International Law," pp. 91–108, in Byers (2001).

Toulmin, S. (1950) *The Place of Reason in Ethics* (Cambridge: Cambridge University Press).

Toulmin, S. (1992) *Cosmopolis: The Hidden Agenda of Modernity* (New York: Basic Books).

Toulmin, S. (2001) *Return to Reason* (Cambridge, MA: Harvard University Press).

Tully, J. (2008) "Two Meanings of Global Citizenship: Modern and Diverse," pp. 15–41, in M. A. Peters, A. Britton, and H. Blee (eds), *Global Citizenship Education: Philosophy, Theory and Pedagogy* (Rotterdam: Sense Publishers).

Tully, J. (1995) *Strange Multiplicity: Constitutionalism in an Age of Diversity* (Cambridge: Cambridge University Press).

Tully, J. (2002) "The Unfreedom of the Moderns in Comparison to Their Ideals of Constitutionalism and Democracy," *Modern Law Review*, vol. 65: 204–28.

Tully, J., M. Kumm, M. Poiares Maduro, and A. Wiener (2009), "Global Constitutionalism," unpublished manuscript, University of Hamburg.

Turner, S. (1994) *The Social Theory of Practices: Tradition, Tacit Knowledge, and Presuppositions* (Chicago: University of Chicago Press).

Turner, S. (2002) *Brains/Practices/Relativism: Social Theory after Cognitive Science* (Chicago: University of Chicago Press).

US Department of State (1952–54) *Foreign Relations of the United States*, vol. 2, pt. 1 (Washington: Government Printing Office).

Ulbert, C., and T. Risse (2005) "Deliberately Changing the Discourse: What Does Make Arguing Effective?" *Acta Politica*, vol. 40: 351–67.

Vandermolen, T. D. (2006) "Molecular Nanotechnology and National Security," *Air and Space Journal*, vol. 20, no. 3: 96–106.

Wæver, O. (2007) "Still a Discipline after all These Debates?" pp. 288–308, in T. Dunne, M. Kurki, and S. Smith (eds), *Theories of International Relations: Discipline and Diversity* (Oxford: Oxford University Press).

Wagner, R. H. (1983) "The Theory of Games and the Problem of International Cooperation," *American Political Science Review*, vol. 77: 330–47.

Walker, N. (2002) "The Idea of Constitutional Pluralism," *Modern Law Review*, vol. 65: 317–59.

Walker, N. (2008) "Out of Place and Out of Time: Law's Fading Co-Ordinates," Inaugural Lecture, delivered at the University of Edinburgh.

Walker, R. B. J. (1988–9) *Ethics, Modernity and the Theory of International Relations* (Princeton: Center of International Studies, Princeton University).
Walker, W. (2007) "Nuclear Enlightenment and Counter-Enlightenment," *International Affairs*, vol. 83: 431–453.
Walster, E., G. W. Walster, and E. Berscheid (1978) *Equity: Theory and Research* (Boston: Allen and Bacon).
Waltz, K. N. (1979) *Theory of International Politics* (Reading, MA: Addison-Wesley).
Waltz, K. N. (1993) "The Emerging Structure of International Politics," *International Security*, vol.18: 44–79.
Waltz, K. N. (1999) "Globalization and Governance," *PS: Political Science and Politics*, vol. 32: 693–700.
Warnock, G. J. (1971) *The Object of Morality* (London: Methuen).
Weber, M. (1988 [1919]) "Wissenschaft als Beruf," pp. 582–613, in Weber, *Gesammelte Aufsätze zur Wissenschaftslehre* (Tübingen: J. C. B. Mohr).
Weber, M. (1994 [1919]) "The Profession and Vocation of Politics," pp. 309–69, in P. Lassman and R. Speirs (eds), *Weber: Political Writings* (Cambridge: Cambridge University Press).
Weber, M. (2004a [1904]) "The 'Objectivity' of Knowledge in Social Science and Social Policy," pp. 359–404, in S. Whimster (ed.), *The Essential Weber: A Reader* (London: Routledge).
Weber, M. (2004b [1921]) "Basic Sociological Concepts," pp. 311–358, in S. Whimster (ed.), *The Essential Weber: A Reader* (London: Routledge).
Weiler, J. H. H. (1999) *The Constitution of Europe: "Do the New Clothes Have an Emperor?" and Other Essays on European Integration* (Cambridge: Cambridge University Press).
Weiler, J. H. H., and M. Wind (2003) *European Constitutionalism beyond the State* (Cambridge: Cambridge University Press).
Weldes, J. (1998) "Bureaucratic Politics: A Critical Constructivist Assessment," *Mershon International Studies Review*, vol. 42: 216–25.
Weldes, J., and D. Saco (1996) "Making State Action Possible: The United States and the Discursive Construction of 'The Cuban Problem, 1960–1994,'" *Millennium*, vol. 25: 361–95.
Wendt, A. (1987) "The Agent-Structure Problem in International Relations Theory," *International Organization*, vol. 41: 335–70.
Wendt, A. (1999) *Social Theory of International Politics* (Cambridge: Cambridge University Press).
Wendt, A. (2003) "Why a World State Is Inevitable," *European Journal of International Relations*, vol. 9: 491–542.
Wendt, A., and R. Duvall (2008) "Sovereignty and the UFO," *Political Theory*, vol. 36: 607–33.
Wiener, A. (2004) "Contested Compliance: Interventions on the Normative Structure of World Politics," *European Journal of International Relations*, vol. 10: 189–234.
Wiener, A. (2008) *The Invisible Constitution of Politics: Contested Norms and International Encounters* (Cambridge: Cambridge University Press).
Wiener, A. (2009) "Enacting Meaning-in-Use: Qualitative Research on Norms and International Relations," *Review of International Studies*, vol. 35: 175–93.
Wiggins, D. (2001) *Sameness and Substance Renewed* (Cambridge: Cambridge University Press).

Wight, M. (1966) "Why Is There No International Theory," pp. 17–34, in H. Butterfield and M. Wight (eds), *Diplomatic Investigations* (London: George Allen and Unwin).

Wight, M. (1978) *Power Politics*, expanded edn (Leicester: Leicester University Press).

Wight, C. (2007a) "Inside the Epistemological Cave All Bets Are Off," *Journal of International Relations and Development*, vol. 10: 40–56.

Wight, C. (2007b) "A Response to Friedrich Kratochwil: Why Shooting the Messenger Does Not Make the Bad News Go Away," *Journal of International Relations and Development*, vol. 10: 301–15.

Williams, M. C. (2007) *Culture and Security: Symbolic Power and the Politics of International Security* (New York: Routledge).

Winch, P. (1990) *The Idea of a Social Science and its Relation to Philosophy*, 2nd edn (Atlantic Highlands, NJ: Humanities Press International).

Windelband, W. (1894) *Geschichte und Naturwissenschaft: Rede beim Stiftungsfest der Kaiser-Wilhelms-Universität Strassburg* (Strassburg: Druck von Heitz).

Wittgenstein, L. (1921) *Tractatus Logico-Philosophicus* (London: Routledge and Kegan Paul).

Wittgenstein, L. (1958), *Philosophical Investigations*, 3rd edn, trans. G. E. M. Anscombe (New York: Macmillan).

Wittgenstein, L. (1980) *Culture and Value*, trans. P. Winch (Oxford: Basil Blackwell).

Wohlforth, W. C. (1999) "The Stability of a Unipolar World," *International Security*, vol. 24: 5–41.

Wyer, R. S. (1969) "Prediction of Behavior in Two-person Games," *Journal of Personality and Social Psychology*, vol. 31: 222–38.

Yee, A. S. (1996) "The Causal Influence of Ideas on Politics," *International Organization*, vol. 50: 69–108.

Yanow, D., and P. Schwartz-Shea (eds) (2006) *Interpretation and Method: Empirical Research Methods and the Interpretive Turn* (Armonk, NY: M. E. Sharpe).

Young, O. (1969) "Professor Russett: Industrious Tailor to a Naked Emperor," *World Politics*, vol.21: 486–511.

Zakaria, F. (2008) *The Post-American World* (New York: Norton).

Zehfuss, M. (2001) "Constructivisms in International Relations: Wendt, Onuf, and Kratochwil," pp. 54–75, in K. M. Fierke and K.E. Jørgensen (eds), *Constructing International Relations: The Next Generation* (Armonk, NY: Sharpe).

Zürn, M., M. Binder, M. Ecker-Ehrhardt, and K. Radtke (2007) "Politische Ordnungsbildung wider Willen," *Zeitschrift für Internationale Beziehungen*, vol. 14: 129–64.

Index